P9-CAE-606

The Rooster's Egg

Jamaica is the land where the rooster lays an egg . . . When a Jamaican is born of a black woman and some English or Scotsman, the black mother is literally and figuratively kept out of sight as far as possible, but no one is allowed to forget that white father, however questionable the circumstances of birth. You hear about "my father this and my father that, and my father who was English, you know," until you get the impression that he or she had no mother. Black skin is so utterly condemned that the black mother is not going to be mentioned nor exhibited. You get the impression that these virile Englishmen do not require women to reproduce. They just come out to Jamaica, scratch out a nest and lay eggs that hatch out into "pink" Jamaicans.

—Zora Neale Hurston

The Rooster's Egg

Patricia J. Williams

Harvard University Press
Cambridge, Massachusetts • London, England • 1995

Library of Congress Cataloging-in-Publication Data
Williams, Patricia J., 1951–
  The rooster's egg / Patricia J. Williams.
   p.   cm.
  Includes bibliographical references and index.
  ISBN 0-674-77942-8 (alk. paper)
  1. Oral communication—Social aspects—United States. 2. Hate
speech—United States. 3. Stereotype (Psychology)—United States.
I. Title.
P95.54.W55 1995
302.2'242'0973—dc20   95-9562

To the memory of Denise Carty-Benia, Mary Joe Frug, and Dwight Greene

Contents

The Rooster's Egg

Scarlet, the Sequel

Mother is a metaphor with power to make the private visible.

—Martha Fineman, *The Neutered Mother*

L ast September I found myself in a motel on the outskirts of Mount Vernon, Ohio, watching television to kill time until my ride back to Columbus. It was a Thursday afternoon, but there seemed to be religious revival meetings on every other channel. The one that riveted me most was a particularly passionate televangelist who screamed and ranted against a government that provides any money at all to women who "fornicate." Welfare is government-sponsored fornication, he shouted, and that's contrary to God's law. There was loud applause and the camera zeroed in on a pink and alabaster family—father, mother, and a quite enchantingly telegenic toddler asleep on Daddy's shoulder.

"Fornication?" I was startled to say aloud. I was a visitor to rural Ohio, from Sin Central itself, New York City, that high-tech Sodom, that cesspool of a Gomorrah. Where's *General Hospital?* I wondered vaguely.

Actually, greater metropolitan New York has as much religious programming as any other part of the country—perhaps more. But with such a truly tough crowd to proselytize, even fundamentalist ministers tend to preach against hipper, more upscale, and definitely less venial sins than mere fornication. But on a crisp autumn day in the pristine apple-growing farm country of Ohio, this television minister did manage to make fornication sound awfully filthy, even to me. I've entered the realm of the Scarlet

Letter, I mused. However would Hester Prynne survive in to-day's sin-obsessed yet multi-orgasmic family circus? Would we find her held up for mockery in the new-age stockades of the Rush Limbaugh show? Would she die in small increments in a homeless shelter, the slow-motion equivalent of a public stoning? Or would she end up like the typical woman on welfare—a young white woman with children who is fully convinced she is not typical but just temporarily down on her luck? And what if poor Hester were black?

As long as there's *Hard Copy,* I suppose we are not wholly back in the times when women who fornicated were obliged to em-broider their own A's branding them adulterers. But witch-hunt-ing misogyny is fiercely recurrent in this nation, even if its forms vary with the ages. Can we be, I wonder, so far from the harshest days of Puritan intolerance if we only imagine that today's scourged women wear a W for welfare, or an S for single, or a B for black, or a CC for children-having-children. Nathaniel Haw-thorne's most widely read novel was, after all, a complex allegory for the state of a nation in which some presume to withhold the benefits of society and others are marked, branded as outcasts in public shaming ceremonies whose very hypocrisy ultimately eats away at the body politic.

Back in New York City, I have remained haunted by that angry televangelist, shouting vengeance and condemnation, cast-ing out women who stray from the path of chastity and then "come searching for a government handout." Let them wander in the wilderness, he cried in a state of near-apoplexy. Reverend Dimmesdale, I sighed to myself, as I boarded a subway the other day, still fixed upon the fury of that sermon. On the subway car there was an old black woman, a bag lady, stooped, asleep or unconscious, her smell overwhelming—so overwhelming that her end of the car was empty, because others who got on gave her a very wide berth. A white man in his mid or late twenties stepped on board and immediately began to fan the air with

3

grand gestures. He said "Oh, God!" loudly and to no one in particular but with great self-importance, his eyes scanning the passengers for someone with whom to complete the drama of his observations. He chose a young black boy of about twelve or thirteen years of age, sweet-faced, gentle-eyed, a knapsack of books on his back, a school kid in a baseball jacket with an adolescent daydream written across his face. The white man looked over at him and scolded in a very loud voice: "You see that? That's why you'd better learn how to work!" Heads turned. The kid looked stricken, then giggled tensely, looked back at the subway car full of those robotic eyes. A wall fell across the introspection of only a moment before, and he smiled a smile of pure incipient rage.

In addition to summoning up the worst ghosts of Puritan intolerance, contemporary attacks on women have blended historical strains of racism, misogyny, and class bias into an unusually potent brew. Aimed particularly at black women, single women, and poor women on welfare, the attacks have handily condensed all three categories into the encompassing figure of "the" black single mother on welfare.

The American rhetoric of single motherhood, from Hester Prynne to Murphy Brown, has always involved a contest between legitimacy and intimacy, convention and form. The offspring of single mothers are traditionally figured as wild cards, pawns of commercial circumstance, as "fatherless" as bees, rather than as fathered by men who, like the Reverend Dimmesdale, have deep stakes in their own, albeit tortured, invisibility. We are also experiencing a mean resurgence of class bias, whose culmination to date is perhaps embodied in a *New York Magazine* cover story of August 24, 1994, "The White Trashing of America," in which the author, Tad Friend, throws around alarmist and alarming condescensions rarely so indulged in the media since *Birth of a Nation:* "Like the urbanites in *Deliverance,* we have found ourselves in the grinning clutches of sexually predatory backwoodsmen. White trash culture commands us to 'squeal like a pig!' And we're oinking." Throw in a few images of lusty black women and, well, you get a mixture that's always been flammable enough to light a fire beneath any given American social issue.

It's instructive to look at an analysis of welfare cases, from the late 1960s to the present, interpreting federal and state AFDC statutes. AFDC, or Aid to Families with Dependent Children, was designed to provide food and nurturance for children in poor families—so that they did not go to school hungry, so that they were not too listless to learn, so that they did not grow up with bowed legs and bad teeth and a host of other problems that were much more common before the advent of AFDC. It is hard to remember, in the blizzard of today's bad press, that AFDC and related welfare programs did at least part of their job well. They didn't wipe out many of the endemic social problems of racism and poverty—problems that long preceded their advent and that we have by and large yet to address—but they did control much of the pervasive hunger, particularly in the South, that had devastated whole communities.

Yet over time AFDC has been slowly and perversely targeted as the *cause* of our larger social problems, as if it were at fault for feeding people who without it would have just starved to death in peaceful oblivion instead of growing up greedy and infinitely more troublesome. Indeed, AFDC guidelines have slowly but surely redefined the actual nutritional needs of children as subsidiary to family structure and work ethic as measures of entitlement and deserving worth.

Somewhere during the Reagan-Bush years the issue of race became more firmly wedded to the notion of welfare than ever before, and the rest is history. We have ascended to the age of workfare and bridefare, with more and more programs containing regulations that require recipients to work or to marry in order to receive some measure of what they need. Women who have borne the brunt of both failed marriages and a failing economy are now to be "taught" the stabilizing, civilizing influences of hard work and a strong male hand around the house. Consider this much-quoted description of a much-lionized welfare official:

> After a decade of national experimentation, no program has done as much to raise the earnings of people on welfare as one here in Riverside County . . .
>
> The philosophy here is unromantic: get a job any job, even a low-paying, unpleasant job. That cuts across the more prevalent national practice, which stresses education and training first, in the hope that people on welfare can earn more later . . .
>
> Riverside's program bears the imprint of its unusual welfare director, Lawrence Townsend, who courts an image of political incorrectness with diatribes against the nation's main welfare program, Aid to Families with Dependent Children.
>
> "Every time I see a bag lady on the street, I wonder, 'Was that an A.F.D.C. mother who hit the menopause wall—who can no longer reproduce and get money to support herself?'" he said.

How pervasive this astonishing mythology has become!—this image of women who prey upon their children, stealing the food from their mouths, leaving the children to fend for themselves and steal in turn from society. We have been rocketed back to some memory-pocket in the collective Victorian brain, when women's problems were measured entirely by the rise and fall of their hormones.

This punitive attitude imagines so much—and eliminates so much else. Perhaps it's time to counter such claptrap with images of women who are trying to negotiate the hardest challenges in our society—women who work around the clock, who are sinking beneath the burden of trying to earn survival wages while raising children, women who are divorced, women who are fired, women who are raped, who are married to the wrong men, or who are married to the right men who happen to be unemployed auto workers.

Statistics show that welfare to single mothers constitutes 1 percent of the federal budget, 3 percent if food stamps are added. Only 38 percent of AFDC recipients are African-American. Of all welfare households, only 8.1 percent are headed by teen mothers. Fifty-two percent of those teenagers are nineteen years old; 31 percent are eighteen. Less than 1.2 percent of all AFDC mothers are minors (under eighteen). Furthermore, studies indicate that approximately 50 percent of women in homeless shelters and 60 percent of all poor women are poor for reasons associated with their having fled abusive relationships. There is, in other words, a remarkable correlation between domestic violence and women's poverty.

But the premises of the mean-spirited welfare war against today's impoverished have grown into industrial-strength clichés, beginning with the one that welfare recipients are oversexed single women who just want to have fun by making babies so they can support themselves on grotesquely huge welfare checks. This is the view of a nation totally uninvested in the humanity of poor children—the total worth of these children, in other words, is supposedly equal to no more or less than the amount of that welfare check. Moreover, this view too often represents the value white taxpayers place on children who are largely imagined to be black. It is a formula that sees nothing to consider other than the annoying, perpetual cost of keeping them alive.

But being on welfare isn't fun. Poor women apply for AFDC because they are the human dimension of our flailing economy— they live in the communities hardest hit by recession/depression. They *are* the unemployment statistics about which there is so much pious political handwringing in the abstract. But then if the war on illegitimacy is indeed a new War on Poverty, it is one in which not poverty but poor people themselves are considered the enemy.

In "The Negro Family: The Case for National Action," Daniel Patrick Moynihan "warned that rising illegitimacy rates and a 'tangle of pathology' posed grave threats to the stability of black families and put at risk the gains in income and equality that blacks had managed to achieve through the civil rights movement . . . a community that allows a large number of young men to grow up in broken families, dominated by women, never acquiring any stable relationship to male authority, never acquiring any set of rational expectations about the future—that community asks for and gets chaos." While explosively controversial when it first appeared in the 1960s, Moynihan's report is enjoying a comeback that reflects the degree to which the nation has let itself off the hook by espousing simple-minded homilies as cures for complex political problems of race and class. Never before have so many been so eager to blame the victims of the legacy of slavery, continuing segregation, homelessness, the withdrawal of public funds for everything from education to condoms, and underground economies of drugs on the one hand and sheer poverty on the other.

From the Republicans to the Democratic White House, from the *National Review* to the *Washington Post,* the message is the same: if only blacks would stop reproducing, stop complaining, and get a father and a job, order would reign once more. The *Post,* which is notorious for its stuck-in-Superfly vision of ghetto life, recently ran an eight-day series on the trials and tribulations of a welfare mother named RosaLee who seemingly had committed every sin the Bible could think of, including, of course, having many children by many different men, setting up her boyfriend to be killed, spreading AIDS, teaching her children to steal, and cheating the welfare system. Despite statistics—as well as record volumes of mail—disputing RosaLee's example as typical of anything, the *Post* articles painted her as generally representative of a "culture" of black pathology whose cure could only come from blacks themselves.

The war on illegitimacy is, to restate the obvious, a way of drawing lines between children who are thought legitimate and those who are not. In terms of its civic consequences, it builds a barrier between legal and illegal children, between those who are all in the family and those who are deemed alien. But what would happen if all these children were assumed to be "legitimate" and yet were still living in poverty? What possibilities could be imagined if this debate were about people the civic circle deemed worthy and deserving?

One of the most alarming features of the current war against welfare is the insidious myth that welfare is a form of affirmative action for the genetically inferior, allowing the least deserving to breed at taxpayer expense. One feature of modern fascist states, from Hitler's Germany to Franco's Spain to Mussolini's Italy, has been a fierce pronatalist sentiment on behalf of some favored category of women as a way to save the ship of state, coupled with an emphasis on the importance of men's role in owning those (or "their") women's reproduction. These movements have frequently coexisted with antinatalist policies against women deemed undesirable, with a corresponding attempt to "disown" them by denying them any notion of legitimate family—legitimacy, of course, depending upon the steadying influence of Real Men.

Our present welfare war is pervaded with the assumption that black women have no business having any more children (its most common expression being the fiction, again, that women on welfare are having more children just to get more money). There are enough children in the world already, black women are told—care to try some Norplant? Yet this anxiety about population control does not seem to extend to middle-class whites, who are encouraged to spend tens of thousands of dollars on artificial means of reproduction if necessary; or to poor white women who have children out of wedlock, who are encouraged to give up their children for adoption and redistribution in the great "white baby shortage."

The syndicated columnist Charles Murray has made his reputation by spreading inflammatory theories of black reproductive "excesses" that must be contained. Where the proportion of "fatherless boys" is high, he opines, "surely the culture must be Lord of the Flies writ large, the values of unsocialized male adolescents made norms—physical violence, immediate gratification and predatory sex. That is the culture now taking over the black inner city." Furthermore, says Murray, genetic inferiority and not despair, misguided notions of equality and not racism, are at the root of all these problems.

I suppose I could spend time here observing how similar Murray's description of black communities is not only to classic nineteenth-century racist and anti-immigrant propaganda but also to nineteenth-century British demonizations of the lower classes (in fact, Murray was commissioned to write just such a diatribe for the *Sunday Times* of London). I suppose I could spend some time talking about unsocialized white male behavior directed against generation after traumatized generation of black families; and I suppose I could spend a great deal of time talking about how this description might also handily be applied to American culture generally.

But all that would be beside the point because the purpose of Murray's diatribe is not to deal with the legacy of racism or uncontrolled guns or unemployment or lack of health care or birth control or the economy of underground drugs or rape or spousal battering or child abuse or education or housing. Rather, Murray's sole focus is on how to stop poor single women from reproducing.

In addition to proposing termination of "all forms" of government economic support for "illegitimate" children, including AFDC and food stamps, Murray suggests that the state stop interfering with "the natural forces" that have rewarded marriage and penalized unmarried women's reproduction "quite effectively for millennia." What might those natural forces be? "Stigma and shotgun marriage," which, he says, "may or may not be good for those on the receiving end, but their deterrent effect

10

on others is wonderful—and indispensable." Moreover, at the same time that he hurls libertarian slogans urging *no* more government programs for the poor, he unblinkingly advocates *more* government support of the things *he* would like to see—"lavish" orphanages and governmental involvement in both encouraging single women to give up their children for adoption and making adoption easier and faster for married couples.

In Murray's depictions, which are currently popular enough to have the attention of Republican and Democratic policymakers alike, the desperate poverty and social isolation of so many black men and women are due solely to the willful abandonment of the institution of marriage and its profits. Moreover, he uses the specter of the black "underclass" to threaten white wombs into good wifeliness: "Either we reverse the current trends in illegitimacy—especially white illegitimacy—or America must, willy-nilly, become an unrecognizably authoritarian, socially segregated, centralized state." This strategy is perhaps most familiar as the Dan Quayle Memorial the State Is Not a Father (But Motherhood Is Nationalism) Move, as when Quayle cited the television sitcom character Murphy Brown's fictional out-of-wedlock birth as the kind of social collapse that caused the Los Angeles riots. This characterization of black social life as the chaotic and erotically charged abyss into which refined white Americans will slip—and whose border is maintained most centrally by the virtue of white women—is a formulation as old as slavery. It is also a formulation that has been used against the women's movement at least since the late 1800s. It is nothing less than tragic to see its divisiveness resurgent in the highest halls of power, with barely a whisper about the tremendous questions of due process, to say nothing of racial and gender equality, that are so urgently implicated.

But, again, Murray believes equality is the source of all our difficulties. Against that backdrop, his proposal of state-run orphanages for the children of women deprived of welfare becomes particularly sinister. Surely even Murray can foresee that orphan-

11

ages might fall prey to the same forces that have resulted in such terrible conditions in inner cities—white flight, withdrawal of services, contemptuous staff who wish they were working in a white neighborhood, or who think they're in the military. What makes him believe orphanages will work if this country can't even staff inner-city schools well enough to teach children to read—schools that are always promised more money, more gimmicky programs, always getting little more than new metal detectors; schools now filled with supposedly fatherless children and, under Murray's ideal, soon to be filled with truly motherless children.

In fact, I don't believe even Murray thinks such a system will improve the lot of its wards. What it will do, however, is confine children, track them, fingerprint them from the get-go, sterilize the unruly ones on their thirteenth birthday. In state-run orphanages you won't have to worry about such troublesome details as parental consent. Eliminating welfare is, after all, part of Murray's vision of how to "manipulate the fertility of people with high and low I.Q.'s." But if Murray thinks black kids are scary and dangerous and resentful now, just try a system effectively jailing them at birth.

This save-the-babies-eliminate-the-mothers ideology is very close in sentiment to that of those anti-abortionists who idealize the fetus into an impossible innocent, a figmented possibility that evil has not yet touched. So this idea of black-babies-in-a-bubble is pumped into the video cyberspace of public policy where all actions can be viewed and controlled, from cradle to grave, by a wiggle of the joystick.

And it is eugenic. It is a worship of the ideal of life, not a worship of life. But even that is rationalized away these days. Take, for example, the influential and provocatively entitled book *Sex and Reason,* by Richard Posner, formerly a University of Chicago law professor and now a Seventh Circuit judge. With remarkable radicalism for someone who generally describes himself as a pragmatist, Posner writes: "Hitler, with his zeal for eugenic sterilization, gave human eugenics a bad name. Before him it was a popular cause, perhaps especially among intellectuals, such as Justice Holmes and Bertrand Russell. The distinguished English geneticist R. A. Fisher expressed profound concern with the infertility of the upper classes, believing that it portended a significant diminution in the quality of the human gene pool. It seems so *logical* that biology should be enlisted in the drive to make a better world."

While acknowledging that there are "serious objections" to the practice of eugenics, Posner echoes Murray in giving lots of room to the laissez-faire accomplishment of that end:

> If poor people tend to have worse genes than rich . . . and if a reduction in the quality of a society's gene pool inflicts an aggregate harm on the society greater than the benefit to the additional poor children who are born, a policy of subsidizing the poor to produce more children would not be optimal . . . The welfare system already subsidizes the production of children by poor people . . . [and] the poor are already having more children than they want because uneducated people (who disproportionately are poor people) find it difficult to use contraception effectively.

And while warning that "we should be alert to policies that have unintended pronatalist or antinatalist effects," Posner is nonetheless famous for advancing his own pronatalist and anti-natalist preferences without any hesitation whatsoever: "Child welfare programs aimed at the poor, such as Aid to Families with Dependent Children, may stimulate births among the poor, while policies aimed at facilitating the entry of middle-class women into the labor market may reduce the middle-class birth rate. Such a combination may leave the overall birth rate unchanged and simply make the population as a whole poorer." So the idea of black-babies-in-a-bubble is pumped this time into the video cyberspace of the free market, into the automat of consumption preference, where all destiny can be bought and sold.

13

"The common denominator of all forms of National Socialist racism," writes German historian Gisela Bock, "was the definition and treatment of human beings according to a differing 'value' defined and ascribed by other human beings. The value criteria were declared to be 'biology,' as was the social and cultural field in which they were embodied: descent and procreation. The common denominator not of all forms of Nazi racism but of its most dramatic forms was the attempt to 'solve' social and cultural problems with means that were also called 'biology': namely by intervening with body and life."

What a bother, that history.

What an irony, these times.

Pansy Quits

"Help me out of these wet things, Pansy," Scarlett ordered her maid. "Hurry." Her face was ghostly pale, it made her green eyes look darker, brighter, more frightening. The young black girl was clumsy with nervousness. "Hurry, I said. If you make me miss my train, I'll take a strap to you."

She couldn't do it, Pansy knew she couldn't do it. The slavery days were over, Miss Scarlett didn't own her, she could quit any time she wanted to.

—Alexandra Ripley, *Scarlett: The Sequel to Margaret Mitchell's "Gone with the Wind"*

D espite the enormous social, political, and legal fluctuations of twentieth-century American life, there has been a remarkable stasis in race relations, an intractability of gender hierarchy, an entrenched power dynamic that has resisted the reorderings of the very best rhetoricians and theoreticians. When Frederick Douglass described his own escape from slavery as a "theft" of "this head" and "these arms" and "these legs," he employed the master's language of property to create the unforgettable paradox of the "owned" erupting into the category of a speaking subject whose "freedom" simultaneously and inextricably marked him as a "thief." That this disruption of the bounds of normative imagining is variously perceived as dangerous as well as liberatory is a tension that has distinguished racial politics in America from the Civil War to this day. Scarcely thirty years after Martin Luther King's dream of a day when his children would be judged by the content of their character alone, the Reagan-Bush presidencies were able to reverse the metaphor of the Freedom Train into a commodity with a high-priced ticket whose fare must be earned in the marketplace.

The transformation of the rationales for enslavement or oppression from one discourse to another is perhaps a more familiar one than we in the United States would at first be comfortable acknowledging. As Walter Benn Michaels has observed:

Imagining the slave as a buyer and seller, the contract at the same time defeudalizes slavery, replacing a social fact that exists independent of the desires of master or slave with a market agreement that insists on and enacts the priority of those desires . . . Hence the "new feudalism" that Progressives . . . feared . . . can never come into being not because conditions as bad as and even worse than those obtaining under "old-fashioned" slavery cease to exist but because the intervention of the market, even when it leaves these conditions intact, alters their meaning. In other words, the apologists for "modern slavery" defended it not by appealing to the usual paternalist ideals but by appealing to freedom, in particular freedom of contract.

Political appeals to "liberty," popular references to "freedom," and legal discussions of "equality" have always been weighted and authorized by very powerful images culled from hotly contested fields of symbolic reference. Who is really included in the notion of "national unity"? What is being negotiated when mass violence is labeled a "war," as opposed to a revolution, a rebellion, a riot, or the hold of some cult leader over innocent followers? When did affirmative action become reverse discrimination? How did we get to the point where no one puts black bodies on the auction block anymore, only healthy white babies? Against what social backdrop is sexual harassment transformed into high-tech lynching? And how on earth did we end up in the best-selling world of *Scarlett: The Sequel,* in which ex-slaves comfort themselves, as the whip descends, with the thought that they can quit at any time?

As the civil rights movement has made claims on the civic circle of participation, those resources located in the public sphere (including not just wealth but such intangibles as political responsibility and general idealism) have been spirited out of reach, as in a shell game between the walnut halves of public and private; as in a shell game among a welter of legal nuts. The debate about equality has shifted to one of free speech; legal

17

discussions involving housing, employment, and schooling have shifted from the domain of civil rights to that of the market and thus have become "ungovernable," mere consumption preference. It serves us well, I think, to observe the ironies as well as the consistencies, the currents of desired investment and unintended disenfranchisement that flow on and on and on beneath the surface of our finest aspirations.

It is useful to attempt to unravel the degree to which powerful negative stereotypes of race and gender play against one another, first in negotiating the subtle, sometimes nearly invisible boundaries of social life, of citizenship, and of entitlement; and then, ultimately, in dictating the very visible limits of the law itself. To study the unreflective resurrection and recirculation of the metaphors of disregard in the United States is to reveal a powerful ideological pattern, a semantic of racism that is nurtured in the hidden spaces of cognitive blind spots. As Professors Nancy Fraser and Linda Gordon have written about the genealogy of the notion of "welfare dependence," the use of overdetermined and taken-for-granted images and keywords "serve[s] to enshrine certain interpretations of social life as authoritative and to delegitimate or obscure others, generally to the advantage of dominant groups in society and to the disadvantage of subordinate ones."

The degree to which such images are influential raises the question of the degree to which they may be manipulated for better or worse ends. Thus the scope of my concern includes the rhetorical strategies by which borders are drawn and community marked, including the cultural theorist Eduardo Cadava's question of "how one's rhetoric may see its way home to the mark when the figures one uses may include, within their history, connotations that lead one's argument away from its intended end," as well as the function of the media in shaping "American" identity—in particular the currently popular configuring of "whites as victims" in the shaping of civic identity and legal outcome.

As I write, it is the fortieth anniversary of *Brown v. Board of Education,* the case that shaped my life's possibilities, the case that, like a stone monument, stands for just about all of the racial struggles with which this nation still grapples. I cite it as a watershed moment, but the *Brown* case was part of a larger story that couldn't, shouldn't be made into private property; it was an exemplary story but far from unique.

My family, like so many black families, worked in the civil rights movement, joined the NAACP, took me to march out in front of Woolworth's before I could read—not because of a great event in their lives but because of all the ordinary daily grinding little events that made life hard in the aggregate. Even though I was raised in Boston during the 1950s and 1960s, I grew up knowing the back-of-the-bus stories, the peanut gallery stories, the having-to-go-the-bathroom-in-the-woods stories, the myriad mundane nearly invisible yet monumentally important constraints that circumscribed blacks, and not only in the South. My father, who grew up in Savannah, Georgia, during the 1920s and 1930s, remembers not only the inconveniences but the dangers of being black under Jim Crow: "You had to be careful of white people, you got out of the way, or you'd get hurt, immediately. If you saw a white person coming, you got off the sidewalk. Don't make too much noise. Know which side of the street to walk on. You were always conscious of the difference. The big conversation in all 'colored' homes was just that, color. It affected everybody."

"But that's exactly why *Brown* is indeed 'our' story," cautioned a friend of mine, who being fifteen or so years older than I was old enough to have gone on enough marches to have worn out many pairs of shoes:

The civil rights movement was all about ordinary people who weren't necessarily on the road to Damascus. If some lent their names, others lent their backs, or their expertise or their lives. It was life-threatening work after all, so nobody did it to get their

19

name up in lights; you did it because there was no alternative. Neither fame nor anonymity existed as issues per se—that's come later, as the country seems to have sorted out who it's going to remember for fifteen seconds and what it will forget. It was about group survival. You were always thinking about what would make it better for the children.

Perhaps part of the difficulty in reviewing the years since *Brown* with anything like a hopeful countenance is that we as a nation have continued to underestimate the complicated and multiple forms of prejudice at work in the United States. Segregation did not necessarily bar all forms of racial mixing; its odd, layered hierarchies of racial attitude were substantially more complicated than that. My grandfather, for example, was a doctor who owned several of the houses in the neighborhood where he lived. "Dad's tenants were white, Irish," says my father, "but I never even thought about where they went to school. We all lived kind of mixed up, but the whole system made you think so separately that to this day I don't know where they went to school." There is an old story that speaks to the profundity of these invisible norms: Three men in the 1930s South set out to go fishing in a small boat. They spent the morning in perfectly congenial and lazy conversation. At lunchtime they all opened their lunch buckets and proceeded to eat, but not before the two white men put an oar across the middle of the boat, dividing themselves from their black companion.

The continuing struggle for racial justice is tied up with the degree to which segregation and the outright denial of black humanity have been *naturalized* in our civilization. An aunt of mine who is very light-skinned tells of a white woman in her office who had just moved from Mississippi to Massachusetts. "The North is much more racist than the South," she confided to my aunt. "They don't give you any credit at all for having white blood." This unblinking racial ranking is summarized in the thoughts of James Kilpatrick, now an editor of the *National*

Review, who stated the case for southern resistance in a famous and impassioned plea:

> For this is what our Northern friends will not comprehend: The South, agreeable as it may be to confessing some of its sins and to bewailing its more manifest wickednesses, simply does not concede that at bottom its basic attitude is "infected" or wrong. On the contrary, the Southerner rebelliously clings to what seems to him the hard core of truth in this whole controversy: Here and now, in his own communities, in the mid-60's, the Negro race, as a race, plainly is not equal to the white race, as a race; nor, for that matter, in the wider world beyond, by the accepted judgment of ten thousand years, has the Negro race, as a race, ever been the cultural or intellectual equal of the white race, as a race.
>
> This we take to be a plain statement of fact, and if we are not amazed that our Northern antagonists do not accept it as such, we are resentful that they will not even look at the proposition, or hear of it, or inquire into it.

Dealing with the intractability of this sort of twisted social regard is what the years since *Brown* have been all about. Legal remedy after legal remedy has been challenged on the basis of assertions of not being able to "force" people to get along, assertions that "social equality" (or, these days, "market preference") is just not something that can be legally negotiated. Jack Greenberg, a Columbia University law professor and one of the attorneys who worked on the original *Brown* case, dismisses these arguments concisely: "You have to wonder how it is that *Plessy v. Ferguson,* which made segregation the law for almost seventy years, didn't come in for the same kinds of attacks, as 'social engineering.'"

Jerome Culp, a Duke University law professor, has observed that the litigators and activists who worked on *Brown* in the early 1950s assumed at least three things that have not come to pass: (1) that good liberals would stand by their commitment to black equality through the hard times; (2) that blacks and whites could come to some kind of agreement about what was fair and just—that there *was* a neutral agreed-upon position we could aspire to; and (3) that if you just had enough faith, if you just wished racism away hard enough, it would disappear.

"Growing up," says my father, "we thought we knew exactly what integration meant. We would all go to school together; it meant the city would spend the same money on you that they did on the white students. We blacks wouldn't be in some cold isolated school that overlooked the railroad yards; we wouldn't have to get the cast-off ragged books. We didn't think about the inevitability of a fight about whose version of the Civil War would be taught in that utopic integrated classroom."

The *Brown* decision itself acknowledged the extent to which educational opportunity depended on "intangible considerations" and relied "in large part on 'those qualities which are incapable of objective measurement but which make for greatness.'" Yet shaking the edifice sometimes brings home just how enormous the edifice really is. Moreover, the task of education in general has become vastly more complicated by the influence of television, and the task of learning racial history has been much confounded by the power of mass media.

"We've become a nation of sound bites," says Cheryl Brown Henderson, the daughter of the late Oliver Brown—the named plaintiff in *Brown*—and the founder of the Brown Foundation, an organization dedicated to teaching the history of the civil rights movement.

> That millisecond of time to determine our behavior, whether it's behavior toward another individual, or behavior toward a product we might purchase, or our behavior with regard to what kind of housing or community we want to live in—I really think we allow that [millisecond] to determine far too much of our lives . . . When you take something that short and infuse it with a racial stereotype, and no other information is given, the young person looking at that—even the older person who spends most of his time watching

television—that's all they know. How can you expect them to believe anything else? They're not going to pick up a book and read any history, do any research, or talk to anybody that may in fact be able to refute the stereotype.

In addition to stereotypes, perhaps the media revolution has exacerbated the very American tendency to romanticize our great moments into nostalgia-fests from which only the extremes of Pollyannaish optimism or Malthusian pessimism can be extracted. For all the biblical imagery summoned to inspire the will to go on with the civil rights struggle in this century, if the waters have parted at any given moment, perhaps it has been more attributable to all those thousands of busy people working hard to make sure Exodus occurred one way or another—just people, just working and just thinking about how it could be different, dreaming big yet surprised most by the smallest increments, the little things that stun with the realization of the profundity of what has not yet been thought about.

My father muses:

> It's funny . . . we talked about race all the time, yet at the same time you never really thought about *how* it could be different. But after *Brown* I remember it dawning on me that I *could* have gone to the University of Georgia. And people began to talk to you a little differently; I remember [the white doctor who treated my family in Boston, where I grew up] used to treat us in such a completely offhand way. But after *Brown,* he wanted to discuss it with us, he asked questions, what I thought. He wanted my opinion and I suddenly realized that no white person had ever asked what I thought about anything.

Perhaps as people like my father and the doctor have permitted those conversations to become more and more straightforward, the pain of it all, the discomfort, has been accompanied by the shutting down, the mishearing, the turning away from the euphoria of *Brown.* "It has become unexpectedly, but not unpredictably hard. The same thing will probably have to happen in South Africa," sighs my father.

Perhaps the legacy of *Brown* is as much tied up with a sense of national imagination as with the pure fact of its legal victory; it sparked our imagination, it fired our vision of what was possible. Legally it set in motion battles over inclusion, participation, and reallocation of resources that are very far from over. But in a larger sense it committed us to a conversation about race that we must move forward with, particularly in view of a new rising Global Right.

We must get beyond the stage of halting conversations filled with the superficialities of hurt feelings and those "my maid says blacks are happy" or "whites are devils" moments. If we could press on to a conversation that takes into account the devastating legacy of slavery that lives on as a social crisis that needs generations more of us working to repair—if we could just get to the enormity of that unhappy acknowledgment, then that alone might be the source of a genuinely revivifying, rather than a false, optimism.

I think that the crisis in universities over what is so snidely referred to as "political correctness" must be viewed as part of the attempt to have such a conversation. The much-publicized campus tensions are an unfortunate but perhaps predictable part of the institutional digestive process of the beneficiaries or demographic heirs of the civil rights movement. The battle for equal rights that is symbolized by the landmark integration of grammar schools in Topeka, Kansas, that was waged also with the integration of high schools and colleges, then professional and graduate schools, then workplaces—that battle is now just about forty years old. The generation of children who entered white schools as a result of the transformative legacy of the Supreme Court's opinion in *Brown v. Board of Education* has grown up, become middle-aged, attained the time of life when careers make their lasting mark. It is not surprising, therefore, that the bitter resistance and powerful backlash that have met every step of integrationist vision should have followed to their current loci, those Steven Carter calls "affirmative action babies." It is not surprising, as more blacks, women, gays, Hispanics, Jews, Muslims, and wheelchair-bound people have entered the workplace, gotten tenure in universities, and risen to political office, that the new generation of fire-hosing tomato-throwers have shifted their aim and their tactics accordingly.

No longer are state troops used to block entry to schools and other public institutions—segregation's strong arm, states' rights, has found a new home in an economic gestalt that has simply privatized everything. Whites have moved to the suburbs and politicians have withdrawn funds from black to white areas in unsubtle redistricting plans. No longer is the law expressly discriminatory (as to race and ethnicity at any rate; this is not yet the case in terms of sexual orientation)—yet the phenomenon of laissez-faire exclusion has resulted in as complete a pattern of economic and residential segregation as has ever existed in this country.

Most of all, the moral currency of the civil rights movement's vocabulary has been under attack. "Integration" itself has been transformed in meaning, now used glowingly by former segregationists like Jesse Helms and Strom Thurmond—and rejected by many former civil rights activists—as having come to mean a form of assimilation that demands self-erasure rather than engagement of black contributions and experience.

This facile deflection has historical precedents in the 1950s incantations of "freedom of association" and "contract," which were used to block discussions of integration. Then, as now, civil rights activists had to respond with lawsuits focusing on substantive equality as a constitutional objective, on the premise that certain groups need not suffer unrestrained stigmatization of their humanity and of their citizenship. In today's world, such efforts have focused on harassment in the workplace, the academic freedom to include or exclude the histories of minority groups in curricula, the redefinition of citizenship to encompass the extraordinary linguistic, ethnic, religious, racial, and physical variety of those of us who are American Citizens Too.

While this particular battle resounds in every aspect of American life, there is no place it has been more visible than in universities; there is no fiercer entrenchment than the line drawn around the perceived property in culture. It is a battle remarkable for the persistence of prejudice: as women are still trying to overcome presumptions that they really *like* getting fondled in the back office, blacks are trying to overcome presumptions that they really *deserve* to be on the bottom of the heap. It is a battle complicated not just by ignorance and denial but by disastrous yet well-intentioned experiments—such as the slavery lesson described in this news item:

> A White first-grade teacher in Atglen, Pa., who asked her only two Black pupils to pretend they were slaves during a class discussion on slavery, recently apologized to the youngsters' parents.
>
> "Teacher put us up on a table," said Ashley Dixon, 6, describing the history lesson by teacher Mary Horning. Ashley said Horning told her that, as a slave, she would be sold for about $10 as a house cleaner.
>
> Zachary Thomas, also 6, said Horning used him to demonstrate how shirtless slaves were chained to a post before flogging.
>
> Horning apologized the next day to the children's mothers and asked them to speak to her class on Black heritage. "I did not view it as racial," she said, adding, "I wanted to teach the children about prejudice. I did not do it with malice or to embarrass anyone."

Such well-meaning but thoughtless scenarios reenact and reinforce a power dynamic in which some people get to *imagine* oppression, and others spend their lives having their bodies put through its most grotesque motions. Reference to "good intentions," moreover, however blunderingly destructive their impact, tends to end all further discussion. The merest whisper of the

26

possibility that a little education, a little history, a little fore-thought might improve things is too often crudely and immedi-ately translated into electrical blizzards of fear of "fascism," "thought control," "hypersensitivity," and "lowered standards."

I can't help wondering what is implied when the suggestion of more knowledge, more history is so persistently misunderstood and devalued as unscientific unknowledge, as untruthful unhis-tory. In fact, the upside-downness of meaning has become a major threat to the ability to address educational inequality in a whole range of contexts. "*Inter*culturalism," said a Swarthmore undergrad firmly and disapprovingly when I used the word "mul-ticulturalism" at a tea given in my honor not long ago. "Huh?" said I, through a mouthful of chocolate cream and crumbs. "Interculturalism," she repeated. "Multiculturalism has too much negative meaning these days."

I guess she was right. Every generation has to go through a purging of language, an invention of meaning in order to exist, in order to be seen. Renaming as fair turnaround; renaming as recapture from the stereotypes of others. Yet . . . somehow . . . it seems I am running out of words these days. I feel as if I am on a linguistic treadmill that has gradually but unmistakably increased its speed, so that no word I use to positively describe myself or my scholarly projects lasts for more than five seconds. I can no longer justify my presence in academia, for example, with words that exist in the English language. The moment I find some symbol of my presence in the rarefied halls of elite institu-tions, it gets stolen, co-opted, filled with negative meaning. As integration became synonymous with assimilation into whiteness, affirmative action became synonymous with pushing out more qualified whites, and of course multiculturalism somehow be-came synonymous with solipsistically monocultural privilege.

While constant rejuvenation is not just good but inevitable in some general sense, the rapid obsolescence of words even as they drop from our mouths is an increasingly isolating phenomenon.

27

In fact, it feels like a form of verbal blockbusting. I move into a large meaningful space, with great connotations on a high floor with lots of windows, and suddenly all the neighbors move out. My intellectual aerie becomes a known hangout for dealers in heresy and other soporific drugs, frequented by suspect profiles (if not actual suspects) and located on the edge of that known geological disaster area, the Slippery Slope.

The roadblock that the moral inheritance of the civil rights movement has encountered in the attack on "political correctness" strikes me as just such rhetorical robbery—it is a calculated devaluation of political property values no less than the "white flight" organized by the National Association of Realtors a few decades ago, which left us with the legacy of the "inner city." It seems to me that the ability to talk about diversity (now synonymous with balkanization) depends therefore on a constant clarification of terms, a determination to leave nothing to presupposition, and a renewed insistence upon the incorporation of multiple connotative histories into our curricula, our social lives, our politics, and our law.

I worry that while the happy universalism of assimilative "neutrality" is a fine ideal, we will never achieve it by assuming away the particularity of painful past and present inequalities. The creation of a false sense of consensus about "our common heritage" is not the same as equality. As the example of the first-grade slave auction demonstrates, the ignorant (or innocent) perpetuation of oppression, even as we purport to be challenging it, can result in situations where empowered people imagine they are learning and even end up feeling pretty good about themselves, yet the disempowered end up feeling pretty awful, bearing the burden of the lessons imparted to the more powerful while learning nothing themselves that is new or helpful. Thus powerful inequities and real social crises are ignored, are made invisible, and just get worse.

Does this mean we eliminate the topic of slavery or sexism or homophobia from our classrooms as too "dangerous" or "divisive" or "controversial"? Do we really want to avoid controversy in education? Or is that even the issue?

I am concerned that the noisy rush to discuss the legalities of censorship and the First Amendment preempts more constructive conversations about how we might reinfuse our pedagogy with dignity and tolerance for all. As I have remarked a number of times before, it is as if the First Amendment has become severed from any discussion of the actual limits and effects of political, commercial, defamatory, perjurious, or any other of the myriad classifications of speech. It is as if expressions that carry a particularly volatile payload of hate become automatically privileged as political and, moreover, get to invoke the First Amendment as a bludgeon of paradox—"I have my First Amendment right to call you a monkey, so you shut up about it." As the legal anthropologist Richard Perry observes, hatred thereby gets to cross-dress as Virtue Aggrieved.

In a much-publicized incident at Harvard University a few years ago, a white student hung a Confederate flag from her dormitory window, saying that to her it symbolized the warmth and community of her happy southern home. This act produced a strong series of public denunciations from many other students, blacks in particular, who described the symbolic significance of the Confederacy as a *white* community forged against a backdrop of force, intimidation, and death for blacks. Eventually one black student hung a sheet with a swastika painted on it out her window, with the expressed hope that the university would force both her and the white student to remove such displays. The university did not, and eventually the black student removed her flag voluntarily because it was creating tension between black and Jewish students.

While the entire debate about this incident predictably focused on free speech issues, what seemed strange to me was a repeated and unexamined imbalance in how the two students' acts were discussed. On the one hand, there was a ubiquitous assumption that the white student's attribution of meaning to the Confederate flag was "just hers," so no one else had any "business" complaining about it. The flag's meaning became a form of private property that she could control exclusively and despite other assertions of its symbolic power. (Those other assertions are just "their opinion"; all's fair in the competitive marketplace of meaning.)

At the same time, there was an assumption that the swastika's meaning was fixed, transcendent, "universally" understood as evil. The black student's attempt to infuse it with "her" contexualized meaning (that of the translated power of what the Confederate flag meant to her) was lost in the larger social consensus on its historical meaning. This larger social consensus is not really fixed, of course, but its monopoly hold on the well-educated Harvard community's understanding is a tribute both to the swastika's overarchingly murderous yet coalescing power in the context of Aryan supremicist movements and to our having learned a great deal of specific history about it. The power of that history understandably overshadowed not only that black student's attempt at a narrower meaning but also the swastika's meaning in aboriginal American religion or in Celtic runes.

The question remains, however, how some speech is so automatically put beyond comment, consigned to the free market of ideas, while other expressions remain invisibly regulated, even monopolized by the channels not merely of what we have learned but of what we have not learned. I do not want to be misunderstood: I do not question our consensus on the image of genocide embodied in the swastika; I wonder at the immovability of the comfy, down-home aura attending the Confederate flag—the sense that as long as it makes some people happy, the rest of us should just butt out. The limits of such reasoning might be clearer if applied to the swastika: without having to conclude anything about whether to censor it, the fact remains that we usually don't cut off discussions of Nazism with the conclusion that it was a way of creating warm and happy communities for the German bourgeoisie.

Let me be clearer still in this thorny territory: I wish neither to compare nor to relativize the horrors of the Holocaust and of the legacy of slavery in the United States. This is not an appropriate subject for competition; it is not a sweepstakes anyone could want to win. I do worry that it is easier to condemn that which exists at a bit of cultural distance than that in which we may ourselves be implicated. And it is easier to be clear about the nature of the evils we have seen in others an ocean away than about those whose existence we deny or whose history we do not know. The easy flip-flopping between "free" and "regulated" signification is a function of knowledge; it underscores the degree to which we could all stand to educate ourselves, perhaps most particularly about the unpleasantnesses of the past. We should not have to rely upon the "shock" shorthand of campus crises, for example, to bring to our public consciousness the experience of black history in the good old days of legalized lynching.

The ability to negotiate the politics of coexistence on college campuses is directly related to how those leaders-of-tomorrow, college graduates, will resolve such problems in "the real world." The fighting in the Crown Heights section of Brooklyn, for example, has been plagued by some of the same symbolic and analytical confusion encountered in the Harvard example. The Crown Heights situation has been relentlessly characterized as signaling a breakdown of friendly relations between blacks and Jews across the political spectrum. Which it surely is doing, but I think that this broad, simplistic characterization of an infinitely more nuanced encounter is itself part of the cause of the break-down. The term "black-Jewish alliance" is commonly used to invoke a specific history of shared struggles in the United States, from the turn of the century onward. These struggles, from the labor movement to the civil rights movement, were social set-tings in which the two groups worked shoulder to shoulder, shoring up and very nearly defining the Left in this nation. As was—and still is—appropriate and efficient in the face of the legalized monolith of U.S. apartheid laws, blacks and Jews focused on their similarities, on the commonalities of the Holocaust and the Middle Passage, so incomparable in one sense yet so suffused with the boundless mandate of never forgetting.

Since the successes of the civil rights movement, however, it is clear that the things that divide blacks and Jews demand addressing also. While they may occupy the same symbolic social space when it comes to the Ku Klux Klan, their divergent histories and daily experiences in the United States make it difficult to presuppose much "sameness" when they deal with each other in more nuanced contexts. For example, while both groups face anguishing issues about members who "pass" as either white or gentile, this assimilative force takes on confusing power in regard to one another. "You're white," hurled blacks in Crown Heights; "Anti-Semites," Jews hurled back. And of course each side was right in terms of the injurious forays of that verbal war. Members of the Hasidic community used insulting racial epithets and characterizations about blacks, terms whose history goes back hundreds of years in the United States. Black residents of Crown Heights stood on streetcorners and shouted that Hitler was right. The use in this context of such shop-worn slogans of hate is testament to the power of even partial assimilation into the ethic of America's race hatred.

At the same time, I could not help wondering if this horrible debacle was really about "black-Jewish relations" in the sense of summoning up the collapse of some historic alliance. The blacks in Crown Heights were, for the most part, not African-American descendants of slavery in the United States, but rather immigrants from various parts of the West Indies and the Caribbean. Similarly, I wonder if the fact that the Jews in Crown Heights were mostly members of a fairly self-enclosed Hasidic community introduces a somewhat different tension than that popularly bandied about: they were not "invisible" minorities in the sense that most American Jews are. Their determination not to blend peaceably into the J. Crew mass of suburban manners, morals, and fashionable dress "marks" them in important and dangerous ways—ways that I think reawaken the sort of unfettered, forcefully unsubtle anti-Semitism that flourished more prevalently only a generation or so ago, when most Jews were somewhat more visible by accent, circumcision in the days before it was widespread, segregation, and so on. And blacks, as participants in this culture, have been no less—nor any more—assimilated into that anti-Semitism than anyone else.

I can't help wondering if the Crown Heights tension is really about "blacks versus Jews" at all. That opposition connotes a rather flattened sense of post–civil rights breakdown, as well as a certain neoconservative vision in which Jews have become "zealous Zionists" and blacks have "lost" their "transcendent moral claim" on national sympathies. Does the construction of the debate in these stereotyped terms contribute anything to the possibility of accord?

Could not the dispute in Crown Heights more fruitfully be recast as one involving Jews who don't feel "white" but who occupy the identity space of whites, particularly as the beneficiaries of certain public services such as police protection; and, at the same time, involving blacks who are unaware of themselves as resonantly Christian in this context, yet who, having evolved a strong survivalist, even fundamentalist, version of Christianity, are implicated in its historical attitudes toward Jews—indirectly, convolutedly perhaps, but implicated nonetheless.

I daresay it would also help the analysis to take at least some stock of the fact that the steadfastly Messianic Hasidic community in Crown Heights is at odds not just with blacks but with much of the rest of the Jewish community in this country. Similarly, much of the black Caribbean community of Crown Heights is not only at odds with the Hasidic community but also at odds with—in some instances even prejudiced against—blacks whose ancestors were slaves in the United States. The issue, in other words, is, at least in part, whether unassimilated immigrant groups can live in peace not just with one another but within a culture that resolutely denies their particularity as just too *unpleasant.*

The way such circumstances derail any constructive discussion is epitomized by a story one of my students told me: at the peak of the Crown Heights tension, one of the local television stations thought it would be a great idea to show a group of black and Jewish teenagers having a conversation that would model tolerance, healing, and general we-are-the-worldness. The plan encountered immediate problems, because the Hasidic boys could not have such a conversation in the same room with girls and the black youth of Crown Heights seemed a little, well, sullen. So the producers fetched a group of Reform Jewish students from Long Island, and some pleasant-faced upper-middle-class black kids from private schools in Manhattan, and had them talk about Crown Heights, *in* Crown Heights, engaging in a "debate" that had less to do with the affected communities than with the modeling of an imagined melting pot bubbling happily away. But the absurdity of importing outsiders to enact a conversation that the actual neighborhood can't have is directly akin to the Allan Bloomian nostalgia for an undifferentiated "American" culture flowing seamlessly from the font of "Western" civilization. Whose anxieties are supposedly redressed by such mythic representations? And is it possible that such representations are not just misleading, but downright oppressive?

I remember when I was a little girl, in the late 1950s, two or three black families moved into our neighborhood where for fifty years my mother's family had been the only blacks. I remember the father of my best friend, Cathy, going from house to house, warning the neighbors, like Paul Revere with Chicken Little's brain, that the property values were falling, the values were falling. The area changed overnight. Whites who had seen me born and baked me cookies at Halloween and grown up with my mother now fled for their lives. ("We'd have to hold our breath all the time because colored people smell different," said Cathy with some conviction. Cathy, who was always a little slow about these things, had difficulty with the notion of me as "colored": "No, you're not" and then, later, "Well, you're different.")

The mass movement that turned my neighborhood into an "inner city" was part of the first great backlash to the civil rights movement. I think we are now seeing the second great backlash, disguised as a fight about reverse discrimination and "quotas" but in truth directed against the hard-won principles of equal opportunity in the workplace and in universities as feeders for the workplace. Universities are pictured as "fortresses" of enlightened and universal values under "siege" by those who are perceived to be uncivilized heathen. (Wherever 3 percent or more of us are gathered, it's a siege, I guess.) The cry has been sounded: The standards are falling, the standards are falling.

The story of my inner-city neighborhood would have been vastly different if Cathy and her family had bothered to stick around to get to know the two nice black families who moved in. Similarly, the future of U.S. universities—particularly in the hoped-for global economy—could be a fascinating one if campus communities chose to take advantage of the rich multiculturalism that this society offers. We face a quite disastrous intellectual crisis, however, if our universities persist in the culture-baiting that has brought us the English-only movement, the brazen assumption that any blacks on campus don't deserve to be there, and the mounting levels of verbal and physical violence directed against anyone perceived to be different or marginal.

This situation makes it easy to spend a lot of time being defensive. We've all heard the lame retorts into which these attacks box us: "I am too qualified!" "Vote for me but not because I'm a woman!" But they don't work. You simply can't dispel powerful cultural stereotypes by waving your degrees in

35

people's faces. (That's precisely the premise of ultraconservative Dinesh D'Souza's much-touted book *Illiberal Education:* that an Ivy League degree just isn't worth what it used to be now that the riffraff has moved in.)

It's hard not to be defensive, of course—talking about race in any other posture is extremely difficult. I recently guest-lectured in the class of a constitutional law professor who was teaching disparate impact cases (cases that consider what if any remedies might correct the racially disparate impact of rules that on their face are race-neutral). As I spoke about shifting demographics and the phenomenon of "white flight," the class grew restless, the students flipping pages of newspapers and otherwise evidencing disrespect. Afterward, the two or three black students congratulated me for speaking so straightforwardly, and for using the words "black" and "white." I later asked the professor: How is it possible to teach cases about racial discrimination without mentioning race? "I just teach the neutral principles," he replied; "I don't want to risk upsetting the black students." (And yet it was clear that those most upset were the white students.)

This tendency to neutralize is repeated throughout the law school curriculum: "core" classes carve off and discard some of their most important parts, such as welfare and entitlement programs from tax policy, consumer protection law from commercial contract. And even though the civil rights movement was one of the most singularly transformative forces in the history of constitutional law, very little of it is taught in basic constitutional law classes. (When I took constitutional law, we spent almost no class time on civil rights.) Some schools—by no means all—pick up the pieces by offering such optional courses as Poverty Law, Law and Feminism, or Race and the Law. It is no wonder that the Rehnquist court has been able to cavalierly undo what took so many lives and years to build: the process of legal education mirrors the social resistance to antidiscrimination principles. Subject matter considered to be "optional" is ultimately swept away as uneconomical "special" interests—as thoughtlessly in real life as it has been in law schools.

Ironically, the smooth conceptual bulwark of "neutral principles" has been turned to the task of evading the very hard work that moral reflection in any sphere requires, the constant balancing—whether we act as voters, jurors, parents, lawyers, or laypeople—of rules, precepts, principles, and context. I have always considered developing the ability to engage in such analytical thought to be the highest goal of great universities. Yet even this most traditional of educational missions is under attack. "Should [parents] be paying $20,000 a year to have their children sitting there, figuring out how they feel about what they read?" asks James Barber, founder of the neoconservative National Association of Scholars at Duke University. His question underscores the degree to which the supposed fear of balkanized campuses is in fact the authoritarian's worst nightmare of a world in which people actually think for themselves.

The necessity of thinking long and hard and aloud about the nature of prejudice was exemplified for me when I was visiting Durham, North Carolina, during the 1990 senatorial race between Jesse Helms and Harvey Gantt (the first black to run for that office since Reconstruction). A friend of mine said she wanted me to see something. Without any explanation, she drove me over to Chapel Hill and dragged me to the center of the University of North Carolina campus. There, right in front of the student union, was a statue entitled *The Student Body*. It was a collection of cast bronze figures, slightly smaller than life-size. One was of an apparently white, Mr. Chips–style figure with a satchel of books on his back, pursuing his way. Another was of a young woman of ambiguous racial cast, white or maybe Asian, carrying a violin and some books and earnestly pursuing her way. A third figure was of a young white woman struggling with a load of books stretching from below her waist up to her chin. Then two white figures: a young man holding an open book with one hand; his other arm floating languidly downward, his hand coming to casual rest upon a young woman's buttocks. The young woman leaned into his embrace, her head drooping on his shoulder like a wilted gardenia. In the center of this arrangement was a depiction of an obviously black young man. He was dressed in gym shorts and balanced a basketball on one finger. The last figure was of a solemn-faced young black woman; she walked alone, a solitary book balanced on her head.

It turned out I was about the only one in the state who hadn't heard about this statue. A gift from the class of 1985, it had been the topic of hot debate. Some students, particularly black and feminist students, had complained about the insensitivity of this depiction as representative of the student bod(ies). Other students said the first students were just "being sensitive" (invoked disparagingly, as though numbskulledness were a virtue). At that point the sculptor, a woman, got in on the act and explained that the black male figure was in honor of the athletic prowess of black UNC grads like Michael Jordan, and that the black female figure depicted the grace of black women. The university, meanwhile, congratulated itself publicly on how fruitfully the marketplace of ideas had been stimulated.

As I stood looking at this statue in amazement, I witnessed a piece of the debate-as-education. Two white male students were arguing with a black female student.

"You need to lighten up," said one of the men.

"But . . ." said the black woman.

"Anyway, black women *are* graceful," said the other.

"But," said the black woman as the white men kept talking.

In the end the black woman walked off in tears, while the white men laughed. There is a litany of questions I have heard raised about scenarios like this: Why should the university "protect" minority students against this sort of thing? Don't they have to learn to deal with it?

Let me pose some alternative questions of my own: Why

should universities be in the business of putting students in this sort of situation to begin with? Since when is the persistent reduction of black men and all women to their physical traits "educational" about anything? How is it that these sorts of ignorant free-for-alls are smiled upon by the same university officials who resist restructuring curricula to teach the actual histories of women and peoples of color?

There is a popular insistence that the solution to the struggle over campus multiculturalism is to just talk about it, one-on-one, without institutional sanction or interference. Free speech as free enterprise zone. But this solution makes only certain students— those who are most frequently the objects of harassment—the perpetual teachers, not merely of their histories, but of their very right to be students. This is an immense burden, a mountainous presumption of noninclusion that must be constantly addressed and overcome. It keeps them eternally defensive and reactive.

This denial of legitimacy is not merely an issue for students. The respect accorded any teacher is only in small—if essential— part attributable to the knowledge inside the teacher's head. (If that were all, we would have much more respect for streetcorner orators, the elderly, and the clear uncensored vision of children.) What makes one a teacher is the force lent to one's words by the collective power of institutional convention. If faculty members do not treat women as colleagues, then students will not treat women as members of the faculty.

I think that the ability to be, yes, *sensitive* to one another is what distinguishes the joy of either multiculturalism or willing assimilation from the oppression of either groupthink or totalitarianism. Empathic relation is at the heart of diplomacy, and a little well-deployed diplomacy can keep us from going to war with one another. But the dilemma many people of color face at this moment in the academic and employment world is this: if we respond to or open discussion about belligerent or offensive remarks—that is, if we pursue the much-touted path of respond-

39

ing to hate speech with "more speech"—we are called "PC" and accused of forcing our opinions down the throats of others. If we respond with no matter what degree of clear, dignified control, we become militant "terrorists" of the meek and moderate middle. If we follow the also-prevalent advice to "just ignore it," then we are perceived as weak, humiliated, ineffectual doormats who ought to have told off our harassers on the spot.

It's great to turn the other cheek in the face of fighting words; it's probably even wise to run. But it's not a great way to maintain authority in the classroom or self-respect in the workplace—particularly in a society that abhors "wimps" and considers "kicking ass" a patriotic duty. In such a context, "just ignoring" verbal challenges is a good way to deliver oneself into the category of the utterly powerless. If, moreover, all our colleagues pursue the same path (insult, embarrassed pause, the world keeps on moving as though nothing has happened), then we have collectively created that peculiar institutional silence known as a moral vacuum.

One of the subtlest challenges we face, if we are not to betray the hard-won gains of the last forty years, is how to relegitimate the national discussion of racial, ethnic, and gender tensions so that we can get past the Catch-22 in which merely talking about it is considered an act of war, in which not talking about it is complete capitulation to the status quo, and in which not talking about it is repeatedly covered up with a lot of high-volume substitute talk about the legalities of censorship and the First Amendment. In the long run, taking refuge in such excuses preempts more constructive conversations about how we might reinfuse our pedagogy with dignity and tolerance for all.

The most eloquent summary of both the simplicity and the complexity of that common task remains W. E. B. Du Bois's essay "On Being Crazy":

> After the theatre, I sought the hotel where I had sent my baggage.
> The clerk scowled.
>   "What do you want?"

Rest, I said.

"This is a white hotel," he said.

I looked around. Such a color scheme requires a great deal of cleaning, I said, but I don't know that I object.

"We object," he said.

Then why, I began, but he interrupted.

"We don't keep niggers here," he said, "we don't want social equality."

Neither do I, I replied gently, I want a bed.

Radio Hoods

It is a hallmark of Limbaugh's commentary to provide blue-collar translations of white-collar conservatism, and in doing so to inflect them with tones of anger and outrage that articulate the resentment of a newly disenfranchised social formation, one that had its wallets emptied by Reaganomics while Reaganism massaged its egos.

—John Fiske, *Media Matters: Everyday Culture and Political Change*

Four years ago, I stood at my sink, washing the dishes and listening to the radio. Howard Stern was a popular deejay in New York City but I had never heard of him; he was not the national celebrity he has since become. I was listening to rock'n'roll so I could avoid thinking about the big news from the day before: George Bush had just nominated Clarence Thomas to replace Thurgood Marshall on the Supreme Court. I was squeezing a dot of Lemon Joy into each of the wineglasses when I realized that two smoothly radio-cultured voices, a man's and a woman's, had replaced the music.

"I think it's a stroke of genius on the president's part," said the female voice.

"Yeah," said the male voice. "Then those blacks, those African-Americans, those Negros—hey, 'Negro' is good enough for Thurgood Marshall—whatever they can't make up their minds they want to be called—I'm gonna call them Blafricans. Black Africans. Yeah I like it. Blafricans. Then they can get all upset because now the president appointed a *Blafrican!*"

"Yeah, well, that's the way those liberals think. It's just crazy."

"And then after they turn down his nomination the president can say he tried to please 'em, and then he can go ahead and appoint someone with some intelligence."

Back then, this conversation seemed so horrendously unusual, so singularly hateful, that I picked up a pencil and wrote it down. I was certain that a firestorm of protest was going to engulf the station and purge those foul radio mouths with the good clean soap of social outrage.

I am so naive. When I finally rolled my dial around to where everyone else had been tuned while I was busy watching Cosby reruns, it took me a while to understand that there's a firestorm all right, but not of protest. In the four years since Clarence Thomas has assumed his post on the Supreme Court, crude, in-your-face racism, sexism, anti-Semitism, and homophobia have become commonplace, popularly expressed, and louder in volume than at any time since the beginning of the civil rights movement. Snide polemical bigotry is everywhere—among my friends, on the street, on television in toned-down versions. Unleashed as the new freedom of "what people are really thinking," it has reached its highest pitch in the wildly proliferating phenomenon of right-wing radio shows. Blaring the battle hymn of the First Amendment, these radio programs enshrine a crude demagoguery that makes me heartsick; I feel more and more surrounded by megawatted expressions of hate and discrimination—the coded epithets, the mocking angry glee, the endless tirades filled with nonspecific, nonempirically based slurs against "these people" or "those minorities" or "feminazis" or "liberals" or "scumbags" or "pansies" or "jerks" or "sleazeballs" or "loonies" or "animals" or "foreigners." American popular culture has suddenly been given a megadose of childish turnaround laced with a very adult kind of verbal brutality.

At the same time I am not so naive as to suppose that this is something new. In clear-headed moments I realize I am not listening to the radio anymore; I really am listening to a large segment of white America think aloud and ever louder—resurgent thoughts that have generations of historical precedent. It is as if the radio has split open like an egg, Morton Downey's clones

44

and Joe McCarthy's ghost spilling out, broken yolks, a great collective of sometimes clever, sometimes small, but uniformly threatened brains—they have all come gushing out. Just as they were about to pass into oblivion, Jack Benny and his humble black sidekick, Rochester, get resurrected in the ungainly bodies of Howard Stern and his faithful black henchwoman, Robin Quivers. The culture of Amos 'n' Andy has been revived and reassembled in Bob Grant's radio minstrelsy, radio newcomer Darryl Gates's sanctimonious imprecations on behalf of decent white people, and Jerry Springer's racially and homophobically charged Punch and Judy shows. And in striking imitation of Father Coughlin and of Jesse Helms's nearly forgotten days as a radio host, the far Right has found its undisputed king in the personage of Rush Limbaugh—a polished demagogue with a daily radio audience of at least twenty million, a television show that vies for the top ratings with David Letterman and Jay Leno, a newsletter with a circulation of 360,000, and two best-selling books whose combined sales exceed seven million copies.

While it is probably true that the media are a reflection of America in general, I resist the temptation to say that they are *just* a mirror. From Churchill to Hitler to the old Soviet Union, it is quite clear that radio and television have the power to change the course of history, have the power to proselytize and to coalesce not merely the good and the noble but also the very worst in human nature. When Orson Welles made his famous radio broadcast "witnessing" the landing of a spaceship full of hostile Martians, America ought to have learned a lesson about the power of radio to appeal to mass instincts and crowd panic.

Radio remains a peculiarly powerful medium even today, its visual emptiness in a world of six trillion flashing images allowing one of the few remaining playgrounds for the aural subconscious. Perhaps its power is attributable to our need for an oral tradition, some conveying of stories, feelings, myths of ancestors, epics of alienation and the need to rejoin ancestral roots, even the ignorant bigoted roots. Perhaps the visual quiescence of radio is related to the popularity of electronic networking. It encourages some deep imaginative blindness of which we are barely aware, the busy embodiment being eliminated from view. Only the voice made manifest, the masked and hooded words that can-not—or dare not?—be seen. Just yet. Nostalgia crystallizing into a dangerous future. The preconscious voice erupting into the expressed, the prime time.

The shape of this electronic voice could be anything. What comes out of the modern radio mouth could be the *Iliad*, the *Rubáiyát*, the griot's song of our times. If indeed radio is a vessel for the American Song of Songs, then what does it mean that a manic, racist, penis-obsessed adolescent named Howard Stern is number one among radio listeners, that Rush Limbaugh's wittily smooth sadism has gone the way of prime-time television, and that these men's books tie for the number one slot on all the best-seller lists—Stern's book having had the largest first printing in publishing history. Professor Andy Herz of Touro College Law School sent me this anecdote:

> In my Jurisprudence class this semester, we were discussing John Stuart Mill's notion that the speech of eccentrics should be pro-tected, even if the majority widely frowns upon their unconventional ideas, because their "ravings" against orthodoxy could ultimately lead society to some deeper understanding. Names like Galileo, Darwin, Pearl S. Buck and other early environmentalists were mentioned as good examples. Then someone (seriously) suggested that Howard Stern might fit the same category: a man who also "rants against orthodoxy" and whose views are looked down upon and even censored by some in the majority. What a vision: Howard Stern as the seer of our future society.

I smiled when I first received this letter. But a few weeks later Citizen Stern became the Libertarian Party's candidate for governor of New York—a candidacy cut blessedly short only by Stern's refusal to disclose his personal finances.

What to make of the stories being told by our modern radio evangelists, and their tragic unloved choruses of "dittohead" callers? Is it really just a collapsing economy that spawns this drama of grown people sitting around scaring themselves to death with fantasies of black feminist Mexican able-bodied gay soldiers earning $100,000 a year on welfare who are so criminally depraved that Hillary's hen-pecked husband or the Anti-Christ-of-the-moment had no choice but to invite them onto the government payroll so they can run the country?

As I spin the dial on my radio, I can't help thinking that this stuff must be related to that most poignant of fiber-optic phenomena, phone sex with Jessica Hahn (who now has her own 900 number). Oral sex. Radio racism with a touch of S&M. High-priest hosts with the power and run-amok ego to discipline listeners, to smack with the verbal back-of-the-hand, to smash the button that shuts you up for once and for all. "Idiot!" shouts Bob Grant—and then the sound of a droning telephone emptiness, the voice of dissent dumped out some trapdoor in the aural space. Rush Limbaugh's "splendidly awful taste" and "delightful offensiveness" have been celebrated in the *National Review*. And Howard Stern remains on the air by popular demand at the highest levels of the FCC, thanks to a seemingly insatiable national appetite for blam! and ker-pow! and make-a-big-bathroom-sound and the earth shakes and you get to giggle afterward.

As I have listened to a range of such programs around the country what has struck me as the most unifying theme of this genre is not merely the specific intolerance of such hot topics as race and gender but a much more general contempt for the world, a verbal stoning of anything different. It is like some unusually violent game of "Simon Says," this mockery and shouting down of callers, this roar of incantations, the insistence on agreement. A disrespect so deep as to be satisfying, I suppose, all those shouted epithets and dashed receivers, like a car crash in a movie except you can stay on the safe side of it if only you agree.

But, ah, if you *will* only agree, what sweet and safe reward, what soft enfolding by a stern and angry radio god, oh leader of a righteous nation. And as an added bonus, the invisible shield of an AM community, a family of fans who are Exactly Like You, to whom you can express, with sheltering call-in anonymity, all the filthy stuff you imagine "them" doing to you. The comfort and relief of being able to ejaculate, to those who understand, about the dark imagined excess overtaking, robbing, needing to be held down and taught a good lesson, needing to be put in its place before the ravenous demon enervates all that is true and good and pure in this life.

The panicky exaggeration reminds me of a child's fear . . . *And then, and then, and then, a huge lion jumped out of the shadows and was about to gobble me up and I can't ever sleep again for a whole week, it was the biggest most dangerous lion in the whole world* . . . The irresistible thread of a good story line; a trail of breadcrumbs to an inevitable ending. Yet the panicky exaggeration is not that of a child but that of millions of adults. And the trail of that story line reminds me of nothing so much as the quietly epic subtitles in that great American cornerstone of the silent screen, *The Birth of a Nation: Drunk with wine and power . . . the negroes and carpetbaggers sweep the state . . . men who knew nothing of the uses of authority, except its insolences . . . want to marry a white woman . . . the town given over to crazed negroes . . . the helpless white minority . . . victims of the black mobs . . . a veritable overthrow of civilization.*

If the statistics are accurate, the audience for this genre of radio flagellation is mostly young, white, and male. (For example, 96 percent of Rush Limbaugh's audience is white, about two-thirds of it white men, and 75 percent of Howard Stern's listeners are white men.) Yet it is hard to take the call-in conversations as a genuine barometer of social relations in any sense other than as a measure of nonrelation and just plain ignorance. Most of the callers, by their own testimony, have spent their lives walling themselves off from any real experience with feminists and gays, they certainly don't have any black neighbors, and they avoid and resent all manner of troublesome "types" in the workplace.

In this regard, it is probably true, as former Secretary of Education William Bennett says, that Rush Limbaugh "tells his audience that what you think inside you can talk about in the marketplace." If only that quality of exorcising "what's inside" were the highlighted feature of that statement. Unfortunately, "what's inside" is then mistaken for what's outside, treated as empirical and political reality. The *National Review* extols Limbaugh's conservative leadership as no less than that of Ronald Reagan, and the Republican Party provides Limbaugh with books, stories, angles, and public support. "People were afraid of censure by gay activists, feminists, environmentalists—now they are not because Rush takes them on," says Bennett. Hooray for the cavalry of bad-boy smash-'em-up audacity, for the cruel cowboy hero gone political.

Our history in the United States has been marked by cycles in which brands of this or that hatred come into fashion and go out again, are unleashed and restrained. If racism, homophobia, jingoism, and woman-hating have been features of national life in pretty much all of modern history, it's probably not worth spending much time wondering if right-wing radio is a symptom or a cause. For at least four hundred years, prevailing attitudes in the West have considered blacks less intelligent than whites. When recent statistics show 53 percent of Americans agreeing that blacks and Hispanics are less intelligent and a majority believing that they are lazy, violent, welfare-dependent, and unpatriotic, it's not as though it's ever been a lot better than that. In other words, it's not as though dittoheads needed Rush Limbaugh to tell them what to think—they can be pretty creative on their own. (Once upon a time, I went on Wisconsin public radio to talk about statistics that showed college-educated black men earning much less than similarly qualified white men. Promptly a male caller phoned in to explain that this was because it took a college degree to bring a black man up to the level of a white high school graduate.)

I think that what has made life more or less tolerable for out-groups has been those moments in history when those "inside" feelings were relatively restrained, when angry or bigoted people more or less kept their feelings to themselves. In fact, if I could believe that right-wing radio were only about idiosyncratic, singular, rough-hewn individuals thinking those inside thoughts, I'd be much less concerned. If I could convince myself, as the Columbia University professor Everette Dennis proclaims, that "Stern and Limbaugh make [radio] a more interactive, more personal experience . . . They make it a better, more vibrant medium. It's the triumph of the individual"—then I'd be much more inclined to agree with *Time* magazine's bottom line that "the fact that either is seriously considered a threat . . . is more worrisome than Stern or Limbaugh will ever be." If, moreover, what I were hearing had even a tad more to do with real oppression, with real depression, with real white *and* black levels of joblessness and homelessness, or with the real problems of real white men, then I wouldn't have bothered to slog my way through hours of Howard Stern's miserable obsessions.

Yet at the heart of my anxiety is the worry that Stern, Limbaugh, Grant, et al. represent the very antithesis of individualism's triumph. As the *National Review* said of Limbaugh's ascent, "It was a feat not only of the loudest voice but also of a keen political brain to round up, as Rush did, the media herd and drive them into the conservative corral." "Rush is God / Rush in '96" reads the body paint slathered across the bare backs of two young male fans pictured in *Time* magazine. And when asked about his political aspirations, New York radio demagogue Bob Grant gloated, "I think I would make rather a good dictator."

Were this only about "conservative" politics, I would not be quite so worried, but Limbaugh's so-called dittohead fans are not really conservative in the best sense of that word. The polemics of right-wing radio are putting nothing less than hate onto the airwaves, into the marketplace, electing it to office, teaching it in schools, and exalting it as freedom. What worries me, in other words, is the increasing-to-constant commerce of retribution, control, and lashing out, fed not by fact but by fantasy and very powerful myth. (The media watchdog organization Fairness and Accuracy in Reporting has issued a series of lists of substantial factual errors purveyed by Limbaugh's show. But is anybody listening to that?)

What worries me is the reemergence, more powerful than at any time since the founding of the Ku Klux Klan and the institution of Jim Crow, of a socio-centered self that excludes "the likes of," well, me for example, from the civic circle, and that would rob me of my worth and claim and identity as a citizen. Dittoheadedess has less the character of individualism (or at least what the conventional political imagination would wish individualism to be) than of a mass-produced group identity that knows itself by denunciation and racialized nationalism. As the *Economist* observes, "Mr. Limbaugh takes a mass market—white, mainly male, middle class, ordinary America—and talks to it as an endangered minority."

I worry about this identity whose external reference is neither family nor religion nor the Constitution but a set of beliefs, ethics, and practices that exclude, restrict, and act in the world on me, on mine, as the perceived if not real enemy. I (that is, the likes of me) am acutely aware of losing *my* mythic shield of protective individualism, in the dittohead cosmos, to the surface shapes of my mythic group fearsomeness as black, as female, as left-wing. "I" merge not fluidly but irretrievably into a category of "them"; I become a suspect self, a moving target of loathsome properties, not merely different but dangerous. And it is precisely this unacknowledged contest of groupness—an Invisible Nation of whites locked in mortal combat with an Evil Empire of rascally carpetbaggers and Know-Nothing Negroes—for which the dominant ideology of individualism has no eyes, no vocabulary, and certainly no remedy, that worries me most.

It is interesting, moreover, to note what has happened as Rush Limbaugh has moved from being a small-time talk-show host with lots of noisy callers to a big-time radio host with twenty million listeners willing to be summed up by a pair of ditto marks, to a television personality, seated behind a schoolmaster's desk with an American flag planted on it, with only an applause-metered audience of onlookers and no call-in voices at all. This is, arguably, a progression away from a conversation among those who styled themselves the Little Guys, on to a mean-spirited populism, and finally to an embodiment of Rush Limbaugh as Über-Little-Guy. And this seems dangerously close to those moments when populism passes into fascism, when the common man is condensed into an aggregation, a mass united in one driving symbol. Limbaugh is hardly just an "irreverent individual" under such circumstances; in invoking the name of the common man, he mines a power that is the "addition of all oneness" and uses it to affirm great, coordinated, lock-step political power.

What happens to the lives of those not in lock step with all this translated license, this permission to be uncivil? What happens to the social space that was supposed to have been opened up by the Reconstruction Amendments' injunction against the badges and incidents of institutionalized stigma, the social space that was supposedly at the sweet mountaintop of the civil rights movement's trail? Can I get a seat on the bus without having to be reminded that I *should* be standing? Did the civil rights movement guarantee us nothing more than the freedom to use public accommodations while surrounded by raving bigots? "They didn't beat this idiot [Rodney King] enough," says Howard Stern in the background.

Not long ago I had the misfortune to hail a taxicab in which the driver was listening to Howard Stern undress some woman.

After some blocks, I had to get out. I was, frankly, afraid to ask the driver to turn it off—not because I was afraid of "censoring" him, but because the driver was stripping me too as he leered into the rearview mirror. "Something the matter?" he demanded, still leering, as I asked him to pull over and let me out at the next corner, well short of my destination. (I'll spare you the full story of what happened from there—trying to get another cab, having lots of trouble as cabs speed by me while stopping for all the white businessmen who so much as scratch their heads near the curb; a nice young white man seeing my plight, giving me his cab, having to thank him, he hero, me saved-but-humiliated, cab driver peeved and surly. I fight my way to my destination, arriving in a bad mood, militant black woman, cranky feminazi, gotta watch out for my type, no pleasing that kind.)

When Yeltsin blared rock'n'roll music at his opponents holed up in the Parliament building in Moscow, in imitation of the Marines trying to torture Manuel Noriega in Panama, it occurred to me that it must be like being trapped in a crowded subway car when all the Walkmen are tuned to Bob Grant or Howard Stern. With Howard Stern's voice a tinny, screeching backdrop, with all the faces growing dreamily mean as though some soporifically evil hallucinogen were gushing into their bloodstreams, I'd start clawing at the doors, begging to surrender, for sure.

Surrender to what? Surrender to the laissez-faire resegregation that is the metaphoric significance of the hundreds of Rush Rooms that have cropped up in restaurants around the country; rooms broadcasting Limbaugh's words, rooms for your listening pleasure, rooms where bigots can capture the purity of a Rush-only lunch counter, rooms where all those unpleasant others just "choose" not to eat? Surrender to the naughty luxury of a room in which a Ku Klux Klan meeting could take place in orderly, First Amendment fashion? Everyone's "free" to come in (and a few of you outsiders do), but mostly the undesirable nonconformist non-dittoheads are gently repulsed away. It's a high-tech world of enhanced choice, you see. Whites choose mostly to sit in the Rush Room; feminists, blacks, and gays "choose" to sit elsewhere. No need to buy black votes, you just pay blacks not to vote; no need to insist on white-only schools, you just sell them on the desirability of black-only schools. No need for signs and police to enforce the separation of gay from straight; non-conformist troublemakers will herd themselves nicely in the face of a din of racist, sexist, homophobic babble. Just sit back and watch it work, like those invisible shock shields that keep dogs cowering in their own backyards.

How real is the driving perception behind all the Sturm und Drang of this genre of radio harangue—the perception that white men are an oppressed minority, with no power and no opportunity in the land that they made great? While it is true that power and opportunity are shrinking for all but the very wealthy in this country (and would that Limbaugh would take that issue on), white men remain this country's most privileged citizens and market actors, firmly in control of almost all major corporate and political power. In contrast, according to the *Wall Street Journal,* "Blacks were the only racial group to suffer a net job loss during the 1990–91 economic downturn, at the companies reporting to the Equal Employment Opportunity Commission. Whites, Hispanics and Asians, meanwhile, gained thousands of jobs." Three years of black gains were wiped out between July 1990 and March 1991, the dates of the last recession. "While whites gained 71,144 jobs at these companies, Hispanics gained 60,040 and Asians gained 55,104, blacks lost 59,479." And while right-wing radio deejays complain that unqualified minorities are taking all the jobs in academia, that white men need not apply, they ignore the degree to which, as a result of the economy, the pool of available academic jobs itself is what has been shrinking, and not just in the United States. Moreover, the number of minority undergraduate and graduate students is declining dramatically: Stanford University, for example, has suffered a 10 percent decline in minority Ph.D. enrollments since 1988, and that statistic reflects a national decline. In fact, there aren't enough people of color in the world to do justice to that expanding balloon of fear felt by white men who think that they have been dispossessed by hordes of the "less qualified."

It certainly cannot be said that minorities are taking over the jobs of radio disc jockeys. In 1993 the *Los Angeles Times* found "only 12 full-time weekday hosts who are members of minority groups among the 1000 or so general-market talk stations. Three of them are on public radio, which tends to be more liberal." And of that small number, a good portion are conservative blacks, although even conservative blacks have trouble in such a race-conscious market: Ken Hamblin, a conservative disc jockey in Denver who rails against "blacks," "black leaders," and the entire civil rights movement, "mentioned on air he was black. The phone lines suddenly went dead, and he had to filibuster his remaining four hours on air."

I think this reaction may be related to the rather fixed way in which all blacks are seen as allied with "radical" causes, no matter what right-wing claptrap they spout. How else can it be that City College of New York professor Leonard Jeffries, who teaches that blacks are sun people and whites are colder, harder, ice people, was held up to be such a symbol of multiculturalism, for example, when his theories revealed him as nothing if not a committed *mono*culturalist? When Khalid Muhammad (the Nation of Islam's national representative) indulged in his notorious anti-Semitic "bloodsucker" rantings, I was curious about why the mainstream media did not just condemn his words, as of course was proper, but condemned them as symbolic of a fearsome black radical Left—this when, except for the fact that he was black, his message was indistinguishable from that of far right-wingers like David Duke.

Similarly, I wonder why Charles Murray's or Richard Herrnstein's or Michael Levin's Nazi-like sociobiological theories of the inferiority of blacks are always so protected from the political vagaries of either Right or Left and graced as "science." And if we can understand what is so upsetting about Louis Farrakhan's famous excesses, one wonders why Senator Ernest Hollings's calling Africans cannibals—in the *Congressional Record* no less—should be received with barely a ho-hum.

What if whites understood Leonard Jeffries not as a "radical" but as a mirror image of a more general American right-winger with a taste for the delicious power of racial pornography? Perhaps some dawning but wrong-headed recognition of this connection motivated *Time* magazine's odd characterization of the call to black leaders to denounce black anti-Semitism as "just another kind of bigotry"—not because such calls single out only black leaders and only when it is black prejudice that is at issue, but because such efforts are purportedly attempts to "enforc[e] racial correctness." My guess is that the author of this astounding bit of moral dismissiveness also might feel that speaking out against white fraternity brothers who stage a slave auction is just another attempt at "enforcing political correctness." As A. M. Rosenthal observed in the *New York Times,* "Not a word did *Time* print to indicate that it ever crossed its collectivized-journalism mind that black leaders who denounced [anti-Semitic] speech really might despise it, that maybe they stood up because they liked that stance in life." Rather than a movement to pressure the full leadership structure of our entire society to look at itself and condemn all forms of bigotry, the intense reductionism in discourse about First Amendment rights in recent years seems to have resulted in an odd formula according to which groups have a *right* to be as racist as they wannabe, and no one else has a *right* to be offended unless they actually get hit.

Unbirthing the Nation

You or I, we'd die, but not a Negro. They're too dumb to go into shock.

—Sergeant Stacey Koon

In his book *Parallel Time*, the *New York Times* editor Brent Staples describes an interview for a job with the *Washington Post* during which he was questioned intensely, not just about his schooling and exemplary employment background, but about the professions, ages, and whereabouts of his parents and siblings:

> These were what I'd come to call The Real Negro questions. He wanted to know if I was a Faux, Chevy Chase, Maryland Negro or an authentic nigger who grew up in the ghetto besieged by crime and violence. White people preferred the latter, on the theory that blacks from the ghetto were the real thing. Newspaper editors preferred them on the theory that they made better emissaries to the ghetto. My inquisitor was asking me to explain my existence. Why was I successful, law-abiding, and literate, when others of my kind filled the jails and the morgues and the homeless shelters? A question that asks a lifetime of questions has no easy answer. The only honest answer is the life itself.

I think very few African-Americans have not had such an encounter—a series of questions from an often very well meaning white person who is not just curious about you but is trying to make you "fit" into some preconceived box of blackness. I remember once being pressed by a student who, despite all my best deflections, asked me a series of increasingly intimate yet clinical questions culminating in the humdinger of whether the house I grew up in was free-standing.

And once the "fit" has been made it's very hard to exist as a real human being in the cage of those too-easy assumptions. The power of de facto segregation in all areas of American life is still so strong that very few African-Americans are not directly affected by poverty, crime, and discrimination. Very few have not seen or known poverty at an intimate level—grown up in it, had relatives who are poor. Very few have not been affected by housing or employment discrimination or the rising rate of hate crimes. Very few, no matter how well off, have escaped the criminal justice system's hypervigilant patrolling for "suspect profiles." Margaret Burnham, a well-regarded Boston lawyer, recently wrote of her young godson's being picked up by police after he got lost on his way to visit her and stopped to ask for directions. A neighbor had called, alleging that a "suspicious-looking black male" was asking questions about the area.

Who are we—middle class or impoverished?—when we are all and everywhere guilty until proven innocent (except perhaps in the fairyland of O. J. Simpson's courtroom, where the presumption of innocence is endlessly intoned like some sardonic knell).

Many whites seem unable to put the realities of such social circumstances together with either the tenaciously held stereotypes of ghetto residents or the nicely dressed, middle-class images of the occasional black person they encounter. "Why should I go campaigning among a bunch of welfare mothers and drug addicts?" asked a candidate for a high Massachusetts public office not long ago; he was speaking of Roxbury, the largely black community where my industrious, sober, and very middle-class parents live alongside a lot of other industrious, struggling, underserved, and dismissed potential constituents. "What could he know of poverty?" a colleague once asked idly, referring to a presentation by Charles Ogletree, a Harvard Law School professor and frequent host of PBS roundtables and civic forums.

"Let's be real," he said. "He teaches at Harvard." Yet, as Sara Lawrence-Lightfoot documents in her magnificent ethnography of the black middle class, *I've Known Rivers,* Professor Ogletree, whose father never completed grammar school, grew up in a family of migrant field workers, in circumstances too many would be too hasty to dismiss as "typically underclass."

Who are we—authentic or faux?—when the very insistence on such division slices like a knife through the intensity and complexity of our life's connections.

If, as Staples says, the only real answer to such impossible dichotomizing is the life itself, then now is perhaps the moment to issue a broad challenge to the popularly purveyed television understandings in which figures like Oprah Winfrey or Bryant Gumbel, who are really more upper middle class or just plain rich, are made to stand as icons of what ordinary blacks could achieve if only they'd work a little harder—thus negating not only the extraordinary talents, luck, and philanthropy of the black upper class but also the existence and vitality of the black working class as a powerful and productive part of American society.

In this vein, Mitchell Duneier's *Slim's Table* offers compelling glimpses of black working-class life and struggle. Duneier's book, an ethnography of black lower-middle-class men who frequent the Valois "See Your Food" cafeteria in the Hyde Park area of Chicago, very effectively pinpoints one of the major flaws in white characterizations of black social life: the blanket elimination from collective consciousness of the black working class. "The prevalent dichotomy between middle class and underclass," Duneier observes, "has resulted in a tendency to associate any 'respectable' behavioral characteristics in black people with a middle-class orientation." Moreover, "Men like the regulars at Valois, who like other members of society are to be sure influenced in some measure by such reports, are themselves prone to talk about the black population in terms of these crude distinctions. They do so as if they themselves are somehow insignificant or exist outside the mass that makes a difference. The prevalent imagery of the black class structure renders the most effective agents of social control in the black community irrelevant in the debate over the future of their own people."

Disregarding this category of black humanity who work so hard at the hardest jobs in America means that blacks who do indeed rise into the middle class end up being figured only as those who were *given* whatever they enjoy, and the black "under-class" becomes those whose sole life activity is *taking*. No work, no earning, no effort. Blacks at either end of this polar configuration thievishly feast on the misbegotten generosities of foolish (white) liberals who'll give away the candy store if you don't watch out.

Furthermore, these characterizations create tensions centered on the myth of "all these middle-class blacks with all this money," usually illustrated by a tiny handful of blacks who, again, are probably better described as upper class—with books on the *New York Times* best-seller list and MacArthur grants and million-dollar businesses. This group is then "modeled" as the blanket prescription for the malaise and dispossession of kids in the projects. But if that were the answer, the *Cosby Show* would have cured world hunger by now.

The myth that the problems of the inner city are due to lack of middle-class role models—as Duneier points out, there are many good, hard-working moral models in black communities even if they don't make quite enough money to be in America's middle class—ignores the well-documented effects of urban blight and displacement that are in far greater measure responsible for fostering the Al Capone-ish, Prohibition-style wars that have ravaged ghettos. John Edgar Wideman describes the decaying neighborhood where his father lives:

> People's energies and hungers tax the structures they inhabit. When natural energies and hungers have no healthy outlet, they feed on their hosts, attack friends and family, the physical environment.

Destroying what's close, the people they should love and probably do love, the walls, the elevators, street lamps, and furniture, the civilized fabric of households, schools, a person sitting on the next bar stool or the guy on his way home from bussing dishes in a fast-food joint, the senior citizen who's just cashed a social security check. What gets torn up is what you can get your hands on.

There is a tremendous lack of clarity about what middle class means when it comes to blacks in any event. As previously mentioned, it's a mushy category that compresses working class with upper class with celebrity super-status—Bill Cosby, Dr. Huxtable, the security guard at my bank, and I are all frequently referred to as middle class. Sometimes, however, it has nothing to do with class as such, and everything to do with skin color or hair "grades" or with whether you speak Received Standard English, or with whether white people feel subjectively comfortable with you, or with whether you're married or "motivated."

Whatever the combination of features attributed to it, the black middle class is almost always used in conventional parlance to teach, to model, to pacify, to instruct in the virtues of endless striving and individualism with maybe a break for group prayer. Paragons, that black middle class. Yet here again there are widely accepted, pervasively inaccurate, romantic fictions about how blacks lived in class-blind harmony under Jim Crow's segregation—poor and rich, side by side, role-modeling up a storm of nostalgia—as opposed to today, when selfish buppie professionals take their skills and move to the suburbs. These images ignore what Duneier points to as the best-detailed survey on the subject of the black middle class, W. E. B. Du Bois's *The Philadelphia Negro*, published in 1899: "They are not the leaders or the ideal-makers of their own group in thought, work or morals. They teach the masses to a very small extent, mingle with them but little, do not largely hire their labor . . . the first impulse of the best, the wisest and the richest is to segregate themselves from the masses."

Nobody who's black doesn't know those old divisions—that's how Clarence Thomas was able to play both ends against the middle during his hearings. Yet the facts as well as the numbers are imagined freely in the thickly swirling stereotypes that surround us. "Most" blacks are middle class when the analysis is convenient: the huge, teeming, overemployed, better-than-ever-off middle class, demanding, insistent, arrogant—dismissed in many of the terms abounding in the rhetoric of anti-Semitism. Then in a flick of the eye, "most" blacks are underclass: innumerably teeming, underemployed,   better-off-than-the-poor-anywhere-on-earth, yet demanding, insistent, cheating and arrogant—dismissed in the same old rhetoric of racism.

Within the black community, the middle class has tradition- ally been composed of the favored sons and daughters of the master, the doctors, lawyers, and undertakers with money or education, the "talented tenth"—usually the light-skinned, al- though an occasional dark-skinned one was "forgiven" for or "saved" from his hue by fervent religiosity, compulsive moral exactitude, and hypercorrected polysyllabic rhetorical skills. Stern, intolerantly self-effacing, dedicated to "uplift" of the race yet implicated as often in the denigration of its neediest mem- bers. So upstanding they're enraged. So exceptional they're des- perately lonely. So virtuous they're bitter with the sacrifice, the never enjoying, the always being on display. So frozen in the viewfinders of racial anxiety they don't move much. Can't afford a single wrong step. The rounded bombast of the eternal spokesmen, the practiced vowels, syllables, words of those per- petually onstage.

The malleability of what "middle class" means runs far beyond the context of black social life, of course. The dictionary conveys some of the complex history of the image of the bourgeoisie, "middle-class" being variously defined as synonymous with thrifty, greedy, smug, conventional, commonplace, respectable, hard-working, and shallow. To understand the stereotypes of black middle-classness, it probably is necessary to look at this contradictory underside of its racialized disparagement, the imported echo of the class wars of England and Europe: middle-classness as the anxious status of those who are snobs, their aspirations outstripping their means, those who are complacent, vain and vulgar, prying, too proud, and utterly absorbed with appearances. In fact, the formula for the stereotype of the black middle class is straight out of Jane Austen when you think about it, but with one important difference: In the United States, blacks are the "unassimilable ethnics," while the very definition of white middle-classness is the complete lack of ethnic markers. What gets eliminated in the black version, therefore, is any subplot of the honest, nose-to-the-grindstone worker: "In the popular imagination . . . only white society has a complete class structure that includes 'respectable' lower classes that work." In the new world order, the only blacks are pimps and thieves or dandies and foolish dreamers. No honest bakers, suffering mill-workers, wronged virgins, stiff-upper-lipped victims of the "marster's" vile temper. Where is Charles Dickens when we need him?

This cultural representation of blacks is complicated: Americans, while purportedly embracing a political ideology of complete classnessness, nevertheless turn to their dark, designated "under"-class for great splashes of ghetto adrenaline. It's better than amphetamines, an injectable *frisson,* like a wake-up call piquing the otherwise silent majority into a raging moral froth: Yonder lies the moral precipice, beware. America just loves that stuff: Rush Limbaugh and verisimilitudinous cop shows like *911* wouldn't be so popular if it weren't for this immense voyeuristic addiction. At the same time, the white world turns to "the black middle class," so designated, for warm hugs of racial reconciliation. Whites seem to reassure themselves that things are just fine but for a few rabble-rousing rioters because after all the black middle class is so darn happy, so well-off, so privileged it positively *whines.*

But as the journalist Ellis Cose warns, "Formidable though the difficulties of the so-called underclass are, America can hardly afford to use the plight of the black poor as an excuse for blinding itself to the difficulties of the black upwardly mobile . . . one must at least consider the possibility that a nation which embitters those struggling hardest to believe in it and work within its established systems is seriously undermining any effort to provide would-be hustlers and dope dealers with an attractive alternative to the streets."

Sometimes I wonder how many of our present cultural clashes are the left-over traces of the immigrant wars of the last century and the beginning of this one, how much of our reemerging jingoism is the scar that marks the place where Italian kids were mocked for being too dark-skinned, where Jewish kids were taunted for being Jewish, where poor Irish rushed to hang lace curtains at the window as the first act of climbing the ladder up from social scorn, where Chinese kids were tortured for not speaking good English.

I think of some Russian neighbors of ours when I was growing up (most of the whites in that section of Boston at that time were working-class first-generation immigrants). There were two girls in the family; the older one was an excellent student and went on to attend college. Her accomplishment, however, was met with great ambivalence within her family, much of it no doubt provoked by her affectation of a bourgeois snobbishness. She cast continual aspersions upon the family for what she perceived as its provincialism and its embarrassing conformity to old ways (cast as lack of conformity to "the mainstream," her term for a naturalized, universalized upwardly mobile middle class). While this young woman's accomplishments were indeed the source of much pride in her family, they were also the source of at least as much anxiety—as her younger sister once expressed it to me, she became a kind of "chafing agent" abrading the family's already insecure sense of how it fit into the social order of the United States.

The elder sister, who lost her rich Russian-inflected accent for a terse version of Boston Brahmin in her first semester of college, was pretty hard to take, I remember, endlessly promoting herself as a Citizen of the World, able to wade in all waters, tasting widely, knowing all, possessing everything. She became suffused with a passion for openness, a compulsion for boundlessness—compulsive because so tied to fear of being bounded, so linked to fear of being made fun of for being "too ethnic," too closed, too ignorant of "the larger society." While this should in no way be taken as a necessarily bad thing, it can signal a lost balance, a sacrifice of appreciation for the bonds, the links, the ties that bind, that make family, connection, identity.

I wonder, in these times of heated put-down, about the genealogy of the sometimes quite irrational fears of what has been labeled "identity politics." Some identity politics is genuinely fearsome, genuinely rooted in neo-fascist tendencies—but the larger measure of concern strikes me as a not-yet-resolved, peculiarly American anxiety about our immigrant, peasant, sharecropper roots. Some of it strikes me as a demand for conformity to what keeps being called the "larger" American way, a coerced rather than willing assimilation in which there is little room for accounts of the Ellis Island variety of the past as contiguous with the present—accounts that are thought to be incompatible with some static image of a monolithic, preexisting rather than vividly evolving American culture.

One day I was shopping for rugs in a store in New York City. The rug salesman was an amiable young man, whose ethnicity I couldn't begin to guess, but who in the assimilative order of most parts of the United States generally would be identified as "white." The rugs I was considering were in a huge heavy heap in the middle of the floor, and the store had positioned two men beside the pile to peel back the layers of rugs for customer viewing. The two rug turners were handsome brown men, perhaps South Asian, but, again, I'm a bad guesser. They spoke very halting English, with a distinct British rather than American inflection. At one point they apparently misunderstood which rug I wanted to see; the salesman curtly corrected them, and then turned to me, rolled his eyes, and sighed in all apparent seriousness: "It's *so* hard to find good help these days."

Now I am definitely the wrong person with whom to lodge such a complaint, but before I could begin what he would have undoubtedly found to be a very annoying disquisition, the salesman reached over and carelessly, messily, flipped back the edge of the top rug. One of the rug turners, who was clearly seething, snapped at him to take his hands off that rug, that that was their job, and then said, very carefully, but with great passion: "What's the matter, don't you understand English?"

I was struck by how quickly and completely the person marked as lower-status had learned to steal the power and thunder of the higher-status person's insult by turning it back on itself. There was something about this exchange that marked a ritual of assimilative initiation: Did someone hurl those words at the salesman's great-grandmother as she scrubbed floors, or did he just hear them in a movie? Will the high sarcasm of the rug turner's remark lose its irony and retain only its demand as the rug turners or their children lose their accents but keep the gesture of power?

One of the unique features of the social positioning of black middle-classness is that for the vast majority of us it is impossible to ever really "pass" into the oblivion of middle-class Yuppiedom, where people are more likely to repress their ethnicity or their religion than, say, their libido. It would be sadly ironic, then, if either blacks or whites missed the lessons of that positioning and failed to grasp the moral insight that comes from being simultaneously in the position to hire the proverbial "help" and in the position of being constantly taken *for* the help.

Sometimes it seems as if the amalgamated "white" middle class of today has lost its sense of derivation from the poor, the tired, the hungry, huddled masses who so threatened the ruling classes of a century ago—an amnesia so complete that the easiest way of gaining access to the United States these days is to buy one's way in by throwing a few million into the business interest of one's choice. If, then, the Statue of Liberty's great motto gets retired just at the point when the homeless, huddled masses of the world are mostly brown and black, perhaps it becomes all the more urgent a calling of the black middle class, those possessed of the precious and painful double vision that W. E. B. Du Bois described as distinguishing blacks living on the edge, to reinfuse the notion of American, and, dare we hope, global, family. "Bring me all of your dreams / You dreamers," wrote Langston Hughes. "Bring me all of your heart melodies / That I may wrap them / In a blue cloud-cloth / Away from the too-rough fingers / Of the world."

Representations of racial and gender inequality in the United States are complicated further by the extent to which Europeans and European-Americans consider and battle among themselves as "minorities." It is easy to allow the relative freedoms found by some European immigrants in the "new world" of the United States to obscure the experiences of terrible discrimination in the "old world" against women, Jews, gays, and certain ethnic groups. And it is easy to overgeneralize from the privileges of this country's great wealth by making money or its lack the explanation for all divisions here. In doing so, however, one underestimates the extent to which markets themselves may be deeply distorted by racial and gender prejudice; one loses sight of the fact that some "successfully assimilated" ethnics in the United States have become so only by paying the high cost of burying forever languages, customs, and cultures. In short, one risks making invisible even the most explicitly biased, irrational, and cruel forms of exploitation by denying the commonalities of a hand-me-down heritage of devalued humanity, even as our specific experiences with that devaluation may differ widely with time and place. The ability to see, and to fully understand, the desperate socioeconomic circumstances of blacks in the United States is, therefore, intricately linked with those evolving histories and the analytical conundrums they present for us all.

Against this backdrop, and in view of the relatively advantaged situation of whites and particularly white men in the United States, the constantly bunkered sense of transgressed rights that appears to be the chief theme of much right-leaning radio and television probably needs more excavation to be understood as the powerfully appealing narrative of "white" (versus ethnic) neonationalism that it appears to have become. I think the appeal is attributable to at least two factors: the persuasive form of the narrative itself; and the ennobling romantic vision of its content, in which tropes of local inclusion or representation are played out against the backdrop of intense global debates about democracy, citizenship, and community.

There are any number of junctures in history where a shift in the boundaries of law or some political movement has been signaled by very particular uses of rhetoric, peculiar twists of the popular imagination. American presidents, for example, routinely attempt to harness the irresistible rhetorical movement of the Puritan jeremiad as a persuasive form by intertwining the language of divine proclamation with that of political mission. At the same time, the appeal for equality, of African-Americans and many others, has always been boosted by the power of great rhetorical moments. During the entire civil rights movement, social activists were at their most effective when they were able to capture certain material events within the metaphoric unfolding of destiny, or of apocalypse, or of nature and "the natural." Martin Luther King's heart-wrenching vision of the mountaintop owes much, of course, to the oral traditions of Africa, but also to the forms of political discourse that influenced the Boston missionaries and New England abolitionists whose words have so necessarily infiltrated the expression of black aspiration.

But it is also true that the deepest of our social divisions have been powerfully perpetuated by precisely such devices. From the earliest Supreme Court cases, the authority of the law was hitched to a myth of compelling mission and a sacred vision, an endowment emanating from God but ultimately speaking through the naturalized logic of positivism. The dispossession of aboriginal people from their land was accomplished by legal opinions that figured the land in question as "virgin," a holy female, a queen whose honor is upheld in the very fact of conquest. The legal awards of "charter" "title," "fee," and "possession" wrested land not from Native American peoples but from "idleness," "wilderness," and "emptiness."

This particular way of imagining is not just How the West Was Won; it has characterized much of the "impersonal" discourse of conquest and exclusion throughout our jurisprudence. If "the wilderness" was a term whose use effectively obliterated the existence of the humans who lived there, "the underclass" is a contemporary device directed to very much the same end. This issue of class is underscored by the vocabulary of the so-called taxpayer revolt, which, while rooted in the sober reality of a stunning national deficit, has found unfortunate expression in a bitter discourse of deservedness in which the deserving are those whose material accumulation identifies them as those who "can't" "keep on" paying taxes, while the undeserving are figured as those who supposedly "don't" pay taxes. Making the streets "safe for taxpaying citizens," for example, has become a rallying point for the criminalization or institutionalization of the homeless in cities as supposedly "liberal" as San Francisco and New York. As Mike Davis has observed in his book *City of Quartz,* "restaurants and markets have responded to the homeless by building ornate enclosures to protect their refuse. Although no one in Los Angeles has yet proposed adding cyanide to the garbage, as happened in Phoenix a few years back, one popular seafood restaurant has spent $12,000 to build the ultimate bag-lady-proof trash cage: made of three-quarter-inch steel rod with alloy locks and vicious outturned spikes to safeguard priceless moldering fishheads and stale french fries."

A friend tells the story of her young niece, who is growing up in New York City. The little girl and a friend were walking into their apartment building when they saw an old man who lived on the street. "Hi, Sam," said my friend's niece, for she and her parents saw him every day and had grown to know him. The other little girl ran at once to her parents and said, very distressed, "You can't call a homeless a name! Mommy, she called a homeless a name!" It is telling, this story, the blanket anonym of "a homeless" revealing the extent to which a whole generation of children are being taught not to see those who live all around them. The very simplest of social exchanges struck this little girl as something like a blasphemous epithet against the safe borders of what exists, of what *can* be known and named.

Similarly, if "underclass" is a way of unnaming the poor, "whiteness" is a way of not-naming ethnicity. And "blackness" has been used as a most effective way of marking the African-American quest for either citizenship or market participation as the very antithesis: blacks are defined as those whose expressed humanity is too often perceived as "taking" liberties, whose submission is seen as a generous and proper "gift" to others rather than as involving personal cost.

The romance of racism, in which professions of liberty and inseparable union could simultaneously signify and even reinforce an "American" national identity premised on deep social division, is, again, the central paradox of our times. D. W. Griffith's filmic paean to the founding of the Ku Klux Klan, *The Birth of a Nation*, ends with all the features of a classic jeremiad, imploring the Invisible Empire of decent white people who care about their daughters to dare to "dream of a Golden Day when the Bestial War shall rule no more. But instead the gentle Prince in the Hall of Brotherly Love in the City of Peace." The last scene of that movie shows a hall full of industrious white citizens attired in togas, in an apparent state of fraternal bliss, a giant, ghostly figure of Jesus Christ hovering above them all. "Liberty and Union, One and Inseparable, Now and Forever!" reads the very last subtitle.

I would like to explore the suggestion that at least part of the sense of victimization of "oppressed" or "trumped" white men is primed by a certain class coding in the appeals of many right-wing political figures and media commentators. I began to take this possibility seriously during the media blare about the attack on the figure skater Nancy Kerrigan, allegedly engineered by the shady retinue of her rival, Tonya Harding. I was startled by mainstream "respectable" print and television media's repeated characterization of Harding and company as "poor white" or even "white trash." Then, weeks into the debacle, I heard an interview with residents of East Portland, Oregon, the neighborhood in which Harding grew up. In the eyes of these people, Tonya Harding was a heroine—and for precisely the reasons for which the dominant media opinion attacked her. She was tough, she was crafty, she had muscles, she could throw back a few beers with the boys, wasn't too fanatic to have a cigarette every now and again; she was *not* America's sweetheart, *not* Cinderella, *not* Pollyanna, this little girl who knew trucks and could handle a chainsaw. What could be better than that?

Indeed, I thought. Might really be handy to be able to overhaul an engine.

With that interview, I began to listen much more closely for insulting and dehumanized depictions of poor whites in the mainstream media, even those too "respectable" to use overt markers like "white trash." The *New Yorker*, for example, ran a piece about the community of Clackamas County, where Harding lives, where her fan club is based, where the rink at which she learned to skate is located. Even as the piece purported to air the felt sense of class division ("'Trailer trash is what they call people out here,' [said a member of Harding's fan club]"), it exudes a profoundly insulting voyeuristic condescension. The author lingers on the physical attributes of everyone she meets: the bodies of the natives range from "meaty" to "fleshy." "Ruddy faces" are set with "pinkish eyelids" which are, in the case of the girls, "rimmed in black liner." Their dispositions run from "weary" to "jittery." Their children are "restless," "shrill-voiced," and "strange." Their hair is "greased-back" or "frosted" or "fading" or "stringy blond." They wear "inexpensive-looking clothing" like "worn-out chambray work shirt[s]" and "plastic windbreaker[s]." Even as the natives insist that Clackamas is a "good neighborhood" and "a very warmy place," the author warns the Gentle Reader that while such words may "make it sound soothing and regular," it's really "more haphazard and disjointed." In fact, every evidence of habitation and community is read right out of existence in this piece: the author finds only a wilderness of "drab rooms," floors that "felt hollow," houses that "look as though they had been built for dolls or chickens," "tumbledown farmhouses," "idle pastures" and "weedy tracts waiting to be seized and subdivided." "There really isn't a town of Clackamas," opines the New Yorker on safari; ". . . there are pockets of businesses having to do with toys and mufflers and furniture, but there really isn't any town to speak of, or even a village to drive through."

Once I developed an eye and an ear for it, I began to see the vast body of sitcoms, talk shows, editorials, and magazines as not just "mainstream" but class-biased and deeply hypocritical. The most interesting aspect of this hypocrisy rests, I think, in the wholesale depiction of poor whites as bigoted, versus the portrayal of enlightened, ever-so-*liberal* middle and upper classes who enjoy the privilege of thinking of themselves as "classless." I can well imagine that this might encourage residents of communities from East Portland, Oregon, to Charlestown, Massachusetts, to hear the word "liberal" as just another synonym for hypocrite.

If I hold in my mind this particular construction of a "powerful liberal media," then I begin to understand how poor whites would feel victimized by their image in the media, in very much the same way as blacks feel victimized by theirs. But blacks, by and large, tend to call the identical phenomenon the product of "conservative" or "right-wing" rather than liberal media, perhaps because no one has ever tried to market bigotry against blacks (as conceivably they have with bigotry against poor whites) as "liberalism." It is instructive to see how the experience of race puts enough of a spin on just this much of the vocabulary that in spite of an arguably shared experience, blacks and poor whites end up on opposite sides of a right-left divide. And looking at it this way gives me some insight into how those who are in one sense aligned with a powerful majority could feel so paradoxically threatened, *as* a "minority" in a world overrun *by* "minorities."

If this has any validity, then the complex ideological overlays of everyday racial dramas can only confound the picture further. In one direction, it might be argued that many African-Americans understand aspects of white blue-collar life as similar to their own. As the media expert John Fiske observes, the cartoon character Bart Simpson's "defiance, his street smarts, his oral skills, together with his rejection, appeared to resonate closely with many African Americans. The Simpsons are a blue-collar family whose class difference from mainstream America is frequently emphasized, and as race is often encoded into class, so class difference can be decoded as racial. Bart's double disempowerment, by class and age, made him readily decodable as socially 'Black.'"

But from the other direction, I think it is very hard for lower-class whites to decode *themselves* as socially black—there is simply too much representational force militating against it. I keep thinking back to the paradigm of *Birth of a Nation,* in which upper-class whites were depicted not merely as suffering at the hands of out-of-control blacks but also as suffering lowered status at the hands of northern "radicals"—a misfortune that eventually brought them to such despair that ladies had to trim their frocks with unprocessed cotton, or "poor man's lace." By the same token, in Margaret Mitchell's *Gone with the Wind,* Scarlett O'Hara is a woman of great "breeding" unjustly reduced by crazed Yankee social engineering, a point made most memorable by her having to tear down the velvet curtains in order to clothe herself according to her lost station. These images tap into powerful myths that invite the average American working-class dreamer—who is, after all, the intended consumer of such romantic pulp—to imagine a great and primeval fall from Edenic upper-class status, *and to do so in racial terms.*

The rhetoric of such southern gothic dramas bears the earmarks of a poor man's jeremiad—the mythic sense of banishment from the classier classes, the pathetic grace of struggle against the odds, the conjunction of just deserts and a clever needle (or a shiny pair of ice skates) saving the day for a brighter tomorrow when North and South, rich and poor shall sit down at the same table and be properly waited on by you-know-who. But it is also a jeremiad in which the borders of the lower-class wilderness are guarded by federally funded "outsiders" who "don't understand" and who block exodus to the promised land by unleashing running-dog hordes of black heathens and criminal "elements" who *belong* in a wilderness.

It is not surprising that empirical information has such a hard time standing up to the passionate desire to don crinoline; and it is not surprising, I suppose, if a badly written rip-off sequel to the badly written original of *Gone with the Wind* can just about outstrip the Bible in worldwide sales, that some savvy disc jockeys spinning the same yarn could capture quite a lot of market share.

Given deep patterns of social segregation and general ignorance of history, particularly racial history, the media remain the principal source of most Americans' knowledge of one another, as well as most of the rest of the world. While the degree to which the media can teach or disinform, entertain or incite, induce passivity or provoke violence is the subject of endless debate, I subscribe to a school that argues that the media do have a significant role to play in both demonstrating and reformulating civic, national, and a host of other allegiances and group identities. While it is beyond the scope of this book and my expertise to try and prove that this is so, a few examples will indicate that even just assuming it for the sake of argument is a valuable exercise.

The most immediate and easiest example is, of course, advertising: whole industries rise and fall on the ability of words and images to sway mass opinions, tastes, and actions. The second example is the more theoretical role of a free press in our political philosophy: the free exchange of information is understood to be not merely influential but central to this country's vision of itself as democratic. Third, the last thirty years have seen a snowballing phenomenon combining these two aspects of media potential: the Madison Avenue marketing of political candidates and causes. Again without having to conclude that the media have any "real" effect at all, it is very clear that billions of dollars have been spent on the likelihood of their propagandistic, even hypnotic power.

If we throw into the calculation the very narrow channels of access to the media, and the very closely held circles of ownership of the media, then the increasing resemblance between the "free press" and a string of infomercials demands close scrutiny indeed. Or, if the media aren't all that important, then at the very least we may need to retheorize the idea of democracy in a system in which a supposedly free, independent, publicly interested press becomes an explicitly privately interested, corporately sponsored, patron-subsidized business-for-profit.

Whether any of this also means that the media alone can actually incite violence or cultural bias is the hottest of debates, as vociferously denied by some as it is proclaimed by others. Examples such as the careful control of the media exercised by the Pentagon during the Gulf War are difficult: some might say that the kind of mass persuasion it takes to coalesce a nation's belief in the possibility of a "computerized," "surgically clean" war is different from the kind of persuasion the Disney Corporation exercises in purveying those fictions of invincibility that permit foolish teenagers to lay down their lives on the center dividers of busy highways. Be that as it may, the media are more openly acknowledged to have at least the capacity to dissuade from violence, to provide a forum for the words of leaders pleading for common sense and calm among the multitudes in times of crisis. In San Francisco, for example, a radio show on KMEL called *Street Soldier* has taken this power as a responsibility with great consequence:

> Unquestionably the show has helped avert violence. When a Samoan teenager was slain, apparently by Filipino gang members, in a drive-by shooting, the phones lit up with calls from Samoans wanting to tell [the hosts] they would not rest until they had exacted revenge. Threats filled the air for a couple of weeks. Then the dead Samoan's father called in, and, in a poignant exchange, the father said he couldn't tolerate the thought of more young men senselessly slaughtered. There would be no retaliation, he vowed. And there was none.

In contrast, we must wonder at the phenomenon of the very powerful leadership of the Republican Party, from Ronald Reagan to Robert Dole to William Bennett, giving advice, counsel, and friendship to Rush Limbaugh's passionate divisiveness. We must wonder at the *Economist*'s contention that "the fate of Mr. Clinton's presidency depends" on whether Rush Limbaugh will garner enough popular support for NAFTA so as to become its "improbable saviour." We must wonder that, in addition to generally boosting approval ratings of Ronald Reagan's politics, Rush Limbaugh's view "that Americans' lifestyles will not seriously hurt the environment boosts voters' assessment of their benign impact on the environment by more than 20 points." If fascist media mogul Silvio Berlusconi can be elected prime minister of Italy and Howard Stern can even *think* of running for any office anywhere in this galaxy, then we must take very, very seriously the rising eminence of the powerful Mr. Limbaugh.

In an era of infomercials, in other words, the media are increasingly used simply to spread (rather than exchange) information about markets (rather than ideas). Television and radio undoubtedly enable people to shop faster and better; it is easier than ever before to stay informed about a wide range of consumer goods and services. (The Supreme Court, in ruling to expand the cable rights of home shopping services, has even declared that home shopping serves the public interest.)

Yet even as they replace libraries (the traditional bastions of our culture), these media do not seem to be serving the same interests or function as libraries. They are not being geared for the sort of browsing where there is no commercial stake. Although electronically conveyed knowledge may indeed be cheaper and easier to obtain in one sense, I wonder about a larger question: the degree to which information itself needs a patron or sponsor to be conveyed in the first place. Our modern-day patrons are no longer popes and princes; they are corporations and philanthropies. The degree to which the major media, the culture-creators in our society, are owned by very few or are subsidiaries of one another's financial interests, must be confronted as a skewing of the way in which cultural information is collected and distributed. The business of television, and the monopolization and regulation of access to airwaves, databases, satellite systems, and telephone lines have the potential to determine, in much the same way churches and states have in the past, not just who may speak the Word but *what* the Word of law is as well.

Thus executives in the communications industry exercise a power that is not merely concentrated but also propagandistic. They make far-reaching choices in a way that few others in our society can. They project their images of the world out into the world—"five hundred channels at a time!" being the latest industry boast; "five hundred channels of *Lucy* reruns" being the ubiquitous retort of a jaded viewing public. The media do not merely represent; they also recreate themselves and their vision of the world as desirable, salable. What they reproduce is chosen, not random, not neutral, not without consequence. To pretend (as we all do from time to time) that film or television, for example, is a neutral vessel, or contentless, mindless, or unpersuasive, is sheer denial. The media, for better and frequently for worse, constitute one of the major forces in the shaping of our national vision, a chief architect of the modern American sense of identity.

It is true that some of the newer forms of groupness fostered by the media are strikingly different from what "group" connotes in, say, a tribal collective or what "group" meant in Greek antiquity, when "family" or "polis" indicated an interactive ethos not merely of shared interests, but of mutual obligation and deeply-felt duty. Perhaps we have already arrived at a day when market-cluster groupings define us as accurately as religion or ethnicity; when, in the enhanced version of the world that AT&T promises, we are all able to "reach out and touch many"; when mail solicitation businesses and political action committees form our new houses of worship, filled not with hymns but with the deep-space, disembodied, virtual-reality reverberations of the e-mail generation.

Even if one assumes that profit-seeking explains all behavior or that materialism is not itself a kind of culture, if the United States is to be anything more than a loose society of mercenaries—of suppliers and demanders, of vendors and consumers—then we must recognize that other forms of group culture and identity exist. We must respect the dynamic power of these groups and cherish their contributions to our civic lives, rather than pretend they do not exist as a way of avoiding arguments about their accommodation. And in our law we must be on guard against

79

either privileging a supposedly neutral "mass" culture that is in fact highly specific and historically contingent or legitimating a supposedly neutral ethic of individualism that is really a corporate group identity, radically constraining any sense of individuality, and silently advancing the claims of that group identity.

This is most emphatically not to say that all women or all blacks or all men see the world in the same way or only according to their cultures. I do not believe that a "pure" black or feminist or cultural identity of any sort exists, any more than I think that culture is biological. I am arguing against a perceived mono-lithism of "universal" culture, whether one that disguises our overlapping variety by labeling nonwhites "separate," "other," even "separatist," or that argues about whether other cultures even exist.

The point is not that whites cannot ever speak for blacks, or that Norwegians would not be interested in issues affecting His-panics. And the point is not, for example, whether a black actor should be able to play the lead in Shakespeare's *Richard III,* or whether white actors can convincingly portray Asian characters, as was so reductively maintained in the much-publicized debate over Actor's Equity's boycott of the initial Broadway version of *Miss Saigon.* While Actor's Equity maintained that they were concerned about the persistent failure of Broadway producers to hire Asian actors, *Miss Saigon* producer Cameron Mackintosh called the boycott "a disturbing violation of the principles of artistic integrity and freedom." The actress Ellen Holly, on the other hand, pointed out that while the Caucasian actor whose role was at stake in the controversy may have been an innocent victim, "he is not a victim of David Henry Hwang, B.D. Wong and the Asian-American theatrical community that, quite cor-rectly, raised a question about his employment here. Rather, he is a victim of a long and profoundly frustrating history in America in which, decade after decade, the ideal world we all long for has functioned so that whites are free to play everything under the sun while black, Hispanic and Asian actors are not only restricted to their own category, but forced to surrender roles *in their own category* that a white desires."

I maintain that a certain institutional skewing has taken place if within a supposedly diverse society it is only men who play women, only children who fill black roles, or only whites who represent Asians. In the *Miss Saigon* controversy, casting director Vincent Liff said that "he was not able to find an Asian actor suitable for the role, one of more or less the right age who could act and sing." Of course, the evaluation of this statement boils down to whether one believes that there really isn't a single qualified Asian actor to be found anywhere in the whole United States. I do not believe it. And if one does believe that there are willing and qualified candidates, then the issue is reoriented from one of racial or other qualification to one of institutional resistance disguised as artistic taste. It was this resistance to which the attempted boycott by Actor's Equity spoke: Chuck Patterson, head of the Committee on Racial Equality of Actor's Equity met with producers of the play and "asked for the opportunity for Asian-Americans to compete; they said absolutely not . . . Equity is willing to admit that Jonathan Pryce is an actor of enormous talent . . . But there are also Asian American actors of enormous talent, and for a producer to say he can't find an Asian American to play the role is absolutely racist."

Similarly, it would suggest a profound social imbalance if only North Americans compose the intellectual canon of South American history. And if rape occurs mostly to women, it seems peculiar to reserve control over the standards for its remediation exclusively to men. In fact, it is precisely these sorts of disrespectful exclusivities that signal the most visible sites of oppression in any society.

In our society, the most obvious means of tearing down such exclusivities is dispersion of ownership. Participation in ownership of anything, but most particularly of broadcast stations or other tools of mass communication, is the gateway to our greatest power as Americans. Ownership does not merely enable one to sell, to buy, to advertise. It provides the opportunity to propagate oneself in the marketplace of cultural images. Participation in the privileges of ownership thus involves more than the power to manipulate property itself; it lends an ability to express oneself through property as an instrument of one's interests.

We think of freedom of expression as something creative, innovative, each word like a birth of something new and different. But it is also the power to manipulate one's resources to sanction what is not pleasing. The property of the communications industry is all about the production of ideas, images, and cultural representations, but it also selectively silences even as it creates. Like all artistic expression, it is a crafting process of production and negation, in the same way that executing a painting may involve choices to include yellow and blue while leaving out red and green.

If we translate this understanding of ownership into the context of broadcast diversification, the issue becomes not only what is sanctioned, but also who is sanctioning. It is not that minorities live in wholly separate worlds, enclaves walled in by barriers of language, flavors, and music; minorities are not languishing on electronically underserved islands, starving for the rap-marimba beat of a feminist Korean-speaking radio deejay whom only like others can understand. Nevertheless, a feminist Korean deejay is more likely to disapprove insulting images of herself and more likely to choose to propagate images of herself that humanize her and her interests. Likewise, it is not that white owners cannot be persuaded not to rerun old *Amos 'n' Andy* shows, in which white actors in blackface portrayed blacks in derogatory if comic ways and which reiterated the exclusive (until recently) image of blacks in the media. Rather, it is that it is much easier—and very likely not even necessary—to persuade Bill Cosby, for example, to choose to run programming that challenges and variegates the perpetual image of blacks as foolish and deviant.

It is this sanctioning dimension that is so important to the claims of underrepresented groups whose interests are not always understood as distinctive or cultural, such as women and gays. Thus the belief of some that the potential contributions of women are limited to programs "geared to the special biological concerns of women—menstruation, childbearing, breastfeeding, menopause, diseases of the female organs" reveals a flatness of imagination that results, I think, from a general suppression of images of women as anything more than the sum of their parts.

In fact, I think that Bill Cosby's very success—as owner, producer, writer, and actor—in projecting an image of at least a certain middle-class segment of blackness into the realm of the "normal," rather than the deviant, has run him up against yet an even more complex (if instructive) level of cultural co-optation. As *The Cosby Show*'s warm, even smarmy appeal made it a staple in homes around the country, black cultural inflections that were initially quite conspicuous (speech patterns, the undercurrent of jazz music, the role of Hillman College as the fictional black alma mater of the Huxtables, hairstyles ranging from dreadlocks to "high top fades") became normalized and relatively invisible.

This process of normalizing, moreover, risks exaggerating perceptions of the black middle class in relation to the white middle class as not merely derivative but identical, so that *The Cosby Show* has been described as little more than a portrayal of blacks costumed in cultural whiteface. The black author Shelby Steele, one of the most controversial proponents of the view that black identity since the 1960s not only has not been cultural, but also has been nothing more than a construct of white guilt, described *The Cosby Show* as "a blackface version of the American dream." This statement implies that the American dream is something other than black and that Cosby's characters are conforming themselves to a fundamentally white behavioral norm. "The

83

Huxtable family never discusses affirmative action," observes Steele. He then concludes that Cosby's "continued number-one rating may have something to do with the (white) public's gratitude at being offered a commodity so rare in our time; he tells his white viewers each week that they are okay, and that this black man is not going to challenge them." While *The Cosby Show* might well be criticized for not having dealt more actively with social issues, this "whitening" of its appeal, albeit refined into the language of "sameness," devalues and even robs the program of its black content.

I acknowledge that there is perhaps a tragically literal and risky aspect of "black comedy" in the very idea of a comedy about blacks at a time when "95 percent of the inmates currently in New York City jails are black or Hispanic." Perhaps under these circumstances, laughter indeed functions as absolution. And there is indeed reason to pause at the fact that *Cosby* was the number one show among white South Africans at a moment when *Dallas* was the number one show in black townships. Nevertheless, I am confounded by suppositions, such as Steele's, that a television program whose black characters, framed entirely by the interior of their own home, never mention white people is therefore "passionately raceless." This notion accepts a vision of black identity as limited either to explicit racial confrontation or to continual conversations about what to do about white people.

Furthermore, as black cultural contributions are absorbed into mainstream culture, they actually come to be seen as exclusively white cultural property, with no sense of the rich multiculturalism actually at work. Quick examples include the judge who, in holding that a young black woman could not wear cornrows to work if her employer didn't want her to, observed that she was "just imitating Bo Derek"; or the young white person who, having attended her first African dance class, announced that it was "nice to see how many moves they've borrowed from aerobics." Ultimately, discussions of minority set-aside policies must address this consuming, unconscious power as well. It is not enough to have one Bill Cosby or two Oprah Winfreys if overall power is so concentrated in one community that it remains inconceivable that power could have any other source.

A more nuanced example is that as American popular music has become pervasively influenced by and imitative of African, Latin, and African-American forms, the notion of "white" music has nevertheless remained the standard. Recently there has been debate in some parts of the country about the degree to which black deejays and owners of radio stations are troubled by pressures from their black audiences to play "white" popular music as part of their programming. One law-and-economics commentator even observed that a "skeptic might interpret these complaints as the managers' unhappiness with the slightly reduced value of their skills at programming for a specialized market." It seems ironic that when blacks express a taste for music that is culturally informed by and expressively imitative of black musical heritage, that propensity is reduced—in the minds of some blacks as well as whites—to merely "black taste for white music." Furthermore, it is downright insulting that the debate among pressured owners and deejays might be dismissed as just the mercenarily-motivated gripings of those whose skills have supposedly been devalued by the incursion of implicitly more valuable "white" cultural property into their "specialized" preserves.

One consequence of a quietly racist aesthetic in which the status quo is made natural is that any change will be felt as unnatural and thus extremely unsettling. The costs of doing anything to alter the known, even when those alterations are matters of both social justice and self-preservation, are inflated to terrifying proportions, the merest tilt toward institutional adjustment turned into a slippery slope of misfortune. The ubiquity of racism is made menacing in its enormity, the recognition of it as a social problem held out as a threat, as a hedge against doing

85

anything at all about it. Rather than being allowed to feel good about tackling it at some level, we are threatened relentlessly with the clatter of domino theories.

A (probably too) concrete illustration may indicate the reconceptualization of equality that is so urgently needed. Imagine a glass half full (or half empty) of blue marbles. Their very hard-edged, discrete yet identical nature makes it possible for members of the community of blue marbles to say to one another with perfect consistency both "we are all the same" and, if a few roll away and are lost in a sidewalk grate, "that's just their experience, fate, choice, bad luck." If, on the other hand, you imagine a glassful of soap bubbles, with shifting permeable boundaries, expanding and contracting in size like a living organism, then it is not possible for the collective bubbles to describe themselves as "all the same." Furthermore, if one of the bubbles bursts, it cannot be isolated as a singular phenomenon. It will be felt as a tremor, a realignment, a reclustering among all.

Marbles and soap bubbles are my crude way of elucidating competing conceptions of how to guarantee what we call "equal opportunity." One conception envisions that all citizens are equal, with very little variation from life to life or from lifetime to lifetime; even when there is differentiation among some, the remainder are not implicated in any necessary way.

The other conception holds that no two of us are the same and although we can be grouped according to our similarities, difference and similarity are not exclusive categories, but are instead continually evolving. Equal opportunity is not only about assuming the circumstances of hypothetically indistinguishable individuals, but also about accommodating the living, shifting fortunes of those who are very differently situated. What happens to one may be the repercussive history that repeats itself in the futures of us all.

White Men Can't Count

I'm sick of the whole goddamn mess . . . I don't think I'm a racist. But they've gone too far with this thing. Blacks are getting privileges I can't get, my kids can't get. They get into schools with lower grades than whites. They get jobs with lower qualifications than whites. This is not equal opportunity. I'm fed up and so is everyone I talk to.

—Frank Martin, computer analyst, as told to Pete Hamill

In 1975 I had already exceeded my parents' wildest dreams. I was black, black was beautiful, and I was graduating from law school, any law school, never mind that it was Harvard. The world had turned upside down in terms of what any of us had ever dared hope was possible, and things would never be the same again.

Only a blink in time before, in 1968, when I was a junior in high school, I was still on the cusp of the old world. I sat down with my guidance counselor and plotted a course that would enable me to become a schoolteacher. My mother was a teacher, and teaching was considered one of the few professions open to black women. The guidance counselor, a wise woman with her ear to the ground, told me that opportunities were opening up for black students and that I should apply to other schools than just Teachers' College. (Affirmative action, it is easy to forget in today's climate, includes such policies as advertising, recruiting, and otherwise spreading the word about an institution's desire to diversify. A newspaper ad saying "So and So is an equal opportunity employer" is a form of affirmative action, as were the letters my guidance counselor received urging her to send candidates to schools previously deemed off limits.)

So I applied to Wellesley College under the early admissions program and was accepted. At first I planned to major in English and then, well, teach . . . juniors in high school maybe. But by the time I got to Wellesley, opportunities for graduate school were also opening up and the visionary dean of students suggested that I consider going on to law school. Suddenly there were options I had never before considered possible. And suddenly affirmative action provided scholarships and fellowships and instructions on where to apply.

I do think I would have been a pretty good English teacher. Instead I am a supremely fulfilled law professor (as law professors go) and I am an ecstatically happy occasional free-lance writer. My life has exceeded not only my parents' but my own wildest dreams. I feel fortunate every day in a hundred little ways.

What I have achieved is undoubtedly the result of my having been among the first generation of affirmative action babies. I know that there are those who would begrudge me this sense of contented accomplishment—as though just because I wasn't poverty-stricken to begin with, I was not deserving of affirmative action and should have just ignored any other kind of limitation in my life. It's the kind of Oliver Twistian advice given frequently to blacks deemed middle class: be grateful for the gruel because children are starving in the inner cities. While it's a fair admonishment not to forsake or forget the fate of my poorer brothers and sisters, making the world a better place is after all why I wanted to go to law school to begin with. In any event, it is no kind of reason to pit my opportunity to participate in the full promise of the American dream against theirs, as though it were some kind of either-or contest. In short, I do not feel apologetic in the slightest for having transgressed at every step of the way the demographic expectations for my "place" or my "type," as female and as black.

Back in high school there were lots of people in my neighborhood who counseled my parents against spending all that money on my education, at a private college no less, what with my being a girl after all. In the immigrant and working-class black, Irish,

Russian, and Italian neighborhood where I grew up, college was generally thought to be a luxury, even a waste, for daughters; even to think of graduate or professional education was considered positively outrageous.

And it wasn't just my neighbors. In 1964, after all, Harvard Law School Dean Erwin Griswold had invited the eleven female members of the five-hundred-person entering class of 1964 to dinner so that he could quiz them about how they justified displacing men whose careers were sure to be more productive (that is, less *re*productive).

By the time I got to law school less than a decade later, there were about forty-five women in the first-year class, and Ladies Day was no longer officially sanctioned, although many of my professors observed it anyway. Ladies Day, by the way, was the one day a month that the professor would call upon the Ladies-God-Bless-Them, lobbing them soft (even fluffy) balls in place of the snarling, bloody, Real Guy drubbing that passed for "Socratic Questions" the rest of the time.

Being black at Wellesley had not prepared me for this aspect of life in the law. But then being black at Wellesley might have been a completely anomalous experience at any moment before or since. I matriculated during a time when many whites were still romanticizing the project of inclusion. There were so few of us blacks that white classmates would come up and apologize to us for all that pain they imagined we were suffering. They wanted to know what it was *like* being black. People wanted to invite you home for the specific purpose of shocking their parents. They would shyly offer to date your brother to show their solidarity with black causes. And Lord knows *their* brothers missed no opportunity to play the Rolling Stones hit "Brown Sugar" over and over and then some again. (The personal as political was kind of a new notion back then.)

If all this was often condescending, it was also quite comical. And if Wellesley College was a little bit of a culture shock, it was also a place that valued, and that actively taught in those days, an ethic of civility, even if the freshman handbook called it Gracious Living. In any event, no one was ever openly impolite for even a moment.

Law school was a completely different matter. Allan Bakke filed the first reverse discrimination suit, against the University of California, during my entering year, and it was bitterly controversial. My professors were constantly cited in the newspapers, some complaining about how blacks were displacing more productive white men, some damning us with faint praise saying it was necessary to give the Blacks-God-Bless-Them their day in court too. It was revealed to the press that Harvard's admissions process was done in two tiers, one for blacks, one for whites, the average black scores being lower than the average white scores. What they didn't mention was that Harvard's admissions process had lots of tiers, such as the one for children of alumni, who were admitted at rates grossly, even obscenely disproportionate to their "scored" worth. Harvard had tiers for women, tiers for veterans, tiers that for whatever reason admitted some good, smart white men with scores far *lower* than those of any good, smart black students. But the public controversy was never that nuanced.

The faculty was exclusively male in those days, and Derrick Bell was not merely the only black man on Harvard's faculty but the only one on the faculty of any major law school in the country. Where there had been less than a handful of black graduates during all of Harvard Law School's two-hundred-odd-year history, my class suddenly had about fifty. This presence seemed to drive some people even further over the edge than those first women had driven Dean Griswold. Black students were automatically assigned black roommates for "their own comfort." White students had no hesitation about asking black students what their LSAT scores had been in very aggressive demonstrations of their disdain for our presence. And when racial woes intersected with gender miseries, you had such low moments as when some black male law students announced that they were not interested in dating black female law students, but were looking for "the more feminine" types, of whom there were rumored to be an abundance at Lesley Junior College just down the road.

Law school, with its frenetic corporate competitiveness, is to some degree miserable for all who enter its portals, regardless of race or gender. At the same time, I think the new presence of black and female students provided fresh meat for the old cruel hazing games that labeled and marked the "mental vegetarians," separating them from the ones who knew how to tear a carcass limb from limb. Racism and sexism were passed off as just "practical jokes," just a device to see who was fittest to survive, just a little collegial jockeying for position, just a test for admission to the inner circles of some ultimate game of the then-popular Dungeons and Dragons.

My first job was in a prosecutor's office in Los Angeles where I was one of four black women, five white women, two black men, and three Hispanic men, all of us hired at the same time, into a bureaucracy where there had been virtually none-of-the-above before. Our hiring had been the result of an affirmative action effort to respond to public criticism of an office that was accused of being insensitive to the needs of a city almost half of whose citizens were either black or Hispanic. I remember sitting around the office one day listening to some of the more senior prosecutors shoot the breeze. They were talking about a case whose charge one of them had just reduced to a misdemeanor. It was a child-molestation case, involving an eleven-year-old girl whose stepfather was the defendant. They were looking at a photo of the little girl and in the most crude and unselfconscious terms they were admiring the state of her physical development—who could blame the stepfather, they said. They decided they'd never convince a jury to convict, so what the hey.

I was so shocked and upset that I got up and went straight into the office of the deputy in charge and reported them. The deputy listened intently and sympathetically to what I had to say, but it was clearly something he had never thought about. It was always up to the attorneys who handled individual cases to decide how to draw up the charges; he seemingly had had little occasion to consider the possibility of abuse of that discretion. His resolution of the matter was to call an office-wide meeting and to have me lecture on child abuse as an offense to be taken seriously. I did some research, gave my spiel, and lo, my reputation as a radical theorist was born.

My career since then has been marked by lots of situations like that. When I left that job, I went into teaching at a school where I was the second black woman ever hired. I have been associated with at least five universities since then, and at every one I was the first black, or the first black woman, ever hired. In each job I have had, there has been some moment where I have protested what I perceived to be some thoughtless or intentional form of bias. And my reputation for either remarkable insight or radical troublemaking has grown accordingly.

Let me say here that I don't think I am either remarkable or a troublemaker. I think that my attempt to share the insights of women, of people of color, of a certain degree of powerlessness is what human beings do—they bring their insights and sensibilities along with their physical presence. And if women enter environments where men have only been talking to men, the conversation is bound to change. If blacks enter spaces where whites have only been talking to other whites, the conversation is bound to grow somewhat more encompassing.

I think this is what all of us affirmative action babies bring to the contexts we have so newly integrated: an inevitable shift in perspective, a more nuanced consideration of the possibility, the probability—though, no, not the guarantee—of other views. This is the process by which sexual harassment policies and laws have come into being, by which handicapped parking came to pass, by which the world has been so transformed since I was in school in 1975.

We still have a long way to go, but when I look at something as random (if lurid) as the O. J. Simpson case, I can't help comparing it to my first foray in a courtroom, as part of a clinical program offered by the Harvard Legal Aid Society. The judge stopped the proceedings and called me up to the bench. He was astonished to see "a little lady" like me "growing up" to be a lawyer. Did I know Ella Williams? he wanted to know. Ella, it turns out, had worked for his family for many years, and although I was no relation to her, he poured on the avuncular praise by comparing my hard work and determination to hers. "Much good luck to you anyway," he sighed before he released me to rejoin my classmates sitting in the front row.

That memory, twenty years old now, provides quite a contrast to the O. J. trial—soap opera though it be. The courtroom is filled with a dazzling array of affirmative action babies, from the integrated jury box (a moment of silence for Emmet Till), to the integrated, mixed-gender lawyer lineup (thank you Myra Bradwell and Charles Hamilton Houston), to the football hero (remember the Negro Leagues) turned movie star (say hey to crossovers Bojangles and Lena Horne), to Judge Lance Ito (for whom Vincent Chin died); with Charlayne Hunter-Gault (who was the first to integrate the University of Georgia's journalism school), Bryant Gumbel, Oprah Winfrey, Connie Chung, Nina Totenberg, and Katie Couric (affirmative action babies all) dutifully churning it into news. Just think of how *really* appalling this might be if we were back in the black and white world of Ozzie and Harriet, Amos 'n' Andy, Charlie Chan, Tonto, and Betty Boop.

We have accomplished much in the last twenty or thirty years that is too easily forgotten. As the reality of Asian-American police officers, women firefighters, close-captioned TV, and a

Caribbean-American general named Colin Powell fade into the backdrop of the "normal," we lose sight of how recent, costly, and precarious this much inclusion has really been. On the day that Senator Alphonse D'Amato made fun of Judge Lance Ito using a mock Japanese accent, I was transported back fifteen years to a presentation I made to a hiring committee at a law school where I was seeking a job. One of the committee members, a white man, had gotten dressed up in a dashiki and tiger-toothed necklace. During my talk, he put his feet on the conference table, scowled vividly and interrupted me, in a bad imitation of black dialect, with a series of silly and off-the-point questions.

Later, it was explained to me that he had been "testing" me for my ability to respond under stress. Since I recall getting perplexed, enraged, and tongue-tied, I do believe I probably flunked. Nevertheless, I got (but did not take) the job. I believe that I got it thanks to the grace of affirmative action. Perhaps the hiring committee took the action of even inviting me to speak because they felt "forced" to invite a black woman. (They were not actually forced. Contrary to lay understanding, very few affirmative action programs that have ever been judicially sustained force employers to hire anyone; this is the difference between goals and quotas, and affirmative action programs set goals not quotas. Other kinds of affirmative action programs encourage searches for candidates, or provide financial incentives for hiring, or set aside investment opportunities or financing breaks for minority businesspeople.)

These days there are those who would urge us to feel insulted by affirmative action programs that provide incentives for companies and schools to seek women and minority candidates, but I can only say thank goodness for the help and it's about time. Alphonse D'Amato's tactics represent the views of too many professors in universities, too many employers in the market, too many politicians who feel their power threatened by imagined hordes of newcomers. The Glass Ceiling Report of 1995 underscores how far we have yet to go before we can make inroads on the biases that underly the enormous disparities between the availability of qualified women and minorities and their rates of hire. The data from that report showed that far from taking over, women and minorities are underrepresented in all spheres except the very lowest service sectors of the economy, the welfare rolls, and the ranks of the homeless. What's more, "many middle- and upper-level white male managers view the inclusion of minorities and women in management as a direct threat to their own chances for advancement . . . Those male managers . . . actually stand no better odds of reaching the top today than they did 30 years ago. But if there has always been competition, the face of it has changed. White men, the report said, have circled the wagons against challengers whom they view not in terms of their merit but in terms of their color and sex."

The more things change, the more they stay the same, I guess, but I do hope that as we slash our public expectations along with our national budget, we could differentiate affirmative action from its evil twin "quotas"—for which it is so frequently mistaken. I hope we can learn to appreciate the universal benefits of affirmative acts-to-include that make our lives so much richer and more informed. I hope we do not lose sight of our long history of negative action that has made *every* effort at inclusion, from abolition to suffrage to affirmative action, so gosh-darn hard. And I pray that the momentum that made my life's possibilities so palpable survive this Howard Stern-ish moment when rough sex and racist humiliation are the new tests for dividing those who rule the castle and those consigned to disappear in the Dungeon.

But these are not simple times. A friend of mine who specializes in the sociology of Eastern Europe was telling me about a recent trip she had made to Poland to study anti-Semitism. Among the data she had returned with was a statistic stating that fully half of all Poles believe there are several hundred thousand

Jews living in that country. In fact, there are fewer than five thousand. What was so disturbing about this, she pointed out, is that it reveals a "They're everywhere" mentality that magnifies the proposition that "All Jews are bad" into a surplus of hate along the lines of "Everything bad must be Jewish."

Not long after that, I attended a professional meeting of commercial lawyers. During a coffee break, I stood with a group of Real Hungry Men, jockeying for position next to a table loaded with nice little cream puffs and fruit-filled cookies. "My wife wants to move to Chicago to be nearer her family," said one, scooping up a plateful of raspberry thins, "but I told her to forget it. Nobody's hiring white guys anymore." As he melted back into the crowd, I suffered a moment of anxious concern for him. Here I'd been feeling lonely and conspicuous, but maybe things had really changed while I wasn't looking and it was he who had become an oppressed minority, poor fellow. Power concedes nothing without a nose count, I thought, so here goes.

I tallied several hundred in attendance all told. There was a modest sprinkling of women in the crowd, perhaps fewer than a third. There were maybe ten Asians. I was one of two black women and, as far as I could tell, there were no black men, no Hispanics, no Native-Americans, and not a single Pacific Islander.

So who is it that's getting hired if not white guys? And if white guys aren't being hired, what on earth makes them think anyone else is?

The Glass Ceiling Report, issued by a bipartisan federal commission that was initiated by Elizabeth Dole and sponsored by Robert Dole, reaffirmed findings that 95 percent of all senior management positions are still held by white men. At the middle management level, black men constitute only 4 percent of managers, and black women make up 5 percent. "Despite three decades of affirmative action, 'glass ceilings' and 'concrete walls' still block women and minority groups from the top." While executives cited "the pool problem"—that is, a lack of qualified minority candidates, whom "they first think of as African Americans"—in fact there has been a 36 percent increase in well-qualified, college-educated African-Americans just since 1982. While the full force of the kind of arrogant entitlement that views any inclusion as "displacement" is generally reserved for blacks in today's affirmative action debates, women still face significant obstacles. In a study conducted by Lani Guinier and three of her colleagues at the University of Pennsylvania Law School, statistics showed that men were more than three times more likely to make it into the top of their class than women who entered with identical scores and predictive indicators.

In fact, there is simply no data anywhere to show that minorities or women have taken over any part of any given institution in America. Certainly not the labor market. Not the colleges and universities, where rates of racist, sexist, and homophobic harassment are rising and rates of minority enrollments are now declining. Not primary and secondary education, where forty-odd years after the Supreme Court's landmark opinion in *Brown v. Board of Education of Topeka, Kansas,* the public schools of America, including those in Topeka, are still not desegregated. Not the housing market, where segregation, financial "redlining," and white flight all flourish as powerfully as ever in our history. Not political life, where the United States lags woefully behind every industrialized nation in the world in numbers of women leaders.

Yet on the very same day that the Dole-sponsored report was published, Robert Dole himself was busy pressing for the elimination of *all* affirmative action programs, using the exploitively expedient tactic of collapsing popular gender programs into unpopular minority programs: "'After nearly thirty years of Government-sanctioned quotas, timetables, set-asides and other racial preferences, the American people sense all too clearly that the race-counting game has gone too far,' Mr. Dole declared."

Back at the commercial law conference, I gazed around the room full of mostly white men, these dismal demographics dancing through my head. *If white males aren't being hired, then just who is?*

I stopped for breath, another cookie, and a reality check. I came up with three theories to explain the lack of white guys moving to Chicago to join their wives' families:

1. They hate their in-laws and are grasping for straws.

2. No one's being hired and Rush Limbaugh has snookered them into thinking that theirs are the only heads on the block. There is a recession going on, after all, and an outright depression in black communities. For all but the top 20 percent of Americans there has been a 17 percent loss in real income over the last fifteen years or so. If white guys talk exclusively to other white guys, I guess you could end up thinking that Your sacrifice was All.

3. They're imagining things. And to me, it is the dangerously stereotyped shape of that imagining that I find most distressing. If every African-American man, woman, and child—only 12 percent of the population, after all—were employed tomorrow, that would not begin to account for the untold numbers of white men who feel that they have been specifically dispossessed by "less-qualified" blacks. And if every woman alive today were to be certified as a genius of the first order, that would scarcely make up for the Charles Murray-ed and Saul Bellow-ed assertions that the course of Western civilization would not have been significantly influenced if women had never been born. (Men, I suppose, would have continued to give birth through that hole in their foreheads, as Zeus produced Athena. Needless to say, worship of the Greeks and their gods is central to what many white guys feel is threatened by "feminazis" and those rabid multiculturalists.)

In my opinion, the current fashion in trumped white males is fed by some combination of all three elements—a recipe of still-to-bescientifically-measured proportions of personal grudge, economic hard times, and phantasmagoric scapegoat. But such a tight braid of resentments, when clung to by those who have no sense of their own great power, can result in abuses of power that ultimately reassert precisely the prejudices that feed the fantasy. That is to say, if white men in managerial positions are circling their wagons against a "takeover" that is in fact imaginary, then this could have devastating consequences for real people who are imagined to be the greedy, undeserving invaders. And, repeatedly, statistics would seem to indicate that that is exactly what is happening. In one study of Boston-area banks, the Equal Employment Opportunity Commission found that between 1990 and 1993 "the number of black officers and managers dropped . . . 25 percent. In the same period, the number of white men who served as officers rose 10 percent . . . Among clerical workers, the number of white employees advanced . . . 10 percent; the number of black employees dropped . . . 15 percent." Figures for women declined slightly in some categories, or held even. "Only white men and Asians registered substantial gains at almost all levels."

I know it is fashionable these days to dismiss even these figures as the result of the reimposition of "standards" and to conclude that the truly deserving are just taking their rightful place in the Darwinian order of things once more. Without getting into the endless debates about "scoring" and "genetic endowment," my experience—in settings ranging from boardrooms to law firms to academia to the employment experiences of hundreds of my students—convinces me that the single most tenacious barrier to women's and minorities' advancement is old-fashioned but newly-coded prejudice. For all the supposed concern about "objective" test results, I guess I've sat through too many meetings where candidates for this or that are evaluated with absolutely minimal reference to such criteria. Rather, the grades, the scores, the number and quality of articles written, the job history are perfunctorily rushed over; and then the discussions settle in for long battles over things like "chemical response" to the applicant, or whether someone has "enough balls" to "play in our sandbox." It's positively poetic sometimes, stuff like the "client-pleasuring" principle or, my personal favorite, the mysteriously-phrased but fiercely dispositive "fire-in-the-belly" factor. (Was it just accidental—or *my* imagination—that all the women and gay men were found lacking this qualification of hot, flickering loins?)

I do not want to imply that I think that it is only white men who are blindered to the potential benefits of a truly diverse world. Our cultural imagination, fueled by segregation and just plain ignorance of one another, operates at much subtler levels than outright vulgar bigotry. So many uncomprehending encounters are licensed by hidden normative understandings posing as "just personal" or "aesthetic" preferences. This is one reason I am so concerned about recent anti–affirmative action discussions that propose barring "preferential treatment" of—that is, preferences for—historically dispossessed groups, without taking into account the extent to which preferences *against* them operate at a million nuanced levels just below the level of overt discrimination.

One basis for recent judicial resistance to affirmative action, I recognize, is the question whether an expanded consideration, both of injury to groups and of remediation that extends beyond the limited life circumstances of a single litigant, is a matter for the courts. But the reflexive referral of all but the most individualized controversies to the legislature obscures the fact that even the narrowest contract or property dispute is never really as private as theory would have it. Courts always have to consider social ramifications that are rarely limited to the named parties, whether that consideration is of "policy"—the contemporaneous society of those similarly situated—or whether the consideration is funneled into issues of "precedent"—the prior or subsequent society of others.

101

Indeed, I think we must begin to appreciate the extent to which courts actually deal in and perpetuate not merely individual employment or property interests but, simultaneously, interests that govern, silence, and empower significant groups of us as citizens. Professor Jules Lobel, referring to the ideas of the constitutional law expert Owen Fiss, writes, "While . . . a public/private dichotomy may have been appropriate in the Jeffersonian era, it breaks down where large monopolistic television stations control our main forms of mass communication, where giant shopping malls replace the public streetcorner as a popular meeting place. As Fiss points out, positing freedom of speech solely in terms of a negative right of private actors to be free from state interference may, in modern society, conflict with our goal of facilitating the communication of ideas."

One device by which courts have traditionally limited challenges to the social status quo is to constrain cases and controversies within a paradigm of private contract law. This insistence amounts to considering all litigation from within a contractarian model that fragments the social contract into a series of little contracts. In the context of cases about civil liberties, this approach can be downright destructive.

As citizens, we tend to think of raw Hobbesian economic interest as being located outside the shrine in which our civil liberties, our freedom, and our humanity reside. Yet lawyers learn that it is not. Our liberty was always and is increasingly complex and contradictory, a symbology framed not just by economic notions in some general sense, but also by specific contractarian ideas of commodification and bipolar exchange. The subjectivity of our civil and political selves is simultaneously objectified by our most distanced, arm's-length transactions.

This can result in a twisted conception of freedom in which the conception of ourselves as "free" becomes transformed into that of "free agent." With this shift, another occurs: we no longer see freedom's inverse as "domination"; rather we see it only as the

102

inverse of free agency. Thus those who by one set of criteria are living in states of cultural, economic, or physical subjugation may be redescribed as inefficient wealth maximizers, mere depoliticized shoppers who are irrational and undeserving by either choice or resistance. A model of constitutional jurisprudence based on this contractarian vision therefore fails to anticipate the situation in which an aggregate of private transactions in a society begins to conflict with express social guarantees: those express protections or ideals are robbed of their force as law and become "external," implicit interference.

Courts' ability to consider these matters is actually not as limited as the current debates would suggest. The impression that such matters are unmanageable is in fact constructed by a variety of rhetorical images, derived from a deflationary war waged on the value of diversity itself and on any evidence that diversity is a good, necessary, or considered goal. The very notion of societal discrimination is labeled "amorphous" and "reflexive"; actual legislative history is deemed too paltry; congressional and agency findings are judged to be without a demonstrable "factual basis." The attempt to defend historically vulnerable interests is reduced to the privileging of "viewpoints"; cultural identity is collapsed into racial "stereotypes," and the judicial responsibility to check the tyranny of any majority is abdicated out of a hypothesized fear of advancing or benefiting special groups.

Beyond this devaluation of the interests at stake, political, judicial, and media discussions are peppered with inexplicably inverted agency, demonstrating that any language of reform may be turned inside out by conflating it with metaphors of negativity, even as its substance is being relentlessly dehistoricized. Whereas segregation and group exclusion were once thought of as the stigma of inferiority, now it is the very identification of blacks and other racial minorities *as* groups that is stigmatizing— despite the fact that the project is inclusion. Moreover, in the charged context of dismantling a system of favoritism that "favored" whites and "disfavored" blacks, the vocabulary of preference has been glibly reversed, so that now presumably it is blacks who are favored and whites who are automatically disfavored. The casual ahistoricism of this reversal implies a causal link between the inclusion of blacks and the oppression of whites. To give an example that would be extreme were it not asked so often, a student recently demanded of me, "Don't you think affirmative action is what creates a David Duke?" (The former Ku Klux Klan leader David Duke lost the 1990 race for U.S. Senator from Louisiana—but only narrowly, with 60 percent of the white vote and, according to one estimate, 70 percent of the white male vote. Polls taken around the time of the election "showed [Duke's] support running at twice the levels among young white males as among the white population as a whole. Thus, today's teenage white males could push Mr. Duke's vote totals higher in the future.") Blacks are positioned in this query as responsible for the bitterest backlash against them, an eerie repeat of the responses—one being the founding of the Ku Klux Klan—to black gains, having nothing to do with affirmative action, during Reconstruction.

In fact, affirmative action and minority set-aside programs are vastly more complicated than this "you're in, I'm out" conception suggests. Nothing in this rigid win-loss dichotomy permits the notion that everyone could end up a beneficiary, that expansion rather than substitution might be possible, and that the favoring of multiple cultures is enhancement of the total rather than a sweepingly reflexive act of favoritism for anything other than the monolithic purity of an all-white nation.

This particular evocation, of a corrupt system of favoritism seesawing between "the deserving" and "the preferred," caters to an assumption that those who are included by the grace of affirmative action systems are therefore *un*deserving. I want to underscore that I do mean that it *"caters to,"* rather than *creates*, an assumption of inferiority, for the assumption of inferiority has a life that precedes and, unfortunately, will probably outlast affirmative action programs. The subtlety of this distinction has frightened even some blacks into distorting the historic assumption of blacks as inferior into the weird acceptance of their exclusion as the counter to such prejudice. Sitting on university admissions committees, for example, I have seen black candidates who write on their applications comments such as, "Don't admit me if you have to lower your standards." I have never seen the same acutely self-conscious disavowals from students who are admitted because they meet some geographical criterion—such as living in Wyoming, or France, or some other underrepresented area—or who are older reentry students, or football heroes, or alumni children. I think this is so because these latter inclusionary categories are thought to indicate group life experiences, whether we call them cultures or not, that "enrich" rather than "lower."

The question, then, becomes not how to undo inclusionary affirmative action programs, but how to undo the stigma of inferiority that not merely resides in the label or designation of race, but that, according to our national symbology, is actually *embodied* in black presence. If eliminating the stigma were truly as simple as erasing labels, then perhaps enough White-Out in our cases and codes would eliminate the problem once and for all. But it is the ferocious mythology of blackness (or otherness) as the embodiment of inferiority that persists whether blacks are inside or outside particular institutions and regardless of how they perform.

The tenacity of this devalued condition is perhaps captured by something I saw not long ago in a five-and-dime store: a huge bin of identically-molded plastic sets of mother and father dolls. Some dolls in the bin were priced at $3.99 a set. Others had been originally priced at $2.99, now marked down to the "Must Sacrifice!" price of $1.99 a set. As a neutral market phenomenon, this obviously makes little sense, and one would assume that a rational vendor would quickly adjust one way or another for the discrepancy. As a less-than-neutral observer, however, I should add that while all the dolls were obviously cast from the same mold, they had not been privileged to share the same dye lot. The higher-priced dolls were white; the dolls priced for sacrificial sale were black. I was struck by how central the information about color was to my analysis of this situation: in a color-blind frame, the pricing was so irrational that I might comfortably assume a laissez-faire approach, confident that market pressures would assure a rapid adjustment. Knowing the dolls' color, however, exposed a more grim social reality: the irrationality of racism not only perpetuated, but also made "rational," by market forces. The absolute necessity of a corrective response to the silent tenacity of this status quo is the heart of what affirmative action is all about.

My point is not just an observation about economics. It is a semantic one as well: unlabeling our divisions is not a cure in itself. Courts—and we all—rename even as we unname. It is distressing therefore to observe the extent to which both liberals and conservatives seem to rely on a conception of affirmative action as favoritism. Wrapping affirmative action in this rhetoric diverts attention from the task of affirmative inclusion of those whose presence is consistently devalued in our society and actually validates a specter of more "valuable" yet "disfavored" whites who will be tossed into the wilderness of dispossession that blacks are now said to occupy.

In the same vein, many employ the half-hearted ambiguity of "benign racial classification" in place of what might be more forcefully described as the principle of *anti*discrimination. Furthermore, antidiscrimination and diversity are polarized, so that it is no longer possible formally to recognize diversity without its being—not merely risking being—discriminatory. The quest for inclusion becomes transformed into the exact equivalent of that which would exclude: the slogan "separate but equal" is called up as the exact equivalent of the newly minted "unequal but benign." In only thirty years, blacks and Bull Connor have become relativized in this soupy moral economy. The focused and meaningful inquiry of strict scrutiny has become a needle's eye through which minority interests are too inherently suspect to pass. Racial and ethnic identification as that against which one ought not discriminate has been twisted; now those very same racial and ethnic classifications are what discriminate. The infinite convertibility of terms is, I suppose, what makes the commerce of American rhetoric so very fascinating. But these linguistic flip-flops disguise an immense stasis of power and derail the will to undo it.

Furthermore, the complication of this rhetoric, and the ironic result of the too-frequent desire to simplify, seem to have resulted in an odd and risky quest to be rid not only of any undue power to discriminate negatively, but also of the very ability to be discriminat*ing* in any sensitive, curious, or moral way. As I have said before, I think that the idea that an egalitarian society can be achieved or maintained through the mechanism of blind neutrality is fallacious. Racial discrimination is powerful precisely because of its frequent invisibility, its felt neutrality. After all, the original sense of discrimination was one of discernment, of refinement of choice, of value judgment—the courteous deflection to the noble rather than the base. It is that complicated social milieu that must be remembered as the backdrop to what are these days so glibly referred to as "preferences." Racism inscribes culture with generalized preferences and routinized notions of propriety. It is aspiration as much as condemnation; it is an aesthetic. It empowers the familiarity and comfort of the status quo by labeling that status quo "natural." If we are to reach the deep roots of this legacy, antidiscrimination must be a commitment not merely to undo the words of forced division, but also to undo the consequences of oppressive acts. As in the old saw about the two horses given "equal" opportunity to run a race, one of whom has a stone in its shoe, the failure to take into account history and context can radically alter whether mere neutrality can be deemed just.

The outright denial of the material crisis at every level of American society, most urgent in black inner-city neighborhoods but facing us all, is a kind of political circus, dissembling as it feeds the frustrations of the moment. We as a nation can no longer afford to deal with such crises by *imagining* an excess of bodies, of babies, of job-stealers, of welfare mothers, of over-reaching immigrants, of too-powerful (Jewish, in whispers) liberal Hollywood, of gays, of gang members ("gangsters" remain white, and no matter what the atrocity, less vilified than "gang members," who are black), of Arab terrorists, and of uppity women; the reality and complexity of our social poverty far exceeds these scapegoats.

The overwhelming response to right-wing excesses in the United States has been to seek an odd sort of comfort in the fact that the First Amendment is working so well—that you can't suppress this sort of thing, look what's happened in Eastern Europe. Granted. So let's not talk about censorship or the First Amendment for now. But in Western Europe, where fascism is rising to power at an appalling rate, suppression is hardly the problem. In Eastern and Western Europe as well as the United States, we must begin to think just a little bit about the fiercely coalescing power of the media to spark mistrust, to fan it into forest fires of fear and revenge; we must begin to think about the levels of national and social complacence in the face of such resolute ignorance. We must ask ourselves what the expected result is, not of censorship or suppression, but of so much encouragement of, so much support for, so much investment in the fashionability of hate. What future is it that we are designing with the devotion of such tremendous resources to the disgraceful propaganda of bigotry?

Town Hall Television

Perhaps 6 April 1989 will go down in history as the first "designer drug raid." As heavily armed and flak-jacketed SWAT commandoes stormed the alleged "rock house" near 51st and Main Street in Southcentral L.A., Nancy Reagan and Los Angeles Police Chief Darryl Gates sat across the street nibbling fruit salad in a luxury motor home emblazoned "THE ESTABLISHMENT." According to the Times, the former first lady "could be seen freshening her makeup" while the SWATs roughly frisked and cuffed the fourteen "narco-terrorists" captured inside the small stucco bungalow. As hundreds of incredulous neighbors ("Hey, Nancy Reagan. She's over here in the ghetto!") gathered behind the police barriers, the great Nay-sayer, accompanied by Chief Gates and a small army of nervous Secret Service agents, toured the enemy fortress with its occupants still bound on the floor in flabbergasted submission. After frowning at the tawdry wallpaper and drug-bust debris, Nancy, who looked fetching in her LAPD windbreaker, managed to delve instantly into the dark hearts at her feet and declare: "These people in here are beyond the point of teaching and rehabilitating."

—Mike Davis, *City of Quartz*

If the pen is mightier than the sword and a picture is worth a thousand words, then a little simple multiplication is all it takes to figure out the enormous propagandistic power that television has to create truth and shape opinion. Within the world of TV land, into which American life has been reduced as well as reproduced, the phenomenon of the talk show has emerged as a genre located somewhere on the spectrum between coffee klatch and town meeting, or perhaps between the psychiatrist's couch and the crowd scene at a bad accident.

Talk-show sets usually resemble the interiors of homes, if not my home; they employ as backdrops what appear to be living rooms or home libraries or other womblike spaces. There are usually some nice comfortable armchairs or a sofa or a round (not square) kitcheny table. Coffee mugs are often strewn about, maybe an artsy bunch of jonquils in a nice vase. Yet these womb-rooms are always sawed in half somehow; they offer 180 degrees of pure schmoozey ambiance and then, at the 181st degree exactly, they open up to an amphitheater of perfect strangers, all of whom always look like my sunny neighbors when I lived in Wisconsin, and none of whom ever look like my lock-jawed neighbors in New York (with the possible exception of the audiences on the old *Morton Downey Show*).

To be a good talk-show host requires a personality that has been similarly sawed in half. "How does it feel," they ask their guests with the soft seduction of a mother cat licking her young; "to know you are feared and loathed by millions of our viewers all over America?" they finish, with the poisonous flick of an impatient rattlesnake. Talk-show hosts act like good parents with an unruly set of teenagers-who-also-happen-to-be-serial-killers: Life's a living hell these days . . . All his friends seem to be going through this phase . . . What's a society to do? Phil as Father-Knows-Best; Oprah as not Mom, because that's too close to Mammy, so Ur-Girlfriend instead.

All of this creates, I think, a very powerful illusion of intimate openness . . . yet . . . objectivity—*sincere* objectivity. It creates an illusion of care mixed with an illusion of rigorous inquiry—a species, I guess, of Tough Love. It creates an imagined world in which there is no permission for anyone's feelings ever to be hurt, even when they ought to be; in which good intentions and great attitude rule the day.

This results in a forum that is very persuasive by virtue of its form alone: an atmosphere of overdetermined consensus, much like the scene of that bad accident, in which everyone rushes forth with a blaze of inconsistent opinions and viewpoints, but everyone goes away agreeing or believing they agree that they saw the same thing. A Rorschach test of response in which a catharsis of agreement emerges—such as, sleeping with your girlfriend's boyfriend is right! or it's wrong!—even though the reasons underlying the consensus of rightness or wrongness are extremely varied or vastly contradictory.

Talk shows are sometimes touted as new-age town halls or mini-courtrooms. I suppose this comparison reveals a certain longing for community that has arisen as the common turf of political and judicial space has become less and less accessible to all citizens as an arena for debate and resolution. But talk-show politics is hardly that summoned up by the image of the soapbox orator holding forth on the Boston Common or the village green: increasingly plugged into the bottom line of market ratings, the shows' ethics have less and less to do with the democratic constraints of fairness, due process, public accountability, or equality of access. If, again, the general expectation is that talk shows function as a way of airing all points of view or resolving disputes in the manner of a public trial, then we must take stock of the fact that the "talk" is managed with more reference to the rules of football than to any principles of justice; we must begin to wonder if the energy for public debate is not being siphoned off into a market for public spectacle. We must begin to unravel the political function of this jumble of stage-direction-qua-civics. Mangled metaphors of level playing fields tussling with invocations of zero-sum games in which the winner takes all. Bashing the stuffing out of each other but at the end, being good sports and shaking hands and agreeing to disagree and nothing is so important we can't go off and have lunch together. "Can you forgive your father for molesting you?" asks Sally Jesse Raphael. *"No,"* sobs the truly bad sport.

Talk shows as town meetings leave one with the impression of having had a full airing of all viewpoints, no matter how weird, and of having reached a nobler plane, a higher level of illumination, of having wrestled with something till we've exhausted it. And maybe that's true for programs that deal with women who drink their own blood or the joys of body piercing. But I am very concerned that when it comes to some of our most pressing social issues such as anti-Semitism and racism, TV talk shows perform an actual disservice, by (1) creating a sense both of false consensus and of false division, and (2) condoning and perpetuating racism, anti-Semitism, and gender stereotypes, even as they supposedly challenge them.

Let me give an example of a Phil Donahue show I saw some time ago. It was a program that purported to be deeply concerned about the rise of anti-Semitism on campuses in general, and the proliferation of Jewish American Princess jokes in particular. "How would *you* feel . . .?" Phil kept asking by way of challenge to the studio audience.

The program opened with an extraordinarily long volley of Jewish American Princess jokes, not merely recited, but written in large block letters across the screen—for the hearing impaired presumably, although there was no other part of the program so emphatically emblazoned. The jokes played on mean-spirited, vulgar stereotypes; they were just plain offensive, even though they were positioned as merely "models" of the subject to be discussed. Although styled as a repudiation, they reenacted the whole problem—over and over and over again. The audience tittered and giggled its way through this opening volley. It was significant, I think, this tittering—after each joke, the cameras focused as intently as a dentist's drill upon the stunned-rabbit faces of the audience, people caught in a not-quite-sure-how-to-respond mode that implicated them as they struggled to be good sports while being broadcast live to millions of people. It was a marvelously assimilative moment; they were like children trying to decide how to be seen at their best. Smile? Frown? Which is the posture of belonging? So they tittered. Nervously.

I think there is a real risk of destructive impact in jokes that make fun of the supposed characteristics of historically oppressed or shunned people. Of course all humor depends on context, but, if it is possible to speak generally, I think that such jokes too frequently are the enactment of a kind of marking process, in which communities are described, kinship delimited, the enemy imagined. An anecdote will illustrate what I mean by marking, how I think the bright innocence of social divisiveness works:

Some months ago I was riding on a train. In between napping and reading the newspaper, I languidly listened to the conversation of a very well-dressed, well-educated family seated across the aisle from me. Here was a family with traditional values *and* Ralph Lauren looks—mother, father, bright little girl, and a big bearded friend of the family who looked like that seafaring guy on the clam chowder label. It was a fascinatingly upper-class conversation, about investments, photography, and Japanese

wood-joinery. It was also a soothingly pleasant conversation, full
of affection, humor, and great politeness. I enjoyed listening to
them, and allowed myself the pleasure of my secret participation
in their companionability. Then they started telling redneck
jokes.

There was no shift in their voices to warn me of it; they spoke
in the same soft, smiling voices as before, with those deliciously
crisp *t*'s and delicately rounded *r*'s.

The little girl, who was probably around seven or eight years
old, asked, "What's a redneck?" No longer napping, I leaned
closer, intrigued by what this moment of sharp but innocent
intervention promised in terms of drawing these otherwise
thoughtful adults up short in glorious contrition and a renewed
sense of social awareness.

"Drinks beer, drives a pickup, low-class, talks bad," came the
unselfconscious reply. Then the three adults told more jokes to
illustrate. Being very bright, the little girl dumped innocence by
the wayside and promptly responded by telling a bunch of blond
jokes and then one involving "black"—but I couldn't hear if she
was talking about hair or skin.

The father told another joke—what's got ten teeth and something I couldn't hear? The answer was the front row of a Willie
Nelson concert.

They were so pleasant and happy. Their conversation was
random, wandering. They showed each other pictures of their
kids, they played word games, they shared hot dogs. And yet they
were transporting a virus.

This process of marking. No wonder it is so hard to get out of
our race and class binds. It occurred to me, as I watched this
family in all its remarkable typicality, that that little girl will have
to leave the warmth of the embracing, completely relaxed circle
of those happy people before she can ever appreciate the humanity of someone who drives a pickup, who can't afford a dentist.
"Rednecks" were lovingly situated, by that long afternoon of

gentle joking, in the terrible vise of the comic, defined by the butt of a joke.

How *givingly* social divisions are transmitted was brought home to me in an essay written by one of my former students. She described her father as a loving family man, who worked six and a half days a week to provide for his wife and children. He always took Sunday afternoons off; that was sacred time, reserved for a "family drive." Yet the family's favorite pastime, as they meandered in Norman Rockwell contentment, was, according to this student, "trying to pick the homosexuals out of the crowd." ("Bill Clinton would have *homosexuals* in his administration!" railed Pat Robertson in his speech to the 1992 Republican National Convention, during which convention homophobic violence reportedly rose by 8 percent in the city of Houston.)

Hate learned in a context of love is a complicated phenomenon. Love learned in a context of hate endangers all our family.

But back to our show. The rest of the *Phil Donahue Show* on Jewish American Princesses was a panoply of squirmy ways of dealing with being marked. Phil's guests included not only a Real Live Jewish Princess, but a Black American Princess, an Italian-American Princess, and a WASP Princess as well. While they were all willing to be called *princesses* of X, Y, or Z flavor, they all denied that they were the *bad* kind of princess. They negotiated this good princess/evil princess dichotomy by at least four different maneuvers:

First of all, there was the "role model" response—yeah, well, I'm proud to be pushy, and I've made it into a positive attribute, look at how creative I am with the lemons life has handed me. Doesn't bother me a bit (even though an unfortunate cost of this survival mechanism would seem to be a rather defensive, cynical edge).

Second, there was the "But I really am a princess!" response—the attempt to remove the sarcasm from it and be taken as literal, real. The Real WASP Princess proclaimed herself as the inheritor of society's privilege and all the other ethnic princesses as mere wannabe imitations of herself; the black princess claimed to have been the real princess of a considerably smaller if warmer realm, in having been the apple of her protective family's eye; and the Italian-American princess claimed that her real name *was* Princess, at least that's what Daddy always said.

Third, there was the move to concede that while some women may be like that awful thing at the butt of all those jokes, "all Jewish women are not JAPs." There was, in other words, a concession of the category as validly descriptive, and then the attempt to exceptionalize oneself from it. This is, I think, a powerfully defeatist move because it concedes the category as given, it allows the stereotype legitimacy. The response to racist labeling is thus locked into the logic of merely defining oneself in or out of the label, rather than focused on challenging the prejudice and judgmentalism of the marking process at all. I think this resort to a "them-us" dichotomy or an "I'm different" strategy is perhaps the most prevalent individual response to bigotry, as well as the most destructive.

Fourth, there is the opposite move—and perhaps the most prevalent institutional response to bigotry—the tendency to generalize rather than to exceptionalize, to make shrill self-absorption a general feature of all women, who are arrayed so as to possess a panoply of generally negative qualities. Women of *all* ethnicities are bitchy, stupid, fluffy, greedy, sacrificial, ran the logic of a narrative that played sexism against anti-Semitism, that played general stereotype against its sub-components. Thus "equal opportunity bimboism" is proffered as an odd model of the way in which tolerating intolerance emerges as the new norm for tolerance itself.

Perhaps the best example of the new tolerance of the same old intolerance is the intriguing fact that Howard Stern's sidekick, Robin Quivers, is a black woman who sounds exactly like the quintessential, self-abasing, totally concessionary but not dumb stereotype of a white woman. A *blond* white woman stereotype at that. A shrewdly submissive "bimbo" in blackface. "Oh, *How*ard," she sighs. This weird component is so manifest that Garry Trudeau parodies it in his *Doonesbury* cartoon, in which a movie is supposedly being made of Stern's book *Private Parts.* Boopsie, Trudeau's blonde update of Betty Boop, is sought to play the part of Robin Quivers. "But Quivers is black," says Boopsie. "Don't worry, it's radio," comes the reply. It is a cartoon that echoes the pre-*really*-weird weirdness of Michael Jackson's Unbearable Lightness of Being—specifically, when he attempted to cast a little white boy to play himself as a child in a Japanese-produced video of his life.

Trudeau's cartoon is a complex commentary on the strange post–civil rights era configuration of what integration seems to have become: to the extent that it exists, it does not merge black and white people as much as it hybridizes troublesome stereotypes of women and minorities. Barbie now has cornrows and six little gold earrings. Ken has two-tone hair, one earring, and for a brief moment in doll-making history sported a necklace with a cock ring hanging from it. (Mattell executives claimed they had no *idea* . . .) If black women are still having trouble breaking into the world of high fashion modeling, the same cannot be said of RuPaul, whose glittering, towering, snap-queen transvestism has made him the toast of the MTV crowd. Mammy dolls have gone Hispanic. The most racially and philosophically conservative justice on the Supreme Court in at least fifty years is a black man. The Victorian image of the "fallen woman gotten with child" has merged with that of the black Jezebel and produced the always-rollicking "welfare queen."

It's an interesting development beyond the time-honored use of blackface makeup to mock black people: just use a black *person.* It's a move that was captured in the casting of the movie version of *The Bonfire of the Vanities;* the role of a judge who spews racist claptrap to black defendants was recast from that of white man in the novel to black man in the movie. Let the black judge deliver the racist rebuke because then it's not racist, seems to be the logic of the day. So confined are black bodies by the rigors of puppeted rebuke and suffocating buffoonery that there is a certain sociopathic logic in Michael Jackson's repeated surgical attempts to escape the stereotype of the societally scourged "black male" body.

The powerful weight of stereotypes about blacks as not seriously human was painfully visible in the (how shall I put this gently) incomprehensibly miscalculated spoof undertaken by the actor Ted Danson of his then-girlfriend Whoopi Goldberg, in which Danson donned blackface, ate watermelon, joked about their sex life and her genitalia, and used the word "nigger" repeatedly. Supposedly mystified by the storm of public reaction, Danson made much of the claim that Whoopi had approved of the material, even helped write it, and that therefore it couldn't be racist.

Only weeks after that fiasco, Goldberg's recipe for "Jewish American Princess Fried Chicken" was published in a book entitled *Cooking in Litchfield Hills.* The recipe "instructs you to 'Send a chauffeur to your favorite butcher shop for the chicken,' 'Watch your nails' when you shake the chicken in a brown paper bag, and 'Have Cook prepare rest of meal while you touch up your makeup.'" Again there was a big debate about whether it was funny or whether it was anti-Semitic (as though these are necessarily oppositional). Again the handwringing about subject position, although I'm sure that's not what people imagined they were doing. "'This is in worse taste (than the Friars Club debacle) because she could get away with that because she is black,' said one Litchfield resident." Let's sidestep for just a moment the complicating detail that Goldberg didn't "get away with" much of anything precisely because she employed the body of Danson as the time-honored comedic vehicle of racial minstrelsy—a white man in blackface mouthing too-familiar-to-be-ironic stereotypes, albeit supposedly written by a black woman to parody herself. Rather, I would like to examine the retort by Goldberg's publicist: "Maybe (the critics) are not aware that Whoopi is Jewish, so she is certainly not anti-Semitic." It's a familiar litany: I heard a Jewish person tell this joke so it's not anti-Semitic. And of course, a Jewish person wrote this joke for me, so I couldn't possibly be anti-Semitic just because I'm trying to lighten things up with a little Holocaust humor. In fact, goes the next line of the argument, *you're* intolerant for claiming intolerance. And a bad sport besides. (It is by a reversed but mirror-image logic, perhaps, that two Oakhurst, California, high school youths who dressed up in the white robes and hoods of the Ku Klux Klan and reenacted a lynching of another student for a Halloween party—and who were rewarded with a prize in the costume competition—sought to justify the event by saying that *no* blacks were at the party so it was okay.)

What does this humor mask? At what point does blackface minstrelsy converge with white-hooded threats? Look at *this* and fear for your life; look at *that* and laugh, just laugh and laugh. "My boot came from the area of lower California and connected with the suspect's scrotum around lower Missouri," wrote the Los Angeles police sergeant Stacey Koon of the arrest of a Latino suspect that occurred before his beating of Rodney King. "My boot stopped around Ohio, but the suspect's testicles continued into upper Maine. The suspect was literally lifted off the ground. The suspect tried to speak, but it appeared he had something in his throat, probably his balls." Where are the borders of this cartooned life and that imprisoned one? Is it all just one long joke without end, amen? And when will someone let up on the laugh-track button and just let me breathe?

The *Washington Post* ran an article after the Whoopi and Ted incident that asked all the wrong questions: Was it funny, why not? Was it offensive and why? Yet I wonder if it is not possible to cross well into the realm of the offensive *and* be "funny." I wonder how line-crossing from not-funny to funny seems to redeem any degree of threat or insult. The *Post* article ends with a quote from Tim Conaway, *Hustler* magazine's humor editor, whose last word is "If you're hurt by a cartoon in a magazine . . . I think you ought to look at the real root of that pain." But in bigotry's insistent blindness, humor is precisely the device by which discussion of the roots of pain is most consistently deflected.

Clarence X

Beneath this oppressive burden it is "the body" that somehow represents the individual's instinctive source of freedom. It is the body that resists, the body that has to be dominated, and ultimately the body that comes to be "the prisoner of the soul" (once the soul has been fabricated by society's discipline).

—David Garland

As a child of the civil rights movement, I do find it amazing to wake up and find that a black neoconservative Supreme Court justice named Clarence Thomas has suddenly become the symbolic guardian of racial justice in America. And as though that weren't amazement enough, it turns out that Clarence Thomas's erstwhile hero is, was, or has been none other than Malcolm X.

It took me a long time to sort out what on earth was going on when the newspapers reported that Malcolm X was one of Clarence Thomas's role models. I just didn't get it: Malcolm, man of the people, outspoken firebrand of his day, religious fundamentalist, and radical black nationalist? And Clarence, lonely disdainer of the group—no matter what group—not outspoken about much of anything he wasn't later willing to disclaim, confused theologian in the church of an undefined, mushy breed of so-called natural law.

A friend tried to reconcile it all for me by saying, "Oh, it's not about politics—it's a male thing. You wouldn't understand." (Maybe. But the sentiment was at least one I could place. When asked to explain why he delivered the eulogy at Malcolm X's funeral, for example, the actor Ossie Davis told a reporter, "You always left his presence with the sneaky suspicion that maybe, after all, you were a man . . . However much I disagreed with him, I never doubted that Malcolm X, even when he was wrong, was always that rarest thing in the world among us Negroes: a true man.")

Then another friend said, "Malcolm represented manhood. It's as simple as that." (This, of course, is the way Ossie Davis characterized Malcolm X in the eulogy itself: "Malcolm was our manhood, our living black manhood! This was his meaning to his people. And, in honoring him, we honor the best in ourselves.")

And then, just to make sure things stayed complicated, a third friend observed, "Malcolm wasn't just a role model; he's become the ultimate pornographic object." Against the backdrop of rumored affidavits that Clarence Thomas had a penchant for the pornographic, I found this last particularly provocative; so I went to the library and started reading and thinking about pornography in this larger sense, in the beyond-role-model sense, as part of a scheme of thought that has no necessary connection to sex.

I started to think about pornography as the habit of thinking that is a relation of dominance and submission. A habit of thinking that permits the imagination of the voyeur to indulge in auto-sensation that obliterates the subjectivity of the observed. A habit of thinking that allows that self-generated sensation to substitute for interaction with a whole other human being, to substitute for listening or conversing or caring. In which the object is pacified, a malleable "thing" upon which to project. In which the object becomes interchangeable with the will of the voyeur, in which the insatiable lust of Wanda the Wench is representational of the insatiable lust of all women. In which Wanda the Wench may profess deepest delight in the unspeakable pain of having unspeakable acts of violence enacted upon her, because she "delights" "in being a real woman" and real women are defined as the sum of their body parts, bared, open, and eternally available for use and abuse. In which Wanda says she would never want to be a feminist because they don't believe

123

in having fun and they emasculate men and besides women should be free to experience the joys of a little bondage.

And from this thinking I began to extrapolate, hypothesize, do a little imagining of my own: Here we have Clarence Thomas, man of the moment, whose biggest appeal is that he will stand in and speak for all black people while speaking exclusively about himself. Not that he will represent their interests, but that he will represent their image. He will be a role model, but more in the sense of a runway model than of a modeler of actions or a propounder of ideas; as a Supreme Court justice, he will be seen but not heard. Clarence Thomas says he loves the good old days when a little oppression was good for the soul and brought black people together and taught them the true meaning of community; Clarence Thomas hangs a Confederate flag in his office and says it makes him think of home. Affirmative action just emasculates him, and besides blacks should be free to experience the self-help joys of a little bondage.

I can't help wondering what Wanda and Malcolm would have to say about all this, if she weren't bleeding and he weren't dead.

Recently I have began to appreciate why there was so much controversy about Spike Lee's film of Malcolm X's life. As Alex Haley recounts, "After signing the contract for [the autobiography], Malcolm X looked at me hard. 'A writer is what I want, not an interpreter.'" So perhaps it doesn't really matter who would do such a movie: the effrontery is the transition from literary imagination to the filmic, the iconographic. As Haley continues, "I tried to be a dispassionate chronicler. But he was the most electric personality I have ever met, and I still can't quite conceive him dead. It stills feels to me as if he has just gone into some next chapter, to be written by historians."

And with that shift of perception, I began to see the extent to which a whole generation of us have grown up pretenders to the Malcolm legacy; I see it in the faces of my friends; I hear it in the inflections of our voices. I see it in myself: iconette in the making, dedicatedly pursuing the path of liberatory potential. Who knows if Malcolm would have approved. But that's the beauty of it all, the achingly postmodern transformativity of the singular imagination, floating somewhere in the misty blue angst of annibus domini 1980–2001. Who knows, who cares. And if the complexity that was Malcolm X survives this moment as only a tee-shirt or a trademark, then it is no wonder that Clarence Thomas has emerged as the perfect co-optive successor—an heir-transparent; a product with real producers; the new improved apparition of Malcolm, the cleaned-up version of what he could have been with a good strong grandfather figure to set him right. Clarence X gone good.

Clarence Thomas is to Malcolm X what "Unforgettable. The perfume. By Revlon." is to Nat King Cole. A sea change of intriguing dimension, like the time Eldridge Cleaver came back from Algeria preaching the good news of free enterprise and started marketing trousers with codpieces, and barbecue sauce. Or the time when Ray Charles proclaimed that, although he sang "America the Beautiful" at the 1988 Republican National Convention, he would have done it for the Democrats "if they had paid me some money. I'm just telling the truth."

Symbolic complication was a feature of Clarence Thomas's entire nomination process, right down to the "symbolic" swearing-in ceremony on the White House lawn, which turned out to be an entirely different event from the "real" swearing-in—so that even the oath-taking to uphold the Constitution that was broadcast to Us the People was a reenactment for prime-time consumption. Many blacks supported him because his success was a symbol of the heights to which a black man could aspire. His strong-but-simple, rags-to-riches stories symbolized triumph over adversity, knowledge over darkness, industry over idleness. His powerful mythology, helpfully concocted by some of the very same public relations people who designed Ronald Reagan's, George Bush's, Ross Perot's, and Jesse Helms's campaigns, presented Thomas as the product of a land where dreams come true, where odds are always overcome, where workers whistle (even at the risk of a few sour *feminists* misunderstanding the bright innocence of it all), and where the rainbow is enuf. Clarence Thomas looked like Horatio Alger, Miss Jane Pittman, and Colin Powell all wrapped into one.

If, as some assert, in sexual pornography men act and women appear, and if in racial pornography white people act and black people appear, a classic instance in the political pornography of the Malcolmized moment was when President Bush invited the Black Caucus, who represent many millions of black and white voters, up to the White House to sit and chat about their concerns for a while. As it turned out, of course, the whole event was a magnificently choreographed photo opportunity, the entire point of which was the images—stills of Bush *looking* as if he were listening—disseminated to the media all over America. Similarly, the entire arrangement of witnesses in the confirmation process—four witnesses for, four witnesses against—replicated a kind of "he said–she said" set-up if there ever was one, and belied the extent to which the witnesses represented complex and vastly differing constituencies. The witness from the NAACP represented a membership of thousands upon thousands, yet was made the imagistic equivalent of the witness who represented the relatively minuscule membership of the black bailiffs' association of Southern California.

A lot has been written about role models and the black community. Some of it undoubtedly is useful. I firmly believe that there is great power in seeing ourselves in others who are likable, respectable, and socially desirable. But models are not enough, and I am increasingly concerned that *all* we are left with is "players" in "roles," rather than substantive, interactive beings—people as labels rather than complexly situated bundles of fluid allegiances. Furthermore, I have a sneaky suspicion that the ideals embodied in "role models" are the forced bright side of stereotyped, or even demographic, images—the Willie Horton–shape of all black men, for example—that displace or engulf the lived body and soul. (Thomas figured his own conservative values as the track to success by contrasting them with the image of his sister, Emma Mae Martin, as an unmotivated, welfare-dependent, lazy hustler. Yet the historian Nell Painter points out that "she was only on welfare temporarily and that she was usually a two-job-holding, minimum-wage-earning mother of four. Unable to afford professional help, she had gone on welfare while she nursed the aunt who had suffered a stroke but who normally kept her children when Martin was at work." The aura that dazzles is matched, in other words, by the shadow that follows. The exceptional profile in courage posed in fingershaking opposition to the suspect profile. The wife to the whore, the younger woman to the ex-wife. The model figure that devalues all others as disfigured.

During the Gulf War, a black friend of mine expressed her unswerving pride in and support of General Colin Powell: "Black people can sleep better knowing that a black man has his finger on the button." (Actually I've been losing a lot of sleep lately: In my dreams, I am toiling endlessly in a world where hard labor is supposed to be eternally ennobling, rather than ever degrading or even just exhausting, where ignorance is glorified, where creativity is vilified as mental disobedience, and cruelty rationalized as preemptive necessity. In *my* dreams, there's just a big button, with this disembodied finger on it.)

I worry about this tendency to indulge in figureheading our ideals. I think that imbuing humans with ideal or essential traits is a formula for either dashed ideals or corrupted ones. It is a formula as well for cynicism on the one hand or intolerance on the other. It prevents us from engagement with the shortcomings of idols; it requires that our public figures be monolithic—saints or sinners. It is no wonder we end up with a lot of liars in public office. Malcolm was both saint and sinner, and for his insistence to just *be*, paid dearly. No one knew better than he how complicated is heroism: how much it is the product of good acts and bad, of bravery, craft, dumb luck, and brilliant insight, all mixed up in serendipitous proportion. If Malcolm had conformed to the politically pornographic imagination of his generation's fixed ideals—even just a little—he would no doubt be alive today, hosting a talk show, lunching with Clarence. But Malcolm never was one for mannered acquiescence.

The substitution of role models for complete understanding of the political implications of certain philosophical doctrines results in the privatization of the political, and shifts focus from the implications of philosophy to the personalities of its proponents. It also makes those proponents *very* authoritative. It cedes to them enormous and total power over the consequences of "their" theories, as though theory had no life beyond birth, no interpretive generative property as taken up and reiterated by others. As though the life of the mind were physical, rigid, bounded as the body—as though you could pick an idea up and lay it down, this concrete, static, three-dimensional club of an idea flung forth like law upon the earth. And as though the idea might die like the man.

Given all that, it is simultaneously true that the ideals embodied in role modeling, like laws themselves, are frequently a way of presenting, and are premised on, certain kinds of statistical probabilities. Thus, when Clarence Thomas's image as a black man was advanced as a reason he should be on the Supreme Court, that supposition was often used by black people to mean that the experience of being black increases the likelihood of being sympathetic to the advancement of particular collective agendas. So it was that many people asked with disarming credulousness of Thomas: How could a once-poor black man turn on his people? (One hears the same sorts of veiled statistical wistfulness at the other end of the political spectrum: Tom Metzger, founder of the White Aryan Resistance, said, "I think David

Duke will make a great politician, because politicians make themselves acceptable to a majority of people.")

We live in a moment in which political ad agencies have perfected the art of exploiting symbolic properties while severing them from the statistical likelihoods that gave rise to them. Thus Clarence Thomas could exploit his roots as a poor black man and simultaneously deny that the poverty and material degradation in which millions of other poor blacks live is anything more than a state of mind. And thus Virginia Lamp Thomas, of all people, could, in the pages of *People* magazine, of all places, exploit the status of rape victim by dressing herself in the language of "survivor"—as a way of denying another woman's allegations of sexual harassment. This entire article in *People* is a fascinating study in the metaphors of embattlement, and weirdly evocative of Malcolm X's stories. Listen, for example, to Malcolm X:

> It was Allah's intent for me to help Cassius prove Islam's superiority before the world—through proving that mind can win over brawn. I don't have to remind you how people everywhere scoffed at Cassius Clay's chances of beating Liston.
>
> This time, I brought from New York with me some photographs of Floyd Patterson and Sonny Liston in their fight camps, with white priests as their "spiritual advisors." Cassius Clay, being a Muslim, didn't need to be told how white Christianity had dealt with the American black man. "This fight is the *truth*," I told Cassius. "It's the Cross and the Crescent fighting in a prize ring— for the first time. It's a modern Crusades—a Christian and a Muslim facing each other with television to beam it off Telstar for the whole world to see what happens!" I told Cassius, "Do you think Allah has brought about all this intending for you to leave the ring as anything but the champion?"

And compare Virginia Lamp Thomas:

> Clarence knew the next round of hearings to begin that day was not the normal political battle. It was spiritual warfare. Good versus

129

evil. We were fighting something we didn't understand, and we needed prayerful people in our lives. We needed God.

So the next morning, Wednesday, we started having these two couples in our home to pray for two or three hours every day. They brought over prayer tapes, and we would read parts of the Bible. We held hands and prayed. What got us through the next six days was God. We shut the kitchen blinds and turned on Christian praise music to survive the worst days.

Later, after two hours' sleep, we walked into the hearing room, and people were lining the hallways, urging him on. "Who are these people?" Clarence asked me, and I said, "I think they are angels."

These kinds of calculated disjunctures, rhetorical rearrangements, and surgical revisionism have resulted in such strange symbolic cyborgs that I sometimes think a President could appoint an outright fascist to the Supreme Court, as long as he could find the right packaging—a black Hispanic lesbian one, say, in a wheelchair. This is, of course, exactly what the voters of Louisiana too nearly did, in their rush to endorse the boyish good looks and the political plastic surgery of the "new" David Duke's new words. "When David Duke entered a hotel ballroom here today, JoAnn Jernigan, a retired nurse and lifelong Democrat, jumped to her feet and applauded . . . 'I've got to see my candidate,' she said of Mr. Duke, the Republican candidate for governor and former grand wizard of the Ku Klux Klan. 'He's so cute. How can someone who looks like that be bad?'" It is what Ross Perot and the Infinity automobile did with their fill-in-the-fantasy-of-your-choice style of mythic, malleable self-promotion. And it is what David Duke himself did when, "under the pseudonym 'Mohammed X,' he wrote 'African Atto,' a martial arts manual for black militants. He later said it was a way to develop a mailing list to keep track of potential black agitators. Under the pseudonym 'Dorothy Vanderbilt,' he wrote 'Finders-keepers,' a dating-and-sex manual for women." This is, after all, pornography's great power: to disguise, to dehistoricize, to decontextualize, to isolate.

Against this backdrop, it seems weirdly fitting that one of the most distinguishing features of Clarence Thomas's judicial philosophy is his wholesale rejection of statistics and other social science data, and with it the dismissal of a range of affirmative action remedies that have been central to blacks' social and economic progress over the last thirty years or so. For all of his quite moving anecdotalizing about his own history, Thomas by this gesture effectively supplants a larger common history with individualized hypotheses about free choice, in which each self chooses her destiny even if it is destitution. Clarence Thomas has not clearly committed himself to taking into account past and present social constraints as infringements on the ability to exercise choice. He ignores the history that gives at least as much weight to the possibility that certain minority groups have not had many chances to be in charge of things as to the possibility that they just don't want to, or that they just can't.

While self-help and strong personal values are marvelous virtues, they are no stand-in for the zealous protection of civil and human rights—that protection being the paramount task of the judiciary in any democracy, and of the Supreme Court in greatest particular. The problem with Clarence Thomas's espousal of these self-help values is that he positions them in direct "either/or" tension with any other value; self-help is presented as bitterly competitive rather than in complete concert with those social measures which would help ever more rather than ever fewer people.

Thomas's insistence on a hyperindividualistic case-by-case analytic in race and gender cases is nothing more than another way of insisting on a very high statistical probability, by narrowing the range of reference and narrowing the number of parties at issue. The difficulty with that, of course, is that while the evidence is narrowed from probabilities in the population at large to the credibility of sometimes a single witness, nothing is done to deal with the unconscious or unexpressed probabilistic presumptions that judges as well as juries bring to the calculation of credibility itself. Blacks are "more likely" to be criminals, for example; Hispanics "probably" steal cars; and women are "undoubtedly" hysterics.

Adducing evidence of disparate impact in a larger population is one very effective way of countering such free-floating presumptions or prejudices. Imagine, for example, how cumulatively powerful it would have been if (that is, *hypothetically*) there had been evidence that 99 percent of the female Yale Law School graduates who worked at the Equal Employment Opportunity Commission during a given director's tenure never advanced beyond the lowest G-level ranking, while (still hypothetically) John Doggett and 99 percent of the rest of the male Yalies sailed to the top within two months. Yet evidence of disparate impact is precisely the sort of stuff that Thomas's judicial philosophy *excludes*—thus, in a very real and ironic way, making sure that the vast majority of complaints about race and gender discrimination don't get past the "he said–she said" stage.

Against this, consider the utter disarray of any data about Clarence Thomas's judicial philosophy—the complete, calculated lack of a basis upon which to form an opinion or fashion a likelihood about what Thomas would do on the Supreme Court. (And contrary to the many careless aspersions about how "politicized" the hearings became, it must be kept in mind that the Constitution expressly makes the senatorial process of inquiry a political one. The Constitution specifies that no nominee shall be confirmed without the "advice and consent" of the Senate.) If the Senate is confronted with a tabula rasa—or even a tabula not-so-clara, a "mystery," as some of the senators openly called Thomas—then there is little basis for either knowledgeable advice or informed consent. And this is a severe threat to the functioning of our tripartite system of government, to the bal-

ance of political input that the involvement of the several
branches of government must provide before someone is placed
into that most sensitive position of discretionary insularity, the
shielded office of highest trust that is the Supreme Court.

In the face of the Senate's duty to inform itself about a judicial
candidate's philosophy, Judge Thomas showed a deeply discon-
certing pattern of either revising or disclaiming many of the most
troubling aspects of his record. If we believe in this epiphanous
recanting, we are left with the disturbing phenomenon of a
Supreme Court nominee who didn't read his own citations, who
misunderstood the legal import of his own obstructionist administrative actions, and who didn't really mean most of what he
said. This disdain for accountability was made even more alarming by being echoed in the CIA director's hearings just down the
hall: "In explanation of his flagging memory, Robert Gates recently told the Senate confirmation committee, 'I have to admit
to you that when I left the CIA in 1989 . . . I did a major data
dump.'"

And if we are not inclined to believe that Clarence Thomas's
keen intelligence could leave him in quite so disingenuous a state
of disarray, then we the people must come to terms with the fact
that we were confronted with an outright, practiced refusal to
answer questions. This is a tremendously serious violation of the
Senate's right to get answers to questions about any nominee's
views and his disposition to uphold precedent as well as to judge
facts and interpret new law. The Senate has a constitutional *duty*
to ensure that the Court remain a place where voices of dissent
and unpopular causes may be heard. Ambiguity is not the standard. A senatorial leap of faith, as the *Philadelphia Inquirer* urged
in an editorial, should not have been good enough. Much of the
vocabulary that even some senators employed during the hearings—"impression," "faith," "instinct," "hope," "trust"—simply did not describe a reasoned choice to support Clarence
Thomas.

(But the truth was, I suppose, that through all the masquerade, there really was lots of evidence about what Clarence Thomas was likely to do on the Supreme Court, just none that anyone ever talked about straightforwardly or sustainedly. We were left instead with the ghostly, enigmatic trace of Senator Thurmond's smile . . .)

"There but for the grace of God, go I," said Clarence Thomas of the prisoners he saw being shuttled back and forth from the District Courthouse in Washington, D.C. These words were uttered during his confirmation hearings, an attempt to reassure senators of his compassion, which was in question. Barely four months later, from his post on the Supreme Court, Thomas wrote, in a dissenting opinion, that a prisoner who was beaten and bloodied and had his teeth loosened by prison guards should have no constitutional claim under the Eighth Amendment proscription against cruel and unusual punishment, even where the violence was undue, wanton, and excessive. In a majority opinion joined in or concurred with by everyone else on the Court but Antonin Scalia, Justice Sandra Day O'Connor chided Thomas's use of this "substantial injury" test, pointing out that if the cutoff for constitutional claims is whether someone requires medical attention, this sanctions forms of torture that stop just short of leaving marks on the body. It's not a constitutional issue, in the world according to Clarence, until they *have* to go to the hospital.

Malcolm X once said, "It didn't take me a week to learn that all you had to do was give white people a show and they'd buy anything you offered them. It was like popping your shoeshine rag. The dining car waiters and Pullman porters knew it too, and they faked their Uncle Tomming to get bigger tips. We were in that world of Negroes who are both servants and psychologists."

And I wonder from the sidelines: if in sexual pornography men act and women appear, and if in racial pornography white people act and black people appear, then what happens in the intersec-

134

tional politics of race and gender, when a black woman suffers sexual abuse at the hands of a black man, against the gladiatorial backdrop of a white theater? In order to win, will he have to act as aggressive racial observer (or "play the race card")? Will he have to appear the sexual victim, malleable and open and available (or "lynched," castrated, skewered)? In order for her to have won, would she, paradoxically, have had to appear sexually assertive? And act racially passive? Or vice versa? Or would any matrix of asserted attributes work in her case, or would she always just disappear? Is the double-binding double burden of her race and her gender simply too great a confluence of appearances for her to ever successfully achieve the role of actor? (As opposed to that sly counterfeit, the "mere actress.") What arrangement of ingredients from the archetypal stewpot would allow her interpretive apotheosis into the cult of true womanhood?

In today's world, discrimination and the deprivation of cherished civil liberties have taken on new forms, unforms, and wordlessness that our labor and civil rights laws are hard-pressed if not outright unable to recognize. One reason is a sociopolitical climate in which both formal and informal burdens of proof make it harder and harder to have anything recognized as discrimination. Another is a kind of calculated confusion and rhetorical gaming, of which the spectacle of Clarence Thomas's hearing was exemplary, and which clouds all discussion of the rights of minorities and women in the United States, and of Thomas himself. In the words of a friend of mine: "Thomas invokes a mythical image of Malcolm X to serve his own needs . . . Thomas's use of X is the theft of a religious icon from a people whose religious and spiritual [ties come not from triptychs or cathedrals, but political] memories . . . In short, Thomas is a thief in the temple."

In today's world, this repeated emptying of all our cultural coffers, of all our sources of both self and unity, has left us much the poorer. It has left us with an atmosphere in which public relations firms, like mean-spirited astrologers, dictate presidential politics, and TV call-in polls divine the course of governance. In which David Duke's plastic surgery is a metaphor for the cosmetizing of Nazi policies made mainstream. In which if calling a black person a nigger is bad, then calling a white person a racist must be exactly the same thing only twice as bad. In which sexual harassment is shrugged off as children playing that annoying little game of "he said–she said," so better for the parents not to get involved. In which parties in relationships of political trust are replaced by game-show contestants for verisimilitude. In which reality is a stranger category than fantasy. In which reality is just a high-priced form of fantasy. In which marketing trend is the new-age demonstration of democracy-in-action. In which there is justice for sale and media moments for all.

A Hearing of One's Own

Within there runs blood,
The same old blood! the same red-running blood!
There swells and jets a heart, there all passions, desires, reachings,
    aspirations,
(Do you think they are not there because they are not express'd in
    parlors and lecture-rooms?)

—Walt Whitman, "I Sing the Body Electric"

Upon receiving the Nobel Prize in literature, Toni Morrison said of blacks in the United States: "Our silence has been long and deep . . . In canonical literature, we have always been spoken for. Or we have been spoken to. Or we have appeared as jokes or as flat figures suggesting sensuality. Today we are taking back our narrative, telling our story."

Nevertheless, taking back the narrative remains a complicated affair in today's world. In June 1993, for example, a little-known libertarian named Clint Bolick, litigation director for the conservative Institute for Justice, described Lani Guinier, President Clinton's nominee for director of the Civil Rights Division of the Justice Department, as a "Quota Queen." In direct contravention of anything Guinier had ever written, Bolick accused her of advocating "racial quotas in judicial appointments" and of attempting to "graft onto the existing system a complex racial spoils system that would further polarize an already divided nation." Within days, Bolick and the Republican Party were able to launch one of the most effective rumor-milled smear campaigns Washington has ever seen.

Despite the fact that Guinier herself is the product of an interracial marriage, and the third generation of lawyers in her family who have fought for a good old-fashioned equal-opportunity vision of an integrated America, she was successfully represented as someone who hated whites and all of Western civilization: "her intellectual response to racial polarization is to polarize it further; to assume that racism is so endemic that electoral gerrymandering has to be supplemented with legislative gerrymandering; to hold that colorblind equality of opportunity has to give way to race-saturated equality of outcomes." She was represented as not believing in majority rule: "Bob Dole of Kansas, the Republican leader in the Senate, said last month that he was shocked that Mr. Clinton would nominate someone who was a 'consistent supporter not only of quotas but of vote-rigging schemes that make quotas look mild.' In addition, the American Jewish Congress and the Anti-Defamation League have also expressed reservations about her theories." It was said that she believed that whites can't govern blacks: "Guinier strongly implies that whites are basically a racist political monolith." And most powerfully, Guinier was depicted as a crazy person—or if she wasn't crazy then she was lying, or if she wasn't lying then she certainly was not in touch with the Real World: "The Guinier nomination is the latest bid by the Clintons to paper the country floor-to-ceiling with leftist crazies."

The degree to which all of this was completely unsubstantiated only began to come out after the nomination had gone down in flames, and Guinier emerged as an impressive and—if belatedly and without the power of office—respected spokeswoman on issues of race. Yet it is worth remembering how completely her voice was obliterated at that moment in history when she came close to assuming a position invested with the power of law. Compare, for a small example, the following footnote from one of her articles with the characterizations it spawned during the campaign against her. The footnote reads:

In Virginia, where Douglas Wilder is the first black elected Governor since Reconstruction, some commentators have interpreted his victory as a "new black politics." But cf. Ayres, "Virginia Governor Baffles Democrats with Crusade for 'New Mainstream,'" New York

139

Times, Oct. 14, 1990, at A22, col. 1 (Wilder considers himself "a governor who happens to be black, not a black who happens to be governor.") . . . Others see Wilder's win as the triumph of a single-issue constituency in the wake of recent Supreme Court decisions on abortion. In either case, given the narrow margin of victory, Wilder's ability to govern on other issues important to the black community is considerably vitiated . . .

The following excerpts refer to that footnote:

From the *Wall Street Journal:* "So even Virginia's African-American governor, Douglas Wilder, isn't 'authentic,' she says, because he was elected with votes of the white majority. He therefore must pursue a mainstream agenda that isn't 'important to the black community.'"

From the *Legal Times:* "Thus, Guinier suggests, a black elected official like Virginia Gov. L. Douglas Wilder might not count as authentically black because he had to appeal to white voters in order to get elected."

From the *New York Times:* "As for the notable and formerly impossible elections of black politicians like Gov. Douglas Wilder of Virginia, she questions whether he is an 'authentic' figure for blacks—because he owes his job to white voters as well."

From the *New York Post:* "She does not think whites can adequately represent blacks—which, if true, means we should unload Mayor Dinkins tomorrow because a black by that logic cannot adequately represent whites."

For those familiar with Lani Guinier's work, this all begins to resemble some drunken party game in which each person whispers a message to his neighbor, each embroidering "the story" until there is no story left, only the leavings of inebriated malice. As if that weren't enough, the most corrupt part is that the message which began all the whispering was not Lani Guinier's but Clint Bolick's.

In a manner painfully reminiscent of characterizations of Anita Hill, Lani Guinier was exiled to a world somewhere apart from the realm of the real, outside the mainstream, and beyond the pale. The more normal she "seemed," warned the Bolick-inspired media, the greater the hidden actuality of her dangerous wily calculation: "In a word, Lani Guinier may appear to be learned, presentable and articulate, but at heart she is a crackpot." The public was warned not to look too closely, as if investing her with the power of truthful speech might release some mythic contagion; as if she were a siren guiding the ship of state onto the shoals of destruction; as if she were Pandora or Eve or Lilith or Jezebel. David Boldt, in the *Philadelphia Inquirer,* warned that if she ever got a hearing, "Real America would see her as a madwoman."

"You can't even pronounce her name," said Linda Chavez on the MacNeil-Lehrer show, in a fit of exoticizing, xenophobic preschoolishness. "Strange name, strange hair, strange writing— she's history," began an article in *U.S. News & World Report.* History, you say? Chopped liver is more like it.

But seriously, this question of history. Throughout, Guinier's own insistence on retaining *her* meaning of *her* words was thrown back at her as "denial" or as evidence of opportunism, shiftiness, lying, or insanity. Since this was accompanied by the failure of anyone in the White House to make the slightest effort to set the record straight, Guinier endured a good month and a half of wild accusation, against which absolutely no defense was ever officially put forward. Her credibility was further compromised by her inability to talk to the press before Clinton sacked her; Guinier, it turns out, was under White House instruction not to talk to the press until the promised hearing, which of course never occurred. This restriction was lifted only once, hours before Clinton withdrew her name, when she went on *Nightline.* Immediately after the *Nightline* appearance, the White House reimposed its censorship of her, for fear that any further statements would whip up public sentiment in her favor, forcing a hearing that would result in a "divisive" public discussion of race. (Sena-

141

tor Biden was reportedly furious at Clinton for putting the Senate in the position of "having" to trash yet another black woman.)

While the White House censorship went under the name of protocol, that protocol of tight-lipped restraint was supposedly premised upon the eventual opportunity to have a public hearing. Add to this the fact that Lani Guinier was provided with no media trainer, no media advice, no media advocate—a fatal lack in today's political world. In the press, even commentators one might expect to be her supporters seemed not to have read her articles themselves, relying on the boilerplate Quota Quotes as the universal starting reference.

(I do not include Bill Clinton, supposedly one of Guinier's oldest "friends," among those who didn't read her articles. Frankly, I find hard to believe his now-famous tearful protestation that "at the time of her nomination, I had not read her writings and I wish I had . . . They clearly lend themselves to interpretations that do not express the views that I expressed on civil rights during the campaign . . . It is not the fear of defeat that prompted this decision. It is the certainty that the battle would be carried over ground I could not defend." What I do believe is that by that time the Bolick definition of her work had run so far amok that Clinton decided it would not be in *his* best interests to pursue it.)

But the silence imposed on Guinier by the White House and the Senate—many members of which were simultaneously having apoplexy over the supposed demise of the First Amendment on college campuses—had the effect of creating a historical record that is powerfully and peculiarly skewed against her. Guinier was in the odd position of trying to describe what she had said and written to people whose only rejoinder was, "Well, the *New York Times* says . . ."

One thing that didn't escape the historical record, of course, was Bill Clinton's pain at having to trample all over Guinier, that pain amplified by his undying and much-advertised affection for

142

her. "I love her," said he. "I think she's wonderful. If she called me and told me she needed $5000, I'd take it from my account and send it to her, no questions asked." The tortured and protracted nature of the White House's relation to Guinier's nomination fed odd, complex, yet frequent comparisons of Lani Guinier to Anita Hill and to Tawana Brawley. In at least some quarters it rekindled an examination of the power of stereotypical depiction—all those loony, out-of-control black women crazed by the repeated spurnings of men they just couldn't let go of. (A Senate aide said they tried to encourage Guinier to withdraw long before it came to a head but "she wouldn't take a hint.") Yet even that examination has been short-circuited by the "oh but of course" national sentiment that *any* public discussion of racism or sexism is itself racist, sexist, and moreover guilt-inducing. Of *course* they're going to say it's racism, runs this line of reasoning. Oh of *course* they're going to blame men . . .

Domestically and in the eyes of the world, this all-knowing dismissiveness prefigures any defense of Lani Guinier as just another example of feminism's or the civil rights movement's "grip" on the American media. The *London Daily Mail*'s frenzied description of American feminists who defended Anita Hill is only one of many examples of this phenomenon:

> [Feminism's] effect on other institutions, such as the judicial system, where it has already successfully lobbied for changes in the rules of evidence based on gender and has curtailed the effectiveness of the Supreme Court by character assassination, can only be described as evil. One doesn't want to make a ludicrous comparison, but it seems fair to say that America today, vis-à-vis feminist thought, is at the point Germany reached before the Nazis took over. The Nazis talked about *gleichschaltung*, the need to co-ordinate mainstream thinking with Nazi ideology. Militant feminists are doing that in America with their political correctness.

While Guinier and Hill have received similarly disgraceful and disrespectful drubbings from public officials, there are important

143

distinctions that arguably make Guinier's treatment much worse than Hill's. One of the most salient is that unlike Anita Hill's supposedly "uncorroborated" allegations against Clarence Thomas, Lani Guinier's statements were published in leading law journals over a period of many years and were easily accessible. Yet they were utterly ignored as authoritative in the debate about who she was and what she meant. While perhaps it's just politics that everyone in Washington gets picked apart for what they say, Lani Guinier was condemned for things she never said and consistently denied. The "he said–she said" of the Thomas hearings gave way to a surreal disempowering game of "she *says* she said." Over and over I saw her picture on television, her lips moving, but the sound being given to a voiceover that described all the awful crackpot things she *meant* when her lips moved like that.

This ubiquitous image of Guinier—lips moving, voiceover confirming your worst fears about what she was supposed to have written, what she was *supposed* to be—ultimately served to depersonalize her. It made her a visual aid reinforcing a stereotype. The ubiquity of her image and the suppression of her words enabled the public imagination to run wild. As "Quota Queen" evoked images of welfare queens and other moochers who rise to undeserved heights, complaining unwarrantedly all the way, Lani Guinier the complex human with a distinguished history was reduced to a far-left "element," not at all an individual but a dangerous "type" whose work was part of a larger "agenda"—the attacks on her splaying out into attacks on "the likes of" her. She became, to whites and even some blacks, akin to that hero of free speech and unfettered megalomania, Leonard Jeffries, the new Right's archetype of new-leftists-in-academia. "What is really scary about Guinier is her belief that blacks elected to office by whites are not really black. This stuff is right out of the Leonard Jeffries melanin-and-ice people school of thought." In such broad strokes as this was her work reconfigured as something

144

flaky, embarrassing, untouchable, not-known-or-we'd-never-have-suggested-her.

In fact, Leonard Jeffries got much more of a hearing than Lani Guinier, his every last explosive utterance endlessly documented, filmed, replayed, discussed, shuddered at. Like the larger-than-life black penis, Leonard Jeffries's big black terrifying tongue has become mythologized as the horrific source of all the evils of the black race. Here is a man who has clearly been swallowed by rage and regret, revenge and despair (not that rage, revenge, and despair are not significant elements in black American experience that must be listened to, but there are much more coherent expressions of it than the manic, sometimes indecipherable ramblings of Mr. Jeffries)—and yet he is given power, a platform, and an audience not just of black City College students but of millions of media voyeurs who listen and listen and listen to him, whipping themselves into a froth of fear that he is the "sort of person [who] will be writing your children's textbooks in the coming multicultural order . . . paranoid, anti-Semite and purveyor of crackpot conspiracy theories."

My grandmother used to say that people hear what they want to. It is interesting to imagine what it is that the mainstream wants when Leonard Jeffries gets not only his rights of free speech protected but all that valuable free airtime, and Lani Guinier can't get a word in edgewise. Yet plunging Guinier into silence as though behind a display window is a setup, as I said, for depersonalizing her, and depersonalizing her is a setup for the pornographic indulgence of random vulgar and ignorant attribution—particularly the ubiquitous attribution of "quota queen."

As an aside, it is interesting to note that Lani Guinier's nomination was bracketed in the news by stories of two other legendary "queens." Guinier's saga of quota queenliness was rapidly followed by the appointment of the so-called Condom Queen, Dr. Joycelyn Elders, to the post of Surgeon General. (At issue was her stated desire to make condoms available in public schools as one

way of possibly slowing the spread of AIDS.) The use of the term
"queen" to describe Dr. Elders, another black woman ultimately
driven from her post in a doggedly-waged smear campaign, high-
lights the extent to which the connotations of the term demand
some explicit consideration. It's become a very racialized term,
even when it was used to describe the hotel "queen" Leona
Helmsley—it began as Helmsley's own advertised appellation,
but got played out in very stereotyped media terms as her trial
wore on, a bad play on insulting notions of "Jewish American
Princesses," a high-income tax-fraudulent version of the black
welfare queen. ("Rhymes With Rich," ran a headline describing
Helmsley in the *New York Post.*) In these contexts, "queen" was
used to connote insatiability, the label a veritable crown of thorns,
the mockery of royalty, the opposite of imperiousness even as it
evoked arrogant, demanding disregard.

The other story involving a queen was that of the death of
Marian Anderson, which preceded Guinier's dis-appointment by
some months. It was interesting that with regard to Anderson,
the term was used repeatedly as a celebration of her humanity,
specifically, a repeated tribute to her for symbolizing (but not
proclaiming) that "race doesn't matter"—even as she did so in a
career-long swirl of dignified but unmistakable racial confrontation. I was struck by the different functions of silence in the lives
of Anderson and Guinier. Unlike Guinier, who tried to speak but
was silenced by the government, Anderson chose to speak very
little about her famous battle to sing at Constitution Hall. And
unlike Guinier's muffled noises, Anderson's deep pool of silence
was praised as dignity, her refusal to parry interpreted as a refusal
to sink "low"; her refusal to speak made her a saint, a queen, a
royal personage. Hers was undoubtedly a powerful and moving
legacy. Her eloquence was the act of her refraining, in all its
myriad layers of meaning.

Yet how could she have spoken? What words would not have
destroyed her dignity? Is there anything she could have said

about it to create her own history of that event? She was seen but not heard in one sense, heard but not seen in another. Her silence was heard perhaps precisely because at the same time she was singing a canny combination of spirituals and classical repertoire. The slave voice, in Received Standard English.

One year after Clinton withdrew her nomination, Lani Guinier did something like "taking back her own narrative" when she published her widely, if sheepishly, acclaimed book, *The Tyranny of the Majority*. It will be interesting to note the long-term impact of this book, for even as its ideas are absorbed by the media, the summary descriptions are positively Marian Anderson–like. Suddenly Guinier is "dignified," "elegant," "graceful," and "restrained." There is much scrambling to make up to her for the "mistakes" in how she was treated, but I am not sure that conferring "star" status on her is the same as engaging in the national conversation about race that she so fervently urges—although in my optimistic moments it does look like a step in the right direction.

This is not to compare Lani Guinier with Marian Anderson in any way that makes one more or less than the other. On the contrary, it is to observe the invisible bounds of permissibility, the social limits of appropriate black speech. What would have happened to Anderson if she had been a little less sonorous, if her talent had not been in compelling the emotions, if she had issued a simple verbal pronouncement of the wrongs of the Daughters of the American Revolution. Would she have been just another complainer, going down in infamy with the first-phase Guinier? Would anybody have heard? Or would she have met the fate of the second-phase Guinier, whose listeners seem charmed and chastened but not yet entirely convinced of the alarming urgency of this country's racial division?

A black friend of mine who serves as an associate dean at a major university once finally expressed her immense frustration at a faculty meeting: "No one's listening to me!" she blurted out.

"That's not true," retorted one of the white men on the faculty. "I've been listening to you speak for years now and I want to congratulate you because your verbs always agree." Is the ability to understand affected by the willingness to understand? Does speech falling alone in the forest make a sound?

Like the poet Phyllis Wheatley, Marian Anderson was considered remarkable not just for the quality of her voice but for her "amazing" and "unnatural" yet "natural" mastery of that highest cultural art form, the classical repertoire. I remember one of my law school classmates expressing similar amazement at Leontyne Price's beautiful voice—it was astonishing to him because he assumed she was "untutored"; he talked about her as though he thought her voice must have been delivered to her, full-blown, as something innate and "natural" in the sense of being located in her body alone rather than in her mind, and therefore miraculous because we all know that mastering opera usually requires both master-y and a mind.

Marian Anderson was a black Beethoven, a Japanese Thomas Jefferson, a white person with rhythm, an embodiment of hip-hop who could perform the ballet, who didn't just talk that talk but who could also speak that speech. Powerful testament to universalism, the greatness of our common human spirit. All to the good.

And yet . . . as Marian Anderson was exceptional, so was she exceptionalized. She was "universal," but not representative—no more than B. B. King is seen as a product of a rigorous classical musical education, his first instrument being the concert violin, he a child prodigy at age four. It will be a long time perhaps before either Guinier or Anderson is extrapolated as an archetypal representative of her particular history: each challenges the neoconservative stereotype of middle-class blacks, who, like welfare queens, are depicted as languishing in petulant ease upon the undeserved, hoarded "spoils" of the civil rights movement's few gains. Each epitomizes the complicated, precarious, tenuous reality of black middle-classness as it snakes through families striking individuals here or there, its status depositing them on an unsteady tightrope of social and financial ambiguity more often than on the cushion-for-life that many whites (at least until recently) have been privileged to expect from middle-classedness. The black middle class is filled with the histories of remarkable "strivers" whose fortunes have always very directly relied upon the sacrifices of those not-so-middle-class kin and friends, as well as upon the affirmative disposition and action of powerful institutions to make real opportunity available. "It means so little when a man like me wins some success," wrote Paul Robeson. "Where is the benefit when a small class of Negroes makes money and can live well? It may all be encouraging, but it has no deeper significance. I feel this way because I have cousins who can neither read nor write. I have had a chance. They have not. That is the difference." The awareness of connection is perhaps one of the saddest social losses of the current climate of relentless exceptionalism, in which the black middle class is understood, and not infrequently understands itself, as a fragmented band of "escapees," refugees rather than relatives of those whose struggle for survival is barely seen until it is taken to the streets.

The inherent irony of black voice: "To speak of a silent voice is to speak in an oxymoron. There is no such thing as a silent voice . . . there is something untenable about the attempt to represent what is not there, to represent what is *missing* or absent . . . Indeed, how can the black subject posit a full and sufficient self in a language in which blackness is a sign of absence?"

Quayle Has a Cow

Who has been to blame for the riots? The rioters are to blame.
Who is to blame for the killings? The killers are to blame . . . I believe the lawless social anarchy which we saw is directly related to
the breakdown of family structure, personal responsibility and social order in too many areas of our society . . . Our cities are filled
with children having children; with people who have not been able
to take advantage of educational opportunities; with people who
are dependent on drugs or the narcotic of welfare. To be sure,
many people in the ghettos struggle very hard against these tides
and sometimes win. But too many feel they have no hope and nothing to lose. This poverty is again, fundamentally a poverty of values
. . . When families fail, society fails. Children need love and discipline. They need mothers and fathers. A welfare check is not a husband. The state is not a father.

—Vice President Dan Quayle, May 19, 1992

At the height of the furor over Lani Guinier's appointment, a colleague described her as comporting herself like "a black Jacqueline Kennedy." Although their circumstances were so very different, I think I understand the temptation to such an analogy. What has made both women not just graceful but great has been their ability to stay focused on the good and meaningful priorities in their lives even while negotiating paths filled with political land mines—and to do so without apparent anger or mean-spiritedness. But it did make me wonder when we will stop turning America's most eloquent, intelligent, and committed women into test sites for the ability to endure abuse elegantly.

The day after the November 1992 presidential election, the German Green Party ran a banner headline in its journal announcing that "Hillary's husband" had just won the U.S. presidency. This play, decentering the husband in question and simultaneously shifting the referential standpoint of First Lady to that of First Person, triumphantly captured what was more generally experienced in this country as the anxiety of impending Gender Trouble. Would this loose unmanaged female, Hillary *née* Rodham *didn't-wannabe* Clinton, sit in on Cabinet meetings? Would she make *his* appointments? Is she a radical lefty crackpot who manipulates her wishy-washy puppet-husband's strings? Isn't there a law of nature that the bigger the wife's brain, the smaller the husband's, because the only way a woman's brain grows like that is when she sucks the common sense out through his ears while he sleeps? And isn't the refusal to bake cookies the surest sign of witchcraft?

The excesses of the 1992 Republican National Convention have died down somewhat in the public memory, but the stereotypes upon which they drew have long been and continue to be a social force of some magnitude. While the debate about Hillary Clinton's public role became ever so much more polite after the election, even during Whitewater-gate, the questions that continued to plague her were just better-modulated versions of Daniel Wattenberg's summary in the August 1992 issue of the conservative *American Spectator:* in a much-cited article entitled "Boy Clinton's Big Mama: The Lady Macbeth of Little Rock," Wattenberg likened Rodham to a "self-detonating explosive" who, by letting her "temple dogs roam free," would cause her husband no end of embarrassment. The article went on to characterize "Hillary's charms" as eluding "most outside of an elite cohort of left-liberal, baby-boom feminists"; Hillary's politics as "hard-left"; and Hillary's "self-generated" image as one of "consuming ambition, inflexibility of purpose, domination of a pliable husband, and an unsettling lack of tender human feeling, along with the affluent feminist's contempt for traditional female roles."

Following the election, the press accommodated itself somewhat to the inevitability of Hillary Clinton in the White House, but the attempts to typecast her First Ladyship remained ludicrously fuzzy-brained. Similarly, efforts to slot her as "another" Eleanor Roosevelt were tinged with a faint concern that she was just a little too vulgarly aggressive, transforming Junior League charity work into its grubby lower-class cousin, social activism. Comparisons with the independence of Jacqueline Kennedy failed miserably amid suspicions that not only would she not redecorate the White House, she wasn't likely to vacuum it in four years. It was hard to think of her with the same long-suffering glow as Mrs. Ford, or the long-suffering silence of Mrs. Nixon, or the cold glamour of Mrs. Reagan, or the southern graciousness of Mrs. Johnson, or the rosy ebullience of Mrs. Carter—in fact, no one seemed to think of Hillary as Mrs. Anything at All. (A psychic on the Joan Rivers show predicted, in addition to global depression, that Hillary was "so domineering" that she and Bill would split up "for sure" within two years.) She was perceived more as an outside agitator than as an inside saboteur—a foreign female, like Raisa Gorbachev, whom Mrs. Reagan once took to task for monopolizing dinner parties by "speaking in whole paragraphs."

This kinder, gentler post-election vilification of Hillary Clinton persistently emphasized certain purported qualities: (1) a mysterious "self-generated" power involving sinister "charms"—possibly even hexes—that surpass all human understanding and for sure political accountability; (2) a "hardness" to her left-leaning proclivities that is somehow sexual in its turgid perversity, and maybe even pornographic if only we knew the whole story, but all we know for certain is that it's somehow related to Bill's "softness" and the squishy-hearted effeminacy of his vulnerability in even trying to make her a wife, while she beats him over the head with "Rodham," and in public, no less; (3) a double-back-flip transgressive rejection of biological destiny, manifested in the first instance by her persistent cross-dressing in britches she's too big for, shoes she's too small for, and pants that rightfully belong to the so-called man of the family, and in the second instance by her manful attempt to cover it all up with a Maybelline makeover, contact lenses, and a page*boy* haircut.

But really, no joke. Three centuries after Salem, what's going on? Why are we still burning witches, or even just low-simmering them to death? Why are these images so powerful? Was it merely her Yale degree (the Wellesley degree alone was probably not enough—girls' school) that turned the election of Bill Clinton

153

into an event that must be understood as having happened either despite or because of Hillary Rodham?

There was a television advertisement for Gitano jeans, aired at the height of the 1992 Republican Convention, that featured a writhing, nubile young woman with full red lips who professed that living with "several men before marriage" (who turned out to be her brothers) was perfectly consistent with traditional "family values." Her voice was full of suggestive spaces and little rises: "When you educate a woman you educate the family," she whispered with a tight, torrid little smile, as the camera panned down the breathtaking slopes of her jeans. As I watched, I kept thinking that if this is a message that has permeated to the pubescent Gitano jeans crowd then it's only a matter of time before you have an advertisement that says, "When you educate a woman at Yale Law School, you educate the world."

But as usual, I was wrong. And not just a little wrong, but a whole lot.

In the first instance, in one of the weirder subtexts of this advertisement, I am told that the serpentine young woman was none other than Marie Osmond, that her brothers are Donny and the boys, and that Marie is now divorced and therefore functionally excommunicated from all possibility of going to Heaven according to the Mormon church of which she is a member. To those who understand the rich complications of theology in late postmodernity—could this be the Mormon construction of Hell?

In the second instance, I continually underestimate the extent to which the education of women has always been, in American myth, a means of refined domestication but domestication nonetheless. As long as educated women confine their educated insights to the hearthside or maybe a few volunteer civic enterprises that, it bears repeating, do not involve being paid, they will maintain their claim on femininity. Woe betide, however, the woman who insists on getting paid for all that brainpower, for lo, she will be treated as a prostitute even as society denies the same with righteousness. For all our pretensions to equality, for example, how is it that in 1993 the U.S. Congress had fewer women than the Iranian parliament—Iran being a country that most Americans do not associate with the empowerment of women?

At stake in this debate is the definition of "family" itself. To what extent does the nineteenth-century proposition endure that "bourgeois men and women . . . tended to see any woman who was sexually [or otherwise] active outside of marriage as a prostitute"? To what extent does "family" encompass any less (or more) than the nucleus of father, mother, and their biological offspring? To what extent is a married woman still the common law extension of her husband's estate? To what extent is it true, as the anthropologist Anna Lowenhaupt Tsing proposes, that the women's movement of the 1960s and 1970s has been met with a backlashing rage reserved for escaped property, a process of monsterization of the liberated middle-class female that is in fact unleashed upon the captive bodies of poor women and women of color?

This last point was illustrated with excruciating clarity in Vice President Dan Quayle's notorious and intriguingly complicated attack on the television program *Murphy Brown*. In Quayle's attack on Brown, a fictional white upper-upper-middle-class newscaster who has a child out of wedlock, the Vice President specifically linked her purported lapse in basic family values to the social collapse in South Central Los Angeles in the wake of the acquittal of the police officers who beat Rodney King. The not very subtle implication of this was, of course, that all those rioters were the unfathered wild children born of loose wombs, not "legitimate" mothers. It bears underscoring that if Quayle had said nothing more than this, his remarks would scarcely have raised an eyebrow, and certainly wouldn't have generated the controversy that actually ensued. But the ingredient that so distinguished Quayle's remarks was his bold equation of Ms.

155

Brown's morals with those attributed to real women of color. What made Quayle's remarks so controversial was his mixture, not mere juxtaposition, of images of white and black women's unmarried bodies: corrupt by virtue of their autonomy, their uncontrollability. It was a challenge, I think, to the usual hierarchy of black women as surrogate vessels, strong-walled if chipped pitchers, subordinated to fragile little white "uterine hostesses" (an unfortunate but evocative term I have heard used in surrogacy cases). The challenge to that hierarchy is seen as profoundly undesirable, the offspring alternately viewed as the innocent but irremediably ruined victim of the wild woman's willful profligacy, or else the riotous, hydra-headed reassertion of it.

Dan Quayle's attack on Murphy Brown made me think of the attacks, some thirty years ago, on Elvis Presley. Elvis's gyrating hips, "Nigra" music, and loose wet lips were widely rebuked as corrupting the (white) youth of America and inciting them to civil insurrection and, worse, disrespect for their parents. No wonder Murphy Brown was so threatening: gyrating up there on national TV to that Negro music (Aretha Franklin, specifically), imitating the morals of those loose Negro women. Does that sort of behavior produce proud statesmen like Quayle or Bush? No it does not, ladies and gentlemen. It incites those women's unruly, illicit, overexcited offspring to RIOT.

"The family" is a complicated affair in America. One in three women and one in seven men have been molested by an adult before they reach the age of eighteen. A forcible rape occurs every five minutes. A violent crime is committed every fifteen seconds in this country, the majority by assailants who are known to their victims. So it should hardly be surprising that violence has become a regular ingredient of family and other intimate relations. While much of this has not yet found its way to the level of constitutional controversy, its trauma is a strong component of our cultural environment. There is a peculiar tension between prudery and prurience in the United States: we Americans are

156

obsessed with the suppression of much sexuality that is voluntary, consensual, spontaneous, and joyful, yet are similarly obsessed with a peeping-tom voyeuristic hunger for the weird, violent, exploitative, and sad. There is widespread resistance, for example, to advertising the effectiveness of condoms in protecting against HIV infection, on the grounds that it might be interpreted as "condoning premarital sex." Yet the fundamentalist puritanism of that public disapproval seems strangely akin to the senatorial and general public mockery—like an eighteenth-century shaming ceremony—of Anita Hill, with its rabidly insatiable appetite for ever more lurid fantasies about what she (wink, wink) *really* wanted.

There is, alive and well in the United States, a culture of humiliation which reveals the most intimate lives of others and a fetishism of control of that which is beyond control. We are a nation in which sex outside marriage is resoundingly disapproved of; yet in which the wholesome girls next door are encouraged to bare themselves on the pages of *Playboy*. Single women who choose to have children are sweepingly portrayed as making a "mockery of fathers." Single women who do not have children are too often depicted as needing to be rescued from their presumptively degenerative man-hating insouciance.

A terrifying promotional advertisement for the movie *Single White Female,* for example, ended with the throaty whisper "Careful, she's crazy!" in one ad, and "Living with a roommate can be murder" in another. One reason I found the advertisement so troubling was the simple straightforwardness of the racial boundary and gender terrorization encoded in it. The plot, as outlined in a few seconds of dramatic camera work, was about a young woman who breaks up with her fiancé and kicks him out of her apartment. She then takes out a newspaper ad worded, as the title suggests, in the intensely unselfconscious and fearfully segregationist tradition of the American housing market. She ends up with a murderously destructive roommate who becomes

157

both literally and figuratively a mirror of herself: single white female, simultaneously prey and killer huntress. This theme is reiterated in one way or another in almost every recent film in which women have been so lucky as to have anything like a major part, from *Basic Instinct* to *The Hand That Rocks the Cradle*. It is no wonder that the movie *Thelma and Louise,* mediocre in every respect except for sheer contrast, was so passionately received by female theatergoers.

It is interesting to ponder what a movie entitled *Single Black Female* might be like: what horrors would the mythmaking stereotype-exploiters in Hollywood conjure that could outdo the literary imagination of Dan Quayle? In some ways the movie industry has not bothered to be as straightforwardly libertine with images of black women as it has with white women, except in pornography and, of course, maid motifs (but then of course it hasn't had to—politicians have filled every conceivable appetite for purveyed fictions of black women). This is not to say that by any stretch of the imagination the movies have presented positive images of black women. Black heroines—or even antiheroines— simply don't exist in film, with the possible recent complication of the comedienne Whoopi Goldberg.

To assert the notion of family as a deep-rooted conception of male property is, in today's bruised political climate, to risk accusations of polemicism. Yet the entire Anglo-American property system of transfer and inheritance rests solidly on historic assumptions of white men as rational contractors and of primogeniture as a rationale for their inheriting everything of importance. Honestly, I didn't make it up. *They* did. All I plan to do here is talk about the tracks with which that legacy has marked us all.

From Revolutionary times forward, white women's lives in the United States became increasingly interiorized, their sphere of influence relegated to the domestic, until by the end of the 1800s the so-called cult of true womanhood had produced a sacralized vision of domesticity that for many was as much prison as "home." Women were privy to a domestic life that was relentlessly idealized—that idealization being the subject of so much of the literature of authors like Kate Chopin and Charlotte Perkins Gilman—and a legal life in which they had limited rights to property, contract, and divorce, no right to vote, and the "right" to be beaten by a stick of no greater thickness than the husband's thumb.

Public life, meanwhile, was masculinized, particularly as the economy became more industrially based, the concept of self-interested individualism replacing conceptions of civic virtue. And, as virtue became domesticated and thus feminized, ideals of republican motherhood were limited to childbearing and childrearing—backdrop for rather than at the forefront of the formulations of citizenship. By the 1820s and 1830s the key element in the American definition of manhood was moral autonomy: control over one's emotions and, most important, economic independence. The perfect citizen was one who mastered his own fate by owning his own property, and by controlling his women and livestock with kindly goading to maximum productivity. This exercise of individual ambition was deemed to further the nation's progress.

A woman, in contrast, furthered the national interest by keeping the table well set, the parlor overflowing with music and clever badinage, and the nursery a soothing and sane greenhouse for young minds. "It was the wife's duty to maintain a home environment free from sensuality, to help protect husbands and sons from dissipation. If men were not properly disciplined, they might lead the country to economic stagnation . . . The man's duty was to extend the asceticism he learned from women at home into the economy."

As Joan Hoff, in her book *Law, Gender, and Injustice,* observes, "This private sphere, despite its infusion of civic virtue, insulated postrevolutionary women from the present, just as the public one occupied by postrevolutionary men propelled them toward the future"—a legacy that Hoff asserts has kept women's political claims functionally anachronistic even to this day. This encoding of the tenses of men's and women's existence also serves as a metaphoric backdrop for understanding discussions of the first and second "Great Awakenings" of the women's movement. These historical struggles, first for suffrage and then for the set of freedoms aimed at but not fully realized in the now-forgotten Equal Rights Amendment, are demarcated by what Hoff refers to as a "broken barometer syndrome," in which there are such great time-lags between the initiation of political action and the ultimate improvement in legal status that "the changes often no longer accurately reflect [women's] present needs because of intervening developments in the political economy, family demographics, and technology."

Consider the many universalizing gestures by which "man" is still entrenched as woman's measure: the repeated sabotage of women's struggles by assimilationist models of civic belonging is an unfortunate phenomenon documented in women's writings from Abigail Adams to Audre Lorde. "We should not forget," Hoff says, "that the newspaper attacks on the Declaration of Sentiments of 1848 were so excessive that many of the original one hundred signers withdrew their names from that 'insane' legal document, prompting Elizabeth Cady Stanton to remark: 'No words could express our astonishment on finding that what seemed to us so timely, so rational, and so sacred, should be a subject for sarcasm and ridicule to the entire press of the nation.'" Perhaps the modern parallel of this is to be found again in the 1992 Republican National Convention, which culminated in a smarmy exaltation of "traditional family values" paired with a poisonous stream of sarcasm and ridicule heaped upon "nontraditional" (that is, insubordinate) women—married or not, from Hillary Rodham to homosexuals (including gay men, figured as despicable because supposedly too much like women) to "the" black single mother. It was fascinating to watch the persistent reassertion of the Victorian ideal of woman as ruler of the home and nursery, fully occupied with the raising of great statesmen; it was played upon endlessly, as in this description by Marilyn Quayle: "Barbara Bush exemplifies our ideal of a strong and generous woman dedicated to her husband, her children and our nation." George Bush, in the same speech, was not cited for his dedication to his wife but was praised as "a leader for all generations . . . who will lead this nation to a brighter tomorrow." By the same token, transgression from the role of women-who-nurture-leaders was firmly rejected: "Most women do not wish to be liberated from their essential natures as women," said Marilyn Quayle. Even many Republicans felt her speech further displaced what ought to have been a focus on Republican women holding elected office, rather than exclusively on "wives of" Republicans.

The whole spectacle reminded me of something a Czechoslovakian acquaintance told me while deprecating the supposed implementation of equality for women under Communism: "The women's seats for trade union officials, for example, were sometimes filled by holding beauty contests." In the United States, during the election campaign, we came very close to holding a presidential bake-off.

Responding to the Convention-al call, Barbara Bush, given unprecedented airtime, portrayed her life as a stream of Little League games, carpooling, scraped knees, and cookie-baking. She described all her labors as devotional tribute to the men in her life—her sons and her husband (if she has daughters, we will never know—and even gave over the last part of "her" talk to her grandson, who praised the nobility of his grandfather.

"Do we really want to replace Barbara Bush as First Lady?" asked Pat Robertson, as though the election were for First Lady rather than president. It was, of course, a thinly veiled attack on the manhood of Bill Clinton, who was consistently figured by the

161

Republicans as not being able to keep his woman safely parked at home. And what is interesting about this is that the matter of family values, as applied to men's morals, seemed to have been measured entirely by the domestic behavior of their women. Thus, by convention time, Great Mothering became nothing less than a diversion from poor statesmanship and nationwide depression. Barbara Bush was so exalted that she rose symbolically from being merely George Bush's wife to the greatest honorific of all, that of being his sainted mother. Thus she could not be betrayed by even the usual infidelities.

Hillary Clinton, in sharp contrast, never rose any higher in the motherhood sweepstakes than Daniel Wattenberg's churlish "big mama"—a clever switch of normative American Motherhood into black-sounding parlance, playing on stereotypes of castrating black women who purportedly reduce their men to perpetual little boys. But for the most part, Hillary Clinton, barely a wife, was never featured as mother to anyone, not even to that poor *lonely* waif, Chelsea. Dear neglected Chelsea: so unbrothered, unsistered, and with no one selfless enough to bake the poor kid a few cookies. In the neo-Victorian script, such a bad wife as Hillary could not be betrayed by the cavortings of a Gennifer Flowers; in fact, it was precisely her wifely inadequacy that *contributed* to the flabbiness of her husband's moral muscle. It was Hillary who betrayed her husband by not carpooling, by speaking other than when spoken to, and by having the uppity audacity to write law review articles. And not just any law review articles, mind you, but those which suggest that children have rights too, that children as well as their mothers ought to be liberated from the common law condition of property. Hillary Clinton's great sin was that she left the nicely wallpapered domestic sphere with a slam of the door, crossed the forbidden threshold, took up public life on her own, leaving big feminist footprints all over the place, and without so much as an apology.

Romanticized nostalgia for Victorian family values distracts us as a nation from the crises that confront real women whenever and however they venture beyond the domestic sphere: poverty, homelessness, physical attack, harassment, lack of shelters for those fleeing domestic abuse, lack of daycare, birth control, and prenatal medical attention, lack of affordable health insurance, no maternity leave, etcetera, etcetera. We must begin examining some of the double standards and stereotypes that have so beleaguered what we used to call the women's liberation movement that many young women in college and high school today actually fear feminism (even as they are its beneficiaries). It is such a contrast to my experience: for me or perhaps for us of the forty-something generation, women's liberation was a mass movement, a kind of joyous willy-nilly festival of physical and intellectual freedom. Those who didn't like it dubbed "libbers" ugly, fat, loud, and loose. There was a degree of witch-hunting, to be sure, but in those brief times witches were definitely "in." But as those idealistic libbers have grown older and more influential, as women's liberation has matured from free-floating social-movement-with-balloons into a distinct and affirmative series of programs for sociolegal change, the attacks have become better coordinated and decidedly more effective in their meanness.

Thus we have arrived at the odd moment in history at which the National Organization for Women is deemed fairly mainstream and Congress has openly acknowledged the importance of considering issues of sexual harassment and bills about violence against women. Yet, ironically, vast numbers of women of high school and college age, according to poll after poll, view feminism as the oppressive domain of hirsute lesbians, irresponsible single mothers, and pushy career women. This trio of relentlessly emasculating harpies are supposedly prone to screaming rape every time they get a compliment and scaring strong good men into sheepish, bleating herds of fathers'-rights groups just for the fun of it.

Such mythology has been remarkably effective in obscuring the history of the entire women's movement—from Sojourner Truth to Gloria Steinem—and in compromising public debate about pressing issues of social equality. Because of its ability to erode the way legal cases are pursued, heard, and presented, I have been trying to think about how this mythology works so well.

In the purely anecdotal world of my conversations with and observation of students at the universities where I have taught, it seems clear that the accusation of being a lesbian is among the most powerful weapons available to young men, and the most fearsome risk to the status of young women, for whom many feminist causes are otherwise very much in their self-interest. It is worth taking a few moments to think about how this accusation engenders such massive and instant capitulation.

Younger women particularly, I suspect, fear that being called lesbian means losing many sectors of ordinary social life at a time in life when such things tend to take on desperate, driving importance. The cold panic of imagining life without another date, another friend, ever. And besides the possibility of isolation, it often means verbal assault and greater likelihood of physical assault. If, moreover, one is indeed heterosexual, the accusation can result in a loss of a part of one's identity that is very hard to reclaim without betraying the interests of lesbian feminists.

For example, few women who have been publicly outspoken on feminist issues have not had the experience of being interrupted by The Question: *Now just hang on a minute, little lady. Are you a lesbian, or what?* This is a no-win question. It is, in fact, not really a question; it is a setup for dismissing whatever was said just before. If the answer is yes, then of course all that equality stuff was just the product of special-interest, un-little-lady-like, man-eating politics. If the answer is no, it is very hard to say without effectively disparaging lesbian women, for in this context, "no" has the rhetorical structure of a disclaimer. In other words, "I am not a lesbian," under circumstances where "lesbian" has just been

164

used as an epithet, has the effect of putting one on the "safe" side of the schoolyard brawl—of excepting oneself—without challenging the stereotype that fuels the use of the label as insult. Moreover, that the strategy of "claiming lesbianism" for this limited purpose of solidarity—such a simple device in one sense—requires not just political commitment but also *courage,* even in a nation where officially such status "doesn't matter," is testament to the weight of pervasive prejudice and deep-seated taboos. It underscores how lesbianism, construed as an insult to men and simultaneously as the equivalent of feminism, is an image that plays not only on the obvious homophobia but also on the denigration of any women who are deemed too demanding by the men around them—or too much *like* the men around them.

During the civil rights movement, the term "nigger lover" had—still has, but more visibly then—very much the same sort of power. In those times of particularly heightened and unresolved dangers surrounding racial taboo, the threatened association with black people had the effect not only of insulting and isolating blacks but of disciplining and regulating sympathetic whites with the threat of lost status, lost identity, lost privilege. With sexism and homophobia, as with racism, the divisive labels that have sent the ranks of would-be feminists scuttling in disarray are designed to suppress important social, legal, and political questions of discrimination and inequality by defining any woman who raises such questions as Not-a-Woman. And Not-a-Woman must mean Man, which is, one must suppose, where the hairiness of feminists usually becomes such a prominent part of the disparagement. It is certainly a reversal that has worked for years in regulating some aspects of men's social behavior: calling a man Not-a-Man is a way not only of invoking the demons of homophobia but of justifying much violence against gays, against women, and also among straight men.

Similarly, feminism's claims for equality in pay and advancement in the workplace are constantly beleaguered by the image

165

of the pushy career woman who is always having her period on company time, who is shrill, tense, humorless, and who sees every playful little pat on the behind as attempted rape. "If I compliment my secretary about her new haircut, I'm afraid she'll scream sexual harassment," said a male acquaintance of mine.

Perhaps it is precisely the inability to distinguish between relative levels of intrusiveness—the inability to sense the differences between a compliment about a hairdo, a smack on the posterior, and a rape—that is the heart of the problem for some (but of course by no means all) men. Learning to make those distinctions will undoubtedly involve not only imagining how it feels to be in someone else's shoes, but *asking*. (I want to leave for others the question of certain workplace or school regulations that would *require* men and women to talk about their sexual overtures—although I must say I am struck by the way even *suggestions* to engage in such conversations are sometimes felt as requirements, as "Stalinist." When the Boston Symphony Orchestra hired a diversity consultant who generated a series of questions about race and gender dynamics for staff to "reflect upon," Jeff Jacoby of the *Boston Globe* loudly lamented that "the diversity engineers are going to reprogram you," that "Americans are being badgered into focussing on their differences," and that the Symphony's "new fixation on workplace diversity will only make it anxiety-ridden and tense.")

I think that the shift from presumption or assumption about one another to explicit questions and then conversation about our expectations and differences is probably the minimal prerequisite for the kinds of respectful exchanges that will productively inform the movement toward racial equality and freedom from sexual harassment. And the willingness to ask about another's feelings (without resentment, without condescension, without sneering—to really ask) is no small social courtesy. I think it is a giant step in the mental process of learning that women, for example, are not men's property and prerogative. It is a great deal easier to convince some men that they should ask if they might sit down when received in their date's living room than to convince them that they should ask if they might vault across it to massage her breast.

If I may be allowed to offer my, again, admittedly very unscientific observation, many of the most publicized confrontations between men and women over the issue of harassment in the workplace occur when men take very stereotyped kinds of verbal or physical license and then have their feelings hurt—often apparently quite genuinely—when things are not as they had supposed. Their indignation at women in this situation—as uppity, pushy, petulant, smothering, or too strong—is a direct product of distorted individual and social images of women as captive, or as geographic space that, like unclaimed territory, must be tamed and occupied.

It is these kinds of cognitive blind spots that are perhaps most visibly at work in the complicated series of attacks on Hillary Clinton: If she's a good lawyer she must be a bad mother. If she's First Lady she can't be a professional and political force in her own right. If she's feminist she can't be feminine, and vice versa. And looming almost always larger than Gennifer Flowers-Gate or Whitewater-Gate or Whatever-Gate is the persistent message that poor Bill is married to Not-a-Woman, which means that he must be Not-a-Man. (Although who knows. Paula-Jones-Gate, the breathlessly breaking scandal-of-the-moment as I write, threatens to prove the president's manhood no less—and maybe even greater—than that of Clarence Thomas.)

The devalued reality of American family life is a psychological crisis, an economic emergency, and a sociological embarrassment. The diffuse hugeness of the problem necessitates programmatic commitment on both individual and political levels, both micro and macro responses. The Willie Horton style of campaign deflects us from the need to do that large-scale, bipartisan grappling. This is the chosen strategy of distraction in election after election: Willie

167

Horton/welfare queen/black single mother/Hillary Clinton/ destroyer of family values/bride-of-Willie-Horton-except-he'd- never-be-so-responsible-as-to-have-a-bride. The poor are poor because they wanna be, and what's more, they're promiscuous, they're diseased, and they carelessly drop unwanted babies into the world.

While the 1992 election is behind us, I worry that the passions it inspired run very deep in our culture and remain a minefield of dangerous backlash. To the extent that unruly women—Murphy Brown, Hillary Clinton, or black single mothers—continue to personify an object for reactionary wrath, other pressing social issues become isolated and forgotten. As with the 1988 Willie Horton campaign, there was a strategy of neatly packaging com- plexity: control *them*, and your problems are solved. And a whole range of social boundaries were drawn, pulling together identity groups formed out of neither common nor self-interest but rather guilty allegiances of the threatened gut: white versus black, men versus women, married versus single, straight versus gay, working mom versus sainted stay-at-home mother (for whites), and working woman versus demonized promiscuous, eternally pregnant welfare queen (for blacks).

I hope that the tactics of the 1992 Republican Convention marked the demise of that sort of political hatemongering and were not merely an object lesson in how low we can go. If, as Garry Wills has observed, we could shift the national debate from bewitched men to de-witching our images of women, then maybe, in another generation or two, we might just begin to chip away at whatever walls keep us locked in the divisive conceptual boxes upon which injustice loves to prey.

The Unbearable Autonomy of Being

None of the secrets of success will work unless you do.

—Fortune cookie received with the author's dinner during the 1992
Republican National Convention

O ne of the least laughable consequences of Dan Quayle's *Murphy Brown* remarks was the breadth of their impact. The vice presidency is, for all the ribbing, among the most powerful offices in the world. The deference given power is notoriously indiscriminate: when the king takes up the fish knife with which to carve his meat, not only do the subjects follow, but they are likely to start a trend. When the smart set takes up fox hunting, foxes have reason to run for their lives. When the vice president of the United States of America took aim at single mothers, then open season was declared.

Living life as the pornographic target of another's fantasies is always a nightmare, even when the fantasy is one of idealized desire—never mind when the fantasy is one of disdainful vilification. Life as a bull's-eye has nothing to do with who you really are, or the statistical realities of the group you represent. The fact that 90 percent of women on welfare have only two children, and that most welfare recipients are white, means nothing to those who indulge in their masturbatory mulling about black welfare queens who purportedly reproduce like rabbits. The fact that AFDC provides virtually no money, never mind incentive, for having additional children on welfare does not alter the common perception that poor women have child after child for the supposed "extra benefits" upon which they will be able to lounge in consummate indolence. The fact that the poor pay proportionally more taxes than anyone else in America does nothing to alter the cynical perceptions of middle- and upper-class policymakers who remain convinced that *they* are the "real" taxpayers upon whose largesse the ungrateful, noncontributory poor feed insatiably. And if Hillary Clinton is an unfit wife and mother, then the black single mother—beyond hope of ever being within the protective grace of "wife," good, bad, or otherwise—becomes presumptively symbolic of she who has just emerged from a simultaneous roll in the hay and a snort at the crackhouse.

I adopted my son exactly one week after Dan Quayle made his *Murphy Brown* speech. My child, in other words, was guided into the world not by the stork or the stars but by the flaring political runway that culminated in the 1992 Republican National Convention. I remember it particularly because family values was the buzzword of the day, and amid all the excitement and joy of the baby's arrival I remained vaguely aware that in some sectors of this nation my use of the word "family" might be seen as purloined. I am so many of the things that many people seemed to think were antifamily—"unwed," "black," "single," everything but "teenage." Add "mother" and it began to sound like a curse. Stand at the mirror and say it to *your*self a few times: I am an (over-the-hill) black single mother.

It bears emphasizing that I am an especially privileged mother—whether single or not. I am a lawyer, pretty well established in my career, and my employer permitted me to take off a few months when the baby arrived. My life is such that I have time enough to sit down and muse about single motherhood in print, and I am well aware of how uncommon a luxury that is.

But what is striking to me is how much social resistance I have encountered despite the tremendous privilege of my shining lawyerly middle-classness. If things are this hard for someone like me who has everything, they have got to be unbearably difficult for women who have much less.

Daycare is the first and most obvious deficiency. Although I had known there was a daycare crisis, I was unprepared for the lack of availability even for someone with relatively few financial woes. I made the rounds of lots of facilities: dirty ones with unresponsive administrators on the one hand, and on the other some perfectly wonderful places filled with peace, efficiency, and smiling faces, but filled. For years to come. Clearly New Yorkers are registering their children before they are conceived; my son would have been too old for some of the programs by the time they had room for him.

This is a situation about which much has been written, particularly since Zoe Baird's tax problems directed new inquiry into the range of options for working women. The lack of decent, accessible daycare facilities is directly linked to the not-so-underground exploitation of poor women who work as domestic servants for scandalously low wages. And I am not convinced that room and board should count as part of what domestic servants are paid, particularly when they have families and children of their own to provide for somewhere off the premises. The conceit that a domestic worker is really being paid $1000 a month to live at "such a fashionable address" must also imagine a status value and a cash value that can be translated into edible benefits for her family and the children she will see only on holidays.

Until such translation into material terms of the daycare crisis for all women takes place, the cost of having children remains prohibitive yet strangely denied, for poor working women and for middle-class women alike—and God help women on welfare. This is so regardless of whether one is married, although the burden obviously falls disproportionately on poor single women.

While eventually I found a suitable part-time program for my son, what so much reliance on occasional babysitting by family and friends meant was that my son came to work with me a lot (yes, another luxury as these things go). For the first seven months of his life he spent much time suffering through all my

172

committee meetings, listening to me tap away on the computer, or snoozing in the Snugli while I droned on about things that bored even me. He even went on live radio with me (hooray for WBAI), burbling once or twice but otherwise calm in the face of my great and foolish faith. "I just wanted to say hello to the baby," called in one kind listener.

All this is, again, the description of a very privileged option, but I wonder if it need be so. Increasing numbers of corporations have experimented with on-site daycare facilities with great success and enhanced productivity of workers. It could be cost-efficient and emotionally reassuring for both parents and children. Yet in a rapidly downscaling economy, I fear that such measures are denied to all but a few management-level employees. "A woman's place is in the home," seems to be the solution of choice, as though women's liberation were responsible for the global economy.

During the Great Depression, "spinsters," widows, and single mothers were allowed more of a certain kind of deference—albeit a condescending, pitying deference—as secretaries, as school-teachers—than in today's business world; by contrast, married women (then the overwhelming majority) were ignored, routinely denied jobs so that "men with families" could be employed. In today's recession/depression, in some inverted reiteration of that old formula, it is increasingly "women with families" who have been most severely penalized, for not aligning themselves more economically under the heading of men's dependents.

This shift in public perception of who deserves what slice of dwindling resources has been accompanied and fed by a growing assumption that single mothers ruin their children. It is an interesting notion, since, at least in some of its aspects, it is quite a new one. The Horatio Alger myth, after all, was about captains of industry who came up the hard but noble way, the proud products of struggling widows, urban single mothers. And peak-ing in the 1930s there was a whole genre of Depression-inspired literature in which single mothers and their resolute sons plowed the fields and wrassled coyotes, milked their bone-dry cows with faith and patience, and told each other stories. Then a miracle would happen and they'd be graced with just the right amounts of rain, hay, and milk.

Somehow the years have eroded this mythology; single mothers, who now bear a greater responsibility than at any time in our history for raising the children of this society, are demonized as never before. Complex economic forces and social migrations are only part of what has contributed to the fragmentation of civic, political, and extended-family systems, not only in this country but around the world. For all the nostalgia for the nuclear family of the 1950s, the notion of nuclear family was itself only the idealized side of what was even by then the loss of settled extended family in an increasingly mobile, industrialized society. The cruel mother-in-law jokes so popular in vaudeville have vastly diminished in popularity, not I would guess because of the women's movement, but because mothers-in-law are so rarely a constant feature of anyone's family life today. Those with a live-in mother-in-law are more often seen as richly blessed with a reliable, tax-free babysitter.

Telling single women to get married in the face of decades of demographic and economic tumult is the silliest, most simplistic of antidotes. Nor does it treat as real the social factors that so often isolate couples as well as single parents. I think that if the children of single women are suffering disproportionately from the effects of poverty, we should be examining the continuing ghettoization of women in the workplace, the continuing disparity between women's and men's salaries, and the direct links between these inequalities and the fact that women fall below the poverty level in greater numbers than men.

Nor should we forget to consider lost jobs, declining standards of living, and poverty as contributing to the breakdown of marital relations. We should be asking not what happened to the two-parent household but what happened to our kinship circles. A friend of mine from Ghana could not even fathom what single motherhood meant: "If a girl has a child, she always has her family to turn to, yes?" No, I answered. "Her tribe?" I shook my head. "Her language group . . .?" he persisted with diminished conviction. "Yeah, sure," I said in my best American idiom.

An important part of what has happened since the Great Depression is that the politics of single motherhood has been racialized. Horatio Alger has turned into Willie Horton, and his regal hard-working mother who always gets her just deserts in the end has turned into a shiftless welfare queen who always gets more than she deserves. This powerful ideological myth has somehow trumped every bit of empirical reality, even in the minds of well-educated policymakers. Most Americans still believe that blacks are having more than their fair share of babies, that blacks account for most welfare recipients, and that women on welfare are "addicted" (as Dan Quayle implied) not just to drugs but to being on welfare—as though welfare were the latest fad in euphoric "high."

Yet, again, the facts are that most welfare recipients are white women, many of whom have come out of bad marriages with bad settlements, and that welfare in New York, for an example of a state that has long been considered "too generous," pays only two dollars a week more in benefits for a new child— a dead loss, and certainly not an incentive. Contrary to public opinion, births among black women have been decreasing since the 1960s; infant mortality rates are scandalously high (higher in Harlem than in Bangladesh); and shortened life expectancy, unattended medical conditions, and lack of health care are such serious problems among blacks that, once women enter their twenties, complication from pregnancy becomes a serious health risk. In other words, it makes biological sense, if not normative social sense, to have one's children while in one's teens under such circumstances.

And while I am all for population control, I'm curious as to the eugenic implications of that concept as it is applied to blacks exclusively, while simultaneously a major industry in fertility has grown up for a principally white clientele, providing more eggs, more motility, more births. I have no problem trying to curb the population explosion—or not—but I think constitutional notions of equality demand evenhandedness no less as to class than as to race if we are to make judgments about who deserves to be a parent and who does not.

I am fascinated by the power of such mythology: it has visited me on occasion, and I am taken aback by the cruelty, condescension, arrogance, and just plain in-your-face-ness I have encountered. When my son was one month old, I engaged in a spirited public debate about the upcoming presidential election. At the end, one of my opponents stood up, shook the hand of the woman on the other side of me and said, "Thank you for being so polite. It's obvious *you* come from a two-parent household." When my son was five months old, I called him "sweetheart" in the presence of a neighbor. My neighbor snapped: "You'd better stop talking to him like that unless you want to see him putting Nair on his legs by the time he's seventeen." When my son was eight months old, a young white male law student chided me publicly for not caring about "young black males" because I had adopted him as a "black single mother."

I cite the personal litany not because of how all this makes me feel—wretched!—but because it seems so prevalent as a political force, and so misguided in terms of its sense of cause and effect. Some people act as though single mothers both are vacuum-sealed in a world without men and live in a perpetual state of sexual overindulgence. No role models, just pimps. While I am not a great fan of idealization of any sort, I have begun to long for just a touch of counter-mythology. Say, the mythic black single mother educates her young'uns against all the odds,

176

wrassles urban coyotes, and all while stretching that two-dollar welfare check over twenty-one meals 'til Sunday.

At some level, all of this is about sex, sin, and what lives are worth living. It is also about disguising the class problems of our supposedly classless society, primarily by filtering them through certain kinds of discussions about race and the shiftless, undeserving, unemployable black "underclass." (Which is most emphatically not to say that we shouldn't be talking about the great power of racism in this society: what I mean to say is that welfare is not primarily a black problem, yet the impression that it is functions to avoid discussion of how broad the scar of poverty truly is.) What results is a powerful schema of thought justifying significant intrusions into the lives of black and white women, but poor young black women in particular. (The intrusions into the lives of poor young black men, of course, deserve a book—a long, tragic book—of their own.)

The wholesale demonization of "the black single mother" is quite focused on black patterns of sexual behavior as deviant from larger social norms. I would like to see this voguish literature concentrate a little less on black women's reproductive and man troubles and more on encounters with those who guard the borders of their isolation—employers, schoolteachers, hospital workers, police officers—the lived encounters that make it hard for them to raise a family at all. I would like to see the high rates of black teenage pregnancy framed less by moralistic attributions of black "social disorganization" and more by comparative patterns of the widespread sexual activity among all teens (or for that matter among all politicians, to name a random population whose social indiscretions might take volumes to describe); I would like to see direct, rather than quite subtly implied, links made between pregnancy rates and the availability of health education and reliable birth control as economic resources. Otherwise, one is left with the impression that the rights to children, intimacy, and privacy are the rewards of wealth; one is left with

177

an image in which mainstream society's punitive and oppressive desire to literally make poor blacks disappear wins acceptance when re-expressed as *their* uncontrolled desire for babies *they* can't afford.

In this sense, much of today's demonization of single motherhood conforms to the kind of theorizing first associated with the anthropologist Oscar Lewis—the assumption of a "culture of poverty" that creates destructive intergenerational behavioral archetypes. The frequent use of these purportedly self-perpetuating archetypes to mask the larger society's perpetuation of its own *stereo*types makes this form of sociology the subject of heated debate.

I have to think that some of this is an unconscious ordering, and quite old in our history. My great-great-grandmother, whom my mother's family called Mammy Sophie, was a twelve-year-old slave when she was impregnated by her master. Sophie bore him a daughter, my great-grandmother Mattie. Her master's white wife, Mary, raised the slave daughter Mattie to be "moral," "Christian," and contemptuous of her mother. My mother, Mattie's granddaughter, grew up thinking of Sophie as immoral because she had been raped by this man starting at the age of eleven. My mother says she grew up resenting Sophie the way his white wife must have resented Sophie—as wild, godless, and disruptive. An embarrassment to "the family," although I wonder just whose. Mary raised the light-skinned black Mattie to be tame, Episcopalian, and a palliative racial mediator. Mattie was married at the age of seventeen to a man named Morgan, also light-skinned and thoroughly bred, and together they were given the task of setting up a black Episcopal church, so that they could intercede like oil upon the waters and spread the word of God to the heathen. Mr. Morgan died of consumption at a very young age, and Mattie was married again, to my great-grandfather, a French-Canadian-Cherokee, a man whom I grew up hearing about only as "the dignified Mr. Ross."

My mother told of the time a neighbor and black contemporary of Mattie's died, having contracted consumption from his white family, like so many servants-who-were-also-family. At the wake, Mammy Sophie said to the widow: "My condolences; I know just how you feel." The widow rose up and said, "I was legally married to a husband. You have no idea how I feel." Then Mattie rose up and spoke against her own mother: "And I've had two legal husbands; you can't possibly know what it's like."

My mother grew up with that as a cautionary tale about how awful Sophie was—how loose and irredeemable, how she produced children without mothering them. My mother, in her turn, taught me that black teenage motherhood was deplorable. It was not until I started writing about it, my mother says, that she started rethinking the valuations embedded in this ordering of the account.

History is filled with mirrors in whose stark reflections we must find the lessons for change. Recently I have been haunted by the story of a twelve-year-old girl who gave birth alone in a corridor of her Brooklyn project house, and threw the newborn down a trash chute. The building's maintenance men heard cries just as they were about to activate the trash compactor, and the baby was saved. According to all the papers, no one knew the girl was pregnant— not her mother, not the neighbors, not the teacher of her sixth-grade slow-learner class. It turned out the father of the baby was her twenty-two-year-old uncle. He was being prosecuted for statutory rape. The prosecutor's office announced its intention to prosecute the twelve-year-old girl for attempted murder.

I think that the current insistence on blaming single mothers for the troubles of this country is a concerted way of not seeing the fiscal, racial, and political catastrophes that so beg for our attention. Poverty and disfunction among single mothers and their children are a symptom, not a cause. The vicious stereotypes with which my son and I have been greeted by significant numbers of random strangers—whether the assumption is that unless I am earning the equivalent of Oprah Winfrey's salary my child will inevitably grow up asking society for handouts and stealing for a living, or that even if I were making Oprah's salary I would still sabotage and "feminize" my son's mythic warrior spirit—are things that have nothing to do with me or my son, who is the most delightful, intelligent young man in the world. These stereotypes, so commonly misunderstood as the "difficulty" with single motherhood, are more accurately seen as part of the daily battle that all parents must wage with the world in order to create the space in which our children may grow into gentle, wise, and loving adults with the emotional resources to do bigger battle than street war. And this is a daily struggle that we all—black, white, female, male, parents or not—ought to be engaged in anyway, whether on behalf of our children or ourselves.

It is time to stop demonizing single mothers or anyone else who makes family where there was none before. Children, in their happy irrationality and complete dependence, are perpetual reminders that we are all members of a larger community, that we can never quite attain the atomistic nuclear status to which the sweet nostalgia of *Happy Days* sometimes tempts us. Raising children, even for black single mothers on welfare, is dependent on the very wonderful belief that community is possible; that there is family not only within but beyond the walls of one's home; that there is regeneration for oneself and a life for one's child in the world at large. This belief is what makes me such a tenacious, annoying, finger-shaking communitarian moralist ("Socialist!" sighs my sister); but perhaps if we could just see that family not only is about individuals acting autonomously within some private sphere but also is communally inspired and socially dependent—if we could just refrain from penalizing the nonformulaic (and unduly deferring to the nuclear formula even when domestic abuse rules the roost)—if we could but act on all this in even modest fashion, then we might begin to imagine communities in which no "single" mother need ever be alone, and no child raised in this supposed "man's world" should be without dozens of good men to look to for protection. Cultivating the extraordinary richness of what children offer us depends neither on a mother nor on a father alone, but is a responsibility that extends to grandparents, friends, neighbors, and civic community—across fences, across religion, across class, and across town.

Black-Power Dream Barbie

A Chinese woman in Mao cap and jacket photographed in b&w but for her bright red painted mouth. The neo-controversial headline reads, "Why 6,000,000 women who used to carry a little red book now carry a little red lipstick."

—Leslie Savan in the *Village Voice*

I was thinking about the matter of cultural archetypes and positive black images as I came out of the subway not long ago. Just ahead of me I saw a little black child of about seven accompanied by her mother. She was wearing a bright pink hat that said "Barbie" in white knit letters, with a little white knit copyright symbol just after the name. I wondered if this might mean there is a black Barbie doll on the market, hunkered down in her Barbie Dream House waiting bravely for Ken. Or if there might even be a black Ken doll out there, clean-shaven, crewcut, with knees that don't bend. What does the black Barbie look like, I suddenly wondered—does she have a Porsche and a sequined bikini and ankle-length hair that can be styled in over a hundred ways? Does she look more like Diana Ross or Janet Jackson? Wouldn't the black Ken have to bear an unfortunate stony-jawed resemblance to Shelby Steele or Clarence Thomas? (And surely it is too much to expect that Janet Jackson and Shelby Steele will ever meet and mate.)

Is Barbie, that anorectic instrument of white women's oppression, *capable* of being black? It's pathetic enough that little white girls yearn so for the conical breasts and vaulted arches of a trophy-wife-in-training; but when little black girls don blond wigs and spike heels they pass home and go all the way to straight-out prostitution.

Am I just too old and cynical these days? The little girl bounced down the subway stairs, chattering happily about her day at school, unafflicted with the sense of social foreboding that has made me such a pain to live with since about the age of three. I take life way too hard, I'm told.

The earliest dolls I remember were in Kenneth Clark's famous study of black schoolchildren who loved their white dolls better than their black ones. I remember my parents and their friends discussing that phenomenon and the *Brown v. Board of Education* decision. Proud "race" people and committed integrationists, they geared themselves up for the Kresge boycotts. Nevertheless, as I recall, the only dolls I ever had were white. I remember my father saying that the black dolls made then were "stereotypical." He was holding out for a Rosa Parks doll.

I guess it's no wonder that my favorite toy ended up being a stuffed dog named Cicero. Is there yet a Rosa Parks doll?

Although the toy industry has certainly improved since the 1950s, certain themes have remained constant: if there was a prevalence of stereotypical mammy dolls back then, there is a striking absence of positive archetypes today. Who is it that little black girls are supposed to grow up to be? President of the United States? To Be Sure. Firemen? But Of Course. But in cross-your-heart-and-hope-to-die, honest-to-god-real-life time, what are we supposed to do? Become mothers? Let's Hope Not!! Models? Well . . . as I ponder this, an advertisement for Revlon lipstick comes on TV, featuring a famous German model. The words "Claudia's Lips!" flash across the screen, and Claudia poufs her lips for the zoom lens and smears what appears to be Red Dye No. 2 on their thick sensuous perhaps-even-surgically-enhanced expanse. I sit for a moment trying, unsuccessfully, to imagine that this heralds a soon-to-be-announced multi-million-dollar campaign on behalf of, let's say, LuWanna's Lips . . .

Oh well, how about we just become astronauts.

184

In fact, not play, the absence of black women from any kind of romantic or professional archetype is a complicated phenomenon. When Marjorie Vincent, a black Duke Law School student, won the 1990 Miss America pageant, she paid a visit to her alma mater, where I happened to be at the time. In the halls I overheard a group of her white male classmates declare that they would not attend the reception for her because there was "nothing to see," that her crown was a "clear case of affirmative action beauty." My distress at this observation did not result from any romanticizing of the value of the romantic gaze; rather I worried that the ruthless process of *de*romanticization can impose significant personal and social costs. Statistics show that most black women will spend most of their lives without a mate; the birth rate among blacks has generally declined over the last thirty years while the death rate has risen; and the birth rate among professional black women is close to zero. At the same time, a distressing number of Americans believe that most black women spend most of their time smoking crack, having addicted babies at great public expense, putting skirts on their male children, and generally plotting the wrack and ruin of Mike Tyson's chances to become as rich as Donald Trump. (Perhaps it is this peculiar combination of social hypervisibility and individual isolation that has made *Waiting to Exhale,* Terry MacMillan's soap-opera fiction of lonely black women, so enormously popular among real black women.)

For black men, the situation is complicated manyfold: not only is there very little in the way of romantic or professional archetype to which they can aspire, but their social lot is made far grimmer by their having been used as the emblem for all that is dangerous in the world, from crime to disease. The conceptual cloak that makes any white criminal anomalous in relation to the mass of decent white citizens is precisely reversed for black men: any black criminal becomes all black men, and the fear of all black men becomes the rallying point for controlling all black people. The dehumanizing erasure of black men's humanity has created a social cauldron of much rage, much despair, and even more denial.

The anthropologist Carlos Vélez-Ibáñez describes the related criminalization and economic isolation of Mexican-Americans in terms of a "distribution of sadness." I think the term is a powerful one because it captures some of the psychic and emotional costs of prejudice in the United States—the free-floating, poisonous enervation that corrupts our ability ever to have that long-over-due national dialogue about race, gender, homophobia, and all the other divisive issues that block the full possibility of American community. The notion of displaced sadness also captures some of the hidden social trauma inflicted upon whites as well as blacks, contained in lost images like the one conveyed to me by a Harvard University psychology professor, Jessica Daniels: in her archival research, she found a photograph of a public lynching from just after the turn of the century. It showed the white citizens of a small southern town turned out to watch a black man hang. Among those assembled was a little white girl, clutching a doll with a noose around its neck.

The close genealogical relation between the trauma and violence of racism in the lives of white people and those all too obvious harms of racism inflicted upon black children living in inner cities is not generally acknowledged. Studs Terkel relays the story of a white woman whose experience embodies the way much white-on-white violence is made invisible in very racialized ways:

> One time we were in a department store by the yard-goods section. My mother, her mother, and her grandmother. Four generations. My great grandmother whispered to my grandmother, "Look over there at that black man. He's looking at little June." . . . I can remember even at that time thinking "My God, this is crazy. I go all the time and tell you Uncle Bill or Dad or these other people are molesting me." No black people had ever given me any trouble. Yet, they were so worried about that.

Similarly, I remember hearing a story on the radio about a man who went down to the nearest bank, pulled a gun on the teller, and got away with about $5,000. As he was scurrying down the street with his ill-gotten gain, a van pulled up beside him, two men stepped out, mugged him, took his bag of cash, and sped off into the distance. The bank robber was so incensed he went straight to his local police station and reported the mugging with great indignation. As I said, I heard this story on the radio, and all the disc jockeys in town were yukking it up: what sort of moron would do that, what kind of fool, what kind of yazoo . . . But I'm always curious when I hear about stories that supposedly make no sense. I'm interested in the social forces that invisibly rationalize irrational behavior. So I called up the police station and asked just one question, and, sure enough, it turned out that the first robber had been white, out to rob his friendly neighborhood bank (all in the family, you know), while the muggers had been black invaders, crossing the bounds of where they "belonged," looming ever so much larger and more dangerous in the racial, if not the criminal, order of things—or do the racial and the criminal not collapse into the same category in stories like this?

There is no doubt that the trauma of racism cuts across all lines. Not long ago some students at New York Law School told me of an experience they had had while teaching a so-called street law class in a public high school. They asked a class of twelfth graders to break up into small groups and imagine that they had to send an expedition to populate a new planet. They were to describe the six new architects of the brand new world, giving their race or ethnicity and their professions. In every group, Hispanics, if they were included, were car mechanics ("They're good at stripping cars" was the explanation some students gave); Asians were included in every group and were always scientists ("They're smart"); whites (including ethnic designations such as French, Italian, and Russian as well as just "white") had the greatest numerical presence and variety of profession. No blacks were included in the new world: the one student who listed a Nigerian doctor thought Nigeria was in Asia. The kicker is that this was a school that was 53 percent black and 45 percent Hispanic—a milieu in which many whites might be surprised to find themselves the object of such double-edged veneration. Moreover, when the law students attempted to discuss the significance of such an impressive skewing, the students—sounding for all the world like the *National Review*—uniformly protested that race had nothing to do with it, and why did the law students (who by the way were white) have to "racialize" everything?

This image of a planet with a hand-picked population is what *Brown v. Board of Education* and the entire civil rights movement was supposed to make better. But the tragic insistence of de facto segregation in the United States has resulted in this recurring reconstruction of an ideal world, this dream of elimination, this assemblage of parts into an imaginary whole, this habit of shopping among the surplus of the living for the luxury of self-effacement. It has resulted in a massively expensive web of idealized sensation and deep resentment, as well as what Jonathan Kozol calls a "romanticized accommodation" adorning apartheid with the trappings of empowerment: "Thus we hear of 'site-based' ghetto schools, 'restructured' ghetto schools, ghetto schools with 'greater input' from parents, ghetto schools with curriculum more relevant to the 'special needs' of those we have encaged. But the cage itself, the institution of the ghetto school as permanent disfigurement upon the body of American democracy, goes virtually unquestioned."

One reason discussing race is so difficult in the United States is that moving past the divide of "black/white" requires juggling so many other factors: color has long been a powerful tool for assimilative erasure of class, religion, history, most ethnicity, gender and sexual orientation, disembodied institutional power, and so on. Moving "past race," therefore, will require an un-precedented national reflectiveness about every aspect of our collective lives, and about complexities rooted in the extraordinary variety of both biological and cultural heredity that "black/white" compresses. Moreover, it will require dealing with the unfortunate fact that for many blacks the historical escape route from being black has been not just to pass into whiteness if physically possible but to construct a nuanced system of color consciousness and enhanced culture grafting that is fueled by denial rather than just a desire to embrace our variety.

The challenge becomes, as the years since the civil rights movement have taught us, how to envision a racially integrated world that will represent not merely the absorption of minority blacks into dominant white society but the fluid hybridity of race, culture, and much, much more. Nevertheless, in an environment where blackness and whiteness are the objects of relentless biolo-gized essentialism, it is not surprising that a frequent prescription for racial harmony, at least since the 1960s, has been the notion of "gray babies." While I understand that a waved banner of aggressive miscegenation is one kind of logical response to the virulent history of anti-miscegenation in the United States, I do worry that life is not that simple.

When Tina Brown's new *New Yorker* blasted its way into its first national controversy, it did so by meshing—I even want to say mashing—embodied symbols of the violent showdown in Crown Heights, New York. The February 14, 1993, issue fea-tured a cover illustration of a Hasidic man kissing a black woman on the lips. The artist, the award-winning cartoonist Art Spiegel-man, whose Maus books are among the most oddly captivating and moving accounts of the Holocaust ever published, explained his intentions as a Valentine's Day wish to New York that life's collisions be as simply resolved as by kissing and making up.

But the *New Yorker* cover offended everyone, it seemed; pleased no one; and for all of Tina Brown's protestations that it was *meant* to spark controversy, the controversy that ensued hardly addressed the problems of Crown Heights or racial confrontation in the United States. As lucidly, even childishly resonant as Spiegelman's wish was on one level, his illustration nevertheless blundered onto a battleground of complicated symbolic meaning. That battleground is fraught with lessons, I think, about the kinds of conversations blacks and Jews need (and need not) to be having with one another, and about the pitfalls that even our best efforts at reconciliation seem to encounter. It underscores, moreover, the urgent necessity of pressing on with the conversation, even when it misfires as dismally as Spiegelman's kiss.

First, it was hard to imagine to whom Spiegelman's fantasy was addressed. To the upscale post-ethnic Manhattanites or wannabe Manhattanites who form so much of the *New Yorker*'s readership? To Hasidic Jews, who are not permitted to touch any but their own spouses and certainly not with the closed-eyed, mouth-to-mouth eroticism of Spiegelman's depiction? (Spiegelman was the first to admit that the woman was most likely not "his wife, an Ethiopian Jew.") To blacks, whose experience with artistic representation by whites has always veered to the erotically transgressive? (And imagine *how* transgressive the Jezebel who could lure a devout Hasidic man from his pursuit of piety.)

This kiss as Spiegelman's chosen metaphor for the kind of complicated political reconciliation that Crown Heights requires strikes me as a sign of how immensely sexualized our culture is—in particular of how sexualized our racial encounters are. (And the kiss depicted was a quite sexual one; if there is any doubt about that, consider the same pose with, say, a Hasidic man and Al Sharpton. Perhaps then, in our sexually titillated but homophobic society, the raw sex appeal, even pornography, of the pose would have been all too exaggeratedly visible.) Gray babies have become the optimist's antidote to everything; the pervasive anti-miscegenist horror of tainted bloodlines that inspires segregation's powerful taboos has been countered time and again by the simplistic antidote of More Miscegenation. (My impatience here parallels my earlier concern with the cheerfully chipper rejoinder that hate speech can be countered by the innocent redemption of More Speech. Neither redemptive sex nor whole droning clouds of More Speech will do much if they fail to grapple with the complex histories and causes of racial hatred and violence.)

But, while intermarriage for political reasons may be noble and good, I think this form of romanticism-as-political-solution misses the point. As Calvin Hernton has noted:

> One of the most interesting aspects of the race problem was formulated [by Gunnar Myrdal] into a schema which he called "The Rank Order of Discrimination." When Myrdal asked white Southerners to list, in the order of importance, the things they thought Negroes wanted most, here is what he got:
>
> 1. Intermarriage and sex intercourse with whites
> 2. Social equality and etiquette
> 3. Desegregation of public facilities, buses, churches, etc.
> 4. Political enfranchisement
> 5. Fair treatment in the law courts
> 6. Economic opportunities
>
> The curious thing about this "Rank Order" was that when Myrdal approached the Negroes, they put down the same items as did the whites, but with one major change—they listed them in reverse order!

Moreover, if the whole world were gray tomorrow, I think the situation in Crown Heights would still exist, because it can't be cured by convincing everyone that we're all related. Crown Heights is about how—or if—we human creatures can live together while observing very different cultural practices. I do not mean to suggest that racism and anti-Semitism are not key dimensions in the dispute, but that resolutions based on innocently assimilative, dehistoricized ideals only blur or aggravate rather than assuage. And that maybe a more respectful—yet perhaps ultimately more difficult—vision would depict a Hasidic Jew and a Caribbean neighbor just nodding and saying good morning as they pass each other on the street they share.

It's a kind of heresy, I know, to suggest that the storybook desire to marry a Capulet and live happily ever after might be oppressive, and again I want to underscore the degree to which, like Spiegelman, I personally believe that the streets of Verona will never be calm until there's a little more love between us. But what concerns me is, again, that the *West Side Story* solution is a blindly depoliticized one, and obscures the possibility that simple cantankerous coexistence may be what we should be aiming for in a democracy based on live-and-let-live.

The Crown Heights situation exemplifies the difficulty of understanding the tensions faced in current race relations: we hear about black/white, black/Jewish, black/brown, black/Korean confrontations. It is only when the tension erupts at the level of international figure skating competitions, perhaps, that we are aware of Irish, Italian, or Chinese gangs, to say nothing of White Aryan Resistance gangs, all battling one another dreadfully. The irreducibility of the category of "black" in racist imagination must be whittled away by persistently detailed descriptions of lived encounters among live neighbors; but it is genuinely hard, in these times, to come up with images that might suggest a model of hybridity that is fluid rather than static, a model of value that does not substitute a facile sociobiology for the actuality of culture. Let me offer an anecdote that, among those to whom I have told it, has inspired endless argument about whether it is an example of cultural hybridity that reasserts a co-optive status quo, or one that exceeds the limits of the body to imagine the harmonious potential of borrowed community.

It all began when I went to a dance class, my preferred form of exercise. I arrived at the studio too late for the jazz class for which I had come. The receptionist suggested the hip-hop class,

192

which was just beginning. I'm more like Motown, I pointed out, way past the hip-hop generation. Don't worry, he answered; these are classes for adults. Great! I said, and dashed off in the direction of studio number two.

Now as to the matter of hip-hop, I had certainly expected to feel old. What I had not expected was to feel both so black *and* so *white*.

When I walked in, everyone was speaking Japanese. The teacher was Japanese and all the other students appeared to be Japanese (indeed, this was a studio that had a scholarship and exchange program with dance students from Japan), although they were outfitted in what I think of as high ghetto gear. They wore baggy, too-long, zoot-suit pants; long sleeveless basketball shirts that said stuff like "Spaulding" up the side; black, red, and green baseball caps worn with the brim pulled low and backward; African trading bead bracelets. The teacher paused in midsentence, waved me in, and recommenced in staccato-fast, Japanese-accented black English. "Okey-doke," said the teacher. "From the top. It's okay to screw up." Thank you very much, I responded, and took my place behind a young woman wearing a tee-shirt that said "We got the funk."

And indeed they did. Within ten seconds I realized that I was in way, way over my head. From the very first exercise, which required mid-air turns, splits, and counterpointed shoulder jabs, I knew that I was in deep hip-hop trouble. Nor could I just walk out; it would have been too impolite. This was one of those situations when I was just going to have to tough out being a humiliated spastic in public.

When the warm-up exercises were over, the teacher instructed us to put on our shoes. I realized I had forgotten my jazz shoes and said so. "No prob," said the teacher; "street shoes are copacetic." It was only after I had donned my little foam-cushioned tan suede loafers that I began to notice what passed for street shoes in this crowd. Everyone else was pulling on their hard black leather Doc Martins with improbable platform soles, steel-toed work boots, gigantic basketball shoes, pumped-up hightops with tongues that reached to their kneecaps.

My country-clubbed feet looked beyond ridiculous, and I decided to dance barefoot. But my shoes were just a small signal of things to come. For the remainder of the class, I danced on the sidelines, barefoot, stumbling, tripping, always several beats to a full measure behind the rest.

When class was over and the music died down, our respective social categories started to wash back over us like a returning tide. The teacher proclaimed gently that I "did good." I thanked him for being so extremely kind, and he and the rest of the class bowed shyly and wished me a happy Easter.

By the time I hit the street I was completely black again.

What on earth was going on? I was just as far removed from "black culture" in that class as any American white person. In fact, for a split second, I felt more Japanese than they, and they certainly looked more American than I. They were, when they danced, so deeply enmeshed in a black cultural form—they weren't just wearing it or acting it; they had studied it, they had become it, it was part of their sense memory, it was a shaping of the body, like all dance forms. I have no doubt it was "real." Yet I couldn't help feeling that it was more "mine" than "theirs," even though I had no claim I can actually describe—to say nothing of no rhythm. At the same time, for a fleeting moment when I walked into that class, I was rather conspicuously black. The Real Thing. I think, I imagine at least, that I could feel something like anxious deference as I threw open the door and took my place, staking out the cultural competition. I can be very commanding when I make an entrance, gloriously long-necked and arrogant in the pride of my bangled black womanhood, although again this could definitely be my imagination at happy play. Once I actually started moving, of course, I could see them loosen up considerably; indeed, some of them nearly passed out in the valiant attempt to smother their giggles.

In retrospect I have to wonder whatever made me even think I could hip, to say nothing of hop. It was familiar, hip-hop. I think of it as mine because I have seen it develop all my life; I grew up watching my parents dance to the musical ancestors of the hip-hop generation. It is familiar because its genealogy was part of my family life, even as a line was maintained between that and knowledge of "classical" music, "high-class" culture. Yet even that line was a muddled one: I had a great-aunt who was known for her mastery and knowledge of classical music, and I had a great-uncle who was a member of W. C. Handy's jazz band. Both of them represented parts of what I grew up thinking of as "my" musical heritage. The assertion of this "my" is not necessarily exclusive, nor is it meant in any (black or white or American) nationalistic sense, although it surely could be heard as either or both depending on the context.

One of the points at which assertions of "my" culture get complicated and polarized is when cultural property becomes, on the one hand, contested legal or intellectual property, or, on the other, so aligned with the aesthetics of power that the survival of less-valued cultural aesthetics, and cultures themselves, becomes a pressing issue. This was one reason for the heated debates around Paul Simon's use of the black South African group LadySmith Black Mambasa's music on his albums; or Sting's "sponsoring" of Brazilian musicians in an American market. What was troubling to many, I think, about Simon's presentation of LadySmith's music was that he was foregrounded, they backgrounded, he was headlined, they parenthetical. However well-informed and well-meaning Simon was, in the theater of public image he played the cosmopolitan artist to their "folkish" traditions, Aaron Copland to their spirituals, Elvis Presley to their blues. Yet as Paul Simon *and* the members of LadySmith protested repeatedly, this was a mutually beneficial venture. Cultures flowing over their boundaries, their rhythms dancing together in one big joyful river: Paul Simon's career got a shot in the arm and LadySmith helped finance anti-apartheid efforts at home. Anyone who could find something wrong with that was pictured as a dangerous Scrooge-like hoarder of outdated images of cultural purity.

But it is one thing to romanticize the notion of culture as fixed and pure, and quite another to ignore the legal and economic consequences of a dominant social gaze that habitually, repeatedly sees its own cultural production in such naturalized yet unreflectively nativistic terms that there is little vision for how much has been borrowed or given, little appreciation for the generosity of our interdependence. My concern, at this moment in history, is the popular force by which dominant societies reward certain artists with respect, copyright protection, and wealth, while relegating those who are considered "sub"-cultural artists to the unremunerative bargain basement of perpetually raided "folk" art, music, literary tradition. For me, the most historically powerful example of this is the tension between white American culture (even as "white" itself erases the enormous variety of ethnic and cultural traditions wrapped up in it) and African-American cultural traditions. But while this particular relationship is my topic here, elements of the same power dynamic—although not perhaps to the same degree—could be said to be at work in tensions between the European Community's standardization of commercial cheese production and French culinary practices; or between the American film industry and the film industry of any other country in the world; or in the growing tendency for indigenous or oppressed groups around the world to raid the past for comforting if sometimes imaginary images of golden empire and cradles of True Civilization of which the dominant culture is but the palest imitation.

James Boyle, a law professor at American University, has observed that those whose civic membership is so configured as to deem them manipulators of property are those endowed with what he calls "romantic authorship." The romantic author is privileged and paid for his "inventions" even when they borrow heavily from that which has gone before, as long as they are perceived as "going beyond the last accepted style, breaking out of the old forms . . . The author is the maker and destroyer of worlds, the irrepressible spirit of inventiveness whose restless creativity throws off invention after invention. Intellectual property is merely the token awarded to the author by a grateful society."

The only glitch in this is the way certain actors are historically deemed capable of aesthetic invention and others are deemed not capable of the lofty arts of creation, invention, mingling their labor and effort with the raw materials of life to produce that most precious bit of Lockean property. The extent to which African music and art forms, for example, are deemed "primitive" is in exact proportion to the extent to which they may be mined as "unused," "common," "traditional," or "folk." The degree to which black artists are seen as involuntary vessels through which those complex riffs just pour, overflowing in rhythmic cascades from their fingers and throats and always-tapping toes—this is the degree to which they simply cry out to be domesticated by the kindly patron. The Kind Patron of the untutored arts brings Raw Talent to a wider audience; he popularizes, channels, imitates, and masters it. All culture is co-optive, he insists—why are you so *controlling*, so insufferably *possessive* (even as the copyright is taken out in the name of the Patron).

But of course the problem with all this is not *just* at the level of who holds the copyright. The real problem is about listening for what it is that particular cultural art forms are signifying, what *information* about people's lives these expressions so preciously contain. To give a very simplistic example of the dynamic that is sometimes so frustrating: I remember going with a racially mixed group of friends to see Charles Barnett's *To Sleep with Anger*, a critically acclaimed but not very widely distributed film told very much in the complex, ambiguous cadences of African-American trickster parables. I loved this film with all my heart; to me it was the one of the richest evocations of African-American life I had ever seen on screen. It didn't have the same resonance for all the whites in the group, although it certainly did for some. With some of the others, I had conversations that made me angry. I should hasten to say that it wasn't anybody's fault that they couldn't see everything I saw in the film, but let me recount the way it felt.

"I loved this movie," I said.

"Yes, weren't the sets great?" agreed my friend. "I wanted to rush right out and get some of that wonderful old-fashioned dark heavy furniture for my house."

I was annoyed because it was as though he had taken the furniture home from the movie and thrown out the experience in a garbage can on the streetcorner. "This is the shape of my history," I wanted to shout at him. "And a really nice shape it is," it felt as if he were responding.

These uncomprehending encounters are something all of us go through from time to time. As one critic said of Bernardo Bertolucci's grasp of Buddhism in the film *Little Buddha,* "it is more than possible, I'm afraid, to grab hold of aesthetic opportunities under the impression that you are striking a serious philosophical pose." I remember being upbraided once by a blonde, blue-eyed Chicana whom I had just met, for remarking that she didn't "look Chicano." I was twenty-three years old, and I had just moved to Los Angeles from Boston, where I had lived between exactly two communities for most of my life: the mostly African-American community of Roxbury where I grew up, and the mostly white community of those with whom I went to school. At the time I moved, Boston was a city that had very well demarcated African-American, Irish, Italian, WASP, and Jewish communities; it had a small Chinatown and a growing Puerto Rican and Haitian presence. Cesar Chavez's union movement was the only circumstance in which I had even heard the word "Chicano." When I arrived in California, in other words, I had a head full of vague stereotypes, romantic commitments, and not a whit of history.

The blonde Chicana gave me an earful of history on the spot, as well as a good piece of her mind. I cried, I remember, saying she wasn't being fair, how was I supposed to know, I hadn't meant anything by it. I suppose I felt a little like those who these days feel so victimized by what they call political correctness. But it was vitally important for me to get past that moment of injured defensiveness: for even as I snuffled into the Kleenex that she thrust impatiently at me with instructions to grow up and stop dripping, I realized that a part of me was pained because I felt as if I had betrayed myself in a way that was deeply humiliating: I was remembering all those bothersome times when people had come up to me and said, "You don't talk like a black person." Or I was too educated or too nice or too middle class or too law-abiding or too something to *really* be from the place they imagined the inner city to be, even as they would simultaneously dismiss the words of people who did "talk black" because black speech is marked in this society as low-status—unless it falls from the mouth of a white person saying tired lines like "Gimmee five, dude-ette."

(Yes, that happened to me, and no I didn't hit them, but may I take this opportunity to issue a general plea: that stuff is not only very annoying to us black people, it makes most of you white people sound ridiculous. Now that I feel better, let me hasten to add that this is hardly about the binarism of us blacks and you whites. A Chicano friend complains bitterly when non-Hispanics affect fractured, macho-aspiring "Spanishisms" like the Terminatoresque "Hasta la vista, baby," which, in a certain genre of filmic art, is employed as verbal accompaniment to a rain of swift blows to the chops of another. An Iranian friend wants me to throw in that she hates being called "Sahib." And a Hindu friend concurs that all such linguistic adornment, not designed to communicate substantively in a particular language but merely to "sound like," should probably be avoided, inasmuch as the risks of such imitative license tend only to hinder rather than help the cause of world peace.)

The hard work of listening across boundaries is not always perceived as necessary for those cushioned within the invisible privileges of racial and other hierarchies of power. But the failure to incorporate a sense of precarious connection as a part of our lives is a way of dehistoricizing, suppressing from view, and, if we are not careful, ultimately obliterating.

As I write, hundreds of thousands of people are being exterminated in the small nation of Rwanda in the wake of an attempted coup that began with the assassination of the presidents of both Rwanda and Burundi. The Secretary-General of the United Nations has issued an appeal for troops to which virtually no Western nation has responded. (The only response came from African nations, but none in a position to provide the weapons and humanitarian aid that are at the nearly exclusive discretion of the great Western powers.) The lack of response is not phrased in terms of open hatred; rather it is justified in terms that reveal that Western nations know nothing—and apparently don't want to know anything—of Rwandan history or culture, except of that presumed universal black anti-culture, the "culture of poverty." "They should learn to practice birth control," say callers-in to radio and television news magazines across the United States. "It's donor fatigue," say relief organizations of a public that apparently believes that it has only given but never *received* anything from Rwanda's existence.

There is virtually no public mention of Rwanda's political history and culture as being intimately connected, for example, to Belgium, of remember-the-Belgian-Congo fame, whose bloody empire once counted Rwanda as one of its wealthiest colonies and whose atrocities committed in the name of removing that wealth to Europe helped set in motion the ethnic feuds still reverberating so tragically today. For its part, Belgium declined the United Nations exhortation as though it were being called to the telephone rather than to a peace-keeping mission, with the petulant announcement that "we have no willingness to have contact with the so-called Government in Kigali, which consists of a gang of murderers." As the journalist Simon Hoggart observed of the British reluctance to become involved: "Rwandans are thousands of miles away . . . Nobody you know has ever been on holiday to Rwanda. And Rwandans don't look like us."

In the United States, the example of Somalia was used as a reason not to get involved in Rwanda. But the Somali situation was made more complicated because the United States military turned those Somalis it was supposedly helping into enemies, first by shooting civilians, including children, and then by not even trying to distinguish one black person from another in the context of a bitter ethnic and factional dispute. The United States so underestimated that bitterness as to seem caught off guard that there really was a war, and not just another riot, going on. My notes from the first ebullient days of Operation Restore Hope foreshadow the attitudes that became actions that became the "swamp" of failure it is now considered:

The United States has invaded Somalia with tons of food and waves of tanks and a jolly Saint Nick riding a camel among the masses of starving Muslim orphans. The major networks run advance patrol, securing the beaches sufficiently to install generators and powerful lights bright enough to film from every conceivable angle the military going through the motions of storming the beaches and securing them. It's a field day of public relations. In Congress, military appropriations are on the line. In a kinder gentler new world order the U.S. military must be humanized, so the monumentally humanitarian mission of feeding Somalia has been militarized. NBC anchor Tom Brokaw calls the locals "ya-

201

hoos" and the Somali soldiers "young warlords proving their manhood." Jeff Gralnick, executive producer of the *Nightly News* with Tom Brokaw, calls Somali factional leader Mohammed Farrah Aidid "an educated jungle bunny and the rest of the jungle bunnies are not like this at all. They're illiterates" (and then offers the explanation that he was just "using a phrase that exists in many people's minds in the United States." No one talks about the cold war politics that brought this unfortunate nation to its present famished state; its history is obliterated by the constant reference to every fragment of institutional Somali power in annihilatingly delegitimizing terms: a visit to the local governor—admittedly unstable, even evil, but governor nonetheless—is described as a visit to a "guntoting thug in his so-called villa." I know—who cares about words when there is such famine, such suffering. What difference does it make, as long as people are fed, that no such Ugly Americanisms and impolitic words have been used to describe the unspeakably genocidal regime in Serbia, again, no matter how unstable or evil. But yet—the utter condescension that renders dignity invisible, the humanitarian aid framed as extended to nonhumans, so that even the noblest gesture dehumanizes.

What was also stunning about the media coverage of Somalia was the calculated propagation of pervasive stereotypes about blacks. The Somalis—all Somalis—were described as "undisciplined," "criminal elements" whose criminality involved "stealing from their own." As in the urban police lingo of the United States, Somali men were referred to as "males" as though blacks were of a different species. On TV a nineteen-year-old white American soldier from Indiana intoned that he's seen "some pretty bad places . . . Compton, Watts, the L.A. riots, but this . . . Those places were nothing compared to this." He ended with something about how good we all have it in the United States yet "we" complain so much. Over and over the subtext comparing the lot of blacks in the United States with the lot of blacks in Somalia and, with a finger-shake, the conclusion that those in this country are ever so much fatter and more ungrateful.

You're lucky to be alive, says the subtext to U.S. black citizens. You could be like those others over there. (And if you're not careful, "we" will just stop paying for the cost of your misbegotten illegitimate orphans, move out of your miserable underclass neighborhoods, surround your ghetto deserts with freeway overpasses, and you yahoos can just starve to death.)

The heart-of-darkness metaphor system that made black communities into African if urban "jungles," and that now is being re-exported to make Africa one big inner city, is pervasive in the media. In a cover story by Robert Kaplan in the *Atlantic* entitled "The Coming Anarchy," West African and African-American communities are chosen as examples of the ecologically depleted, disease-ridden, crime-infested, morally bankrupt cesspools that will threaten civilization as we know it. "Dying regions," Kaplan says of West Africa and parts of Asia (no country in particular). The inhabitants come in "hordes" and are analogized to "loose molecules in a very unstable social fluid." If they're dying like flies it's because of their "loose family structures" and "animist beliefs not suitable to a moral society" and levels of rampant crime that give "you some sense of what American cities might be like in the future."

Kaplan seems totally impervious to the anger that this sort of rhetoric necessarily inspires, blind to the racism he indulges in, unconscious of the history he tramples, unaware of the invasions of generations of people who have erased and despised the African continent so much that every intervention has produced only more death—to the extent that the only ones left in some nations are the very young people, those whom Kaplan so dismissively described as "Soweto-like stone-throwing adolescents." He goes to what *he* thinks of as a slum in Turkey, and finds it ever so much more advanced than slums in Africa, which "terrify and repel the outsider." He enters "one house" in Ankara and finds a "home—order, that is, bespeaking dignity. I saw a working refrigerator, a television, wall cabinet with a few books and lots of family pictures, a few plants by the window, and a stove." This dignity he then attributes not to his own rising level of comfort in the presence of these consumer goods, but to a "civilization with natural muscle tone."

This article makes me question not just the author but the whole social valuing that would permit this expression of blatant ignorance of West African kinship systems, politics, religion, and suffering not only to be the cover story of one of the most influential and supposedly "middle-of-the-road" magazines in the world but also to be touted in the editorial notes as a combination of "scholarship, on-the-ground reporting and a deep regard for the past." The only past it incorporates is that of the worst brands of exploitative colonialism, a lesson in purposively applied ignorance that condemns us to relive the bloodiest paths of history.

This genre of Africa-imaging has been making a powerful resurgence recently, even suddenly. Kaplan's article was shortly preceded by a cover story in the *New York Times Magazine*, "Colonialism's Back—And Not a Moment Too Soon," in which the author, Paul Johnson, urged new-age colonialism as the answer to the world's problems. Johnson's premise was that some people just aren't able to govern themselves and it's about time the wise strong hand of greater minds intervened. Surprise, surprise, most of those unruly masses happen to live in Africa. At first I thought that the piece was a parody—it was such a calculated rehash of that ugly genre The White Man's Burden (also known as The Negro Problem, The Jewish Problem, The Indian Problem, etcetera), dating at least back to the 1500s, in which unfitness for governance, or parasitism on it, characterizes "the lesser races." Updated only to the degree that the word "thugs" was substituted for "savages," Johnson's piece employed time-honored rhetorical strategies of Kiplingesque Great White Fatherhood: the plea of a mythologized Noble Native to the European to rescue him from the darkness of himself; the "primitive" nature of undifferentiated and unnamed "attempts" at self-rule; the beneficent, stiff-upper-lipped commitment to the Greater Good of God, Reason, and the idealized nation of the author's birth—all so inexorably compelling the establishment of this or that "protectorate."

Kaplan's article in the *Atlantic* reiterated all of these ingredients, including the pleading Noble Native voice of an unnamed "top-ranking African official whose life would be threatened were I to identify him more precisely," who bemoans the irrational practices of his people. While Kaplan does not overtly urge protectorates of the have-nots as the solution, his sense of urgency seems more turned toward the "inevitability" of increased encapsulation of the civilized few, self-enclosed protectorates of the haves, as the remaining outposts of civilization. If Johnson's article imagined the United States and Europe as powerful father figures, Kaplan's description deployed something of a Puritan Errand of the Star Trek generation, with tiny but heroic "former" Americans, survivors-against-the-odds banished into a dark space fraught with alien monsters, looking for a safe place to land that has a little fresh water and some oxygen.

Anticipating disagreement among his readers—particularly, it seems, among those elite African-Americans who read the *Atlantic,* Kaplan is ready with a deflective explanation:

The sensitivity factor is higher than ever. The Washington, D.C., public school system is already experimenting with an Afrocentric curriculum. Summits between African leaders and prominent African-Americans are becoming frequent, as are Pollyanna-ish prognostications about multiparty elections that do not factor in crime, surging birth rates, and resource depletion. The Congressional Black Caucus was among those urging U.S. involvement in Somalia and Haiti. At the *Los Angeles Times,* minority staffers have protested against, among other things, what they allege to be the racist tone of the newspaper's Africa coverage, allegations that the

205

editor of the "World Report" section . . . denies, saying essentially
that Africa should be viewed through the same rigorous analytical
lens as other parts of the world.

With this gesture Kaplan invokes the coded framework of the
reactionary semantics of "political correctness" to minimize and
dismiss the entire range of critical African-American voices. It is
a device that has been historically used against Jews: when the Ku
Klux Klan calls Congress a Jewish-occupied territory, it plays
upon very old notions of Jews as rabid Zionists, whose allegiances
are always suspect, who spend their time sympathizing with
interests that will pollute the body politic. "Rigorous" analysis is
sacrificed to specious, self-interested claims of racism.

In the United States, Africa is not covered, period, never mind
with a rigorous analytical lens. The only way Kaplan can get away
with such a claim is that few in the United States have the faintest
inkling about history, never mind African history. One might
well ask where all the hardwood from all those stripped forests he
cries over is going (is it true that not a few rooms at the *Atlantic*
are paneled in the Victorian splendor of exotic tropical woods?),
and where all the cocoa, coffee, fish, and minerals end up. What
centuries of history are struggling to speak from Kaplan's silent
images of black men in Africa *and* the United States tapping
desperately at the windows of limousines, begging for "tips"?
What histories are suppressed in Kaplan's images of happy Turk-
ish paysans who smoke their hashish and sip their coffee in peace?
Where is any mention of the environmental racism that has made
it "profitable" for West African countries to become dumping
grounds for the world's industrial toxins? Where is any condemnation of World Bank policies and International Monetary Fund
interventions that have had disastrous effects on local economies
and cultures, fueled by the kind of genocidal hypothesizing exemplified by the notorious memo, leaked to the *Economist*, in
which Clinton's economic advisor Lawrence Summers wonders
if industrialized powers oughtn't be considering more directly

the cost-effectiveness of dumping more industrial waste products in those countries where the life expectancy is already so short that people don't live long enough to manifest the full-blown effects of the kinds of cancers and diseases that long-term exposure to these poisons is known to cause?

We have seen this picture drawn before. The ideological map-making in which sovereign states are called "countries," *in quotes*. In which genocide is pursued while the rage is bulldozed under as "hypersensitivity" or "crime." It may not be the fault of this generation, but there is a price to be paid, by those who mindlessly treat three-quarters of the planet as though it were a *different* planet.

It is in this unfortunate tradition that Kaplan, in the style of a classic jeremiad, "imagines new nations" in which the bullet-proof limousine is a trope for the vehicle of errand, mission, forward movement, through the present dangers into the future. In a socio-Darwinian ordering, Kaplan condenses the immense variety and circumstances of most of the world's poor, indigenous, and unindustrialized people into the label "First Man"—a.k.a. Hobbes's nasty, short-lived brute. A well-groomed virtual-reality superhero whom Kaplan calls "*Last* Man" (evoking Francis Fukuyama's neo-Malthusian *End of History*) and who shows a civilized profile inside that limousine, is implicitly white, well-ordered, and plugged in at all times to the artificial intelligence of his computer and fax machine.

I suppose I could simply relabel this little bit of theater the story of Sun Man and Ice Man in order to underscore for the truly culturally blindered why this political reductionism is so appallingly offensive, but let me stick to the terms Kaplan employs. The fact that First Man and Last Man live on the planet at the same moment in history both implies a sociobiological ranking of development and naturalizes Kaplan's conclusion that First Man won't survive or is already extinct. The future will be reserved, in other words, for a small colony of Last Men who had the will, the morality, and the technology to survive in the wilderness supposedly generated by First Men. The scenario structures panicky incentives for Kaplan's Last Man to positively cringe at the very *existence* of those who are figured as other life forms. The deep cultural stereotypes that Kaplan draws upon precisely invite the cruel passivity that has characterized the world's response of sitting back and watching Rwandans die. Their demise is both their fault and our salvation—such is the logic of such a piece. AIDS, genocide, depleted resources, and fascism have nothing to do with Us, and, after all, it's only natural that the Last One in the game wins whatever's left.

In June of 1994 the *New York Times Magazine* ran a series of photographs of the horrendous consequences of the Rwandan massacres. "Yet there is something deeper even than historic horrors and tribal hatreds in all this," ran the legend beneath a picture of water-bleached bodies floating downriver to Victoria Falls. "It owes more to evolutionary biology than to history; it reaches into hearts of darkness located far beyond Africa. Under certain circumstances, not always predictable, people will do almost anything to one another." (If anything *is* predictable on this planet, it is that the *New York Times* will dismiss the angry letter I dashed off in response to the article as unanalytical, lacking rigor, and probably evolutionarily traceable to some biologically miscoded neural electrical storm. If the Zulus haven't even produced a Tolstoy, surely the Tutsis or the Hutus couldn't have produced a *methodical* murderer like Hitler. And that recurrently troublesome little military machine in Haiti? Must be just another random, innate black-on-black thing.)

Our kinship on this earth is such an ambiguous affair, a little of this, a little of that, an exercise in how we can invent ourselves to be seen today and see tomorrow.

Many years ago, a friend invited me to her home for dinner. As it turned out, her husband was a survivor of Auschwitz. He had been an artist before he was captured by the Nazis, and, while he had made his living in an entirely different field since coming to the United States, his wife told me that he still painted as a hobby. She took me to their garage and showed me an immense collection of his work. There he had stored paintings that probably numbered in the hundreds—circus-bright land-scapes with vivid colors and lush, exquisitely detailed vegetation. Yet in every last one of them there was a space of completely bare canvas, an empty patch in the shape of a human being. "He never finishes anything," my friend whispered, but I could hardly hear her, for I had never seen such a complete representation of the suppression of personality, the erasure of humanity that the Holocaust exacted.

A few weeks after this, my sister sent me a microfiche copy of a property listing from the National Archives, documenting the existence of our enslaved great-great-grandmother. The night after I received my sister's letter, I dreamed that I was looking at my friend's husband's paintings, all those vivid landscapes with the bare body-shapes, and suddenly my great-great-grandmother appeared in the middle of each and every one of them. Suddenly she filled in all the empty spaces, and I looked into her face with the supernatural stillness of deep recollection. From that mo-ment, I knew exactly who she was—every pore, every hair, every angle of her face. I would know her everywhere.

I retell this story not for its own sake but to reflect on how difficult it has been to tell at all, mostly because it almost always affects my relationships with those with whom I share it, and in ways that I can never predict. Not necessarily in bad ways, but powerfully. Recounting it on an informal basis to a number of my friends, I have been startled by the range of responses to its blended image of historical oppressions. Some have found the story moving, some have been angered by what they perceive as either the flattening or the co-opting of someone else's story, and for some it has been the ultimate proof that I am not cut out for life in the real world. Yet by telling it I have learned a great deal about my friends—I have learned the *why* of their varied responses, the unexpected, invisible connections of "their" stories to "my" story.

Once I recovered from being put off by the ways people were "taking" *my* story, I began to get inklings of the rarely discussed, sometimes painfully suppressed cultural histories of friends who for the most part identified themselves in the laconic categories of the census—as "white" or "Asian" or "black" or "all mixed up" or "American" or "nothing in particular." This one was the grandchild of a German Lutheran artist killed by the Nazis. That one's mother had fled from North Vietnam to Laos to Cambodia to France. Someone else was Romany but "passing" because "people don't trust gypsies." I learned a lot about wars in Armenia, potato famines in Ireland, civil war in Ghana, oppression in Latvia, electoral fraud in Palau, independence movements in Scotland, and the literary tradition of magical realism in South America. The whole history of the last three centuries of global displacement of indigenous peoples began to unfold from beneath the serene facades of these all-very-American friends with their Georgia locutions and New York accents and midwestern vowels and San Fernando Valley inflections—the rich, painful, nuanced, complex, compressed amalgam that is American culture in its most generous sense.

It's complicated, this creation of cultural property. While I understand, to go back to my earlier example, hip-hop music and dance most clearly as an urban black art form, I appreciate that its movements are no less clearly influenced by Chinese, Japanese, and Korean martial arts movements than by Afro-Caribbean rhythmic patterns. Its appeal need be limited, I suppose, by none of the above. Beethoven is no less black than Thomas Jefferson is Japanese, I think sometimes, but knowing that if I publish this I will receive yet another angry volley of mail insisting that Jesus Christ was not, repeat not, an Afrocentric nut-case like me.

The creation of cultural property is perhaps a more complicated investment than mere words can capture. As I write these words, my son, at eighteen months, rolls on the floor of my office, chattering happily to himself. He eyes the floor-to-ceiling bookcases of African literature and Japanese poetry and *Encyclopedia Britannica*s and Hindu art with satisfaction, turning his body this way and that, examining the literary landscape now sideways, now upside-down. He is so extremely comfortable, fascinated, acquisitive. By his gaze, he makes "my" world his. He invests himself, he becomes part of this room. He rolls and sighs and examines and pats his stomach. He is learning where he belongs, and that sense of belonging will make a certain property of the familiar.

The familiar is the property of belonging, I guess.

A Ghanaian student, years ago, asked me about the anonymity that I must suffer because of my slave heritage. He could not conceive of such rootlessness, the not-knowing that afflicts both whites and blacks in America. It frightened him. He described the songs by which he could trace his family, his tribe, his ancestors back for generations. He portrayed it as a system in which there was great respect not just for one's lineage but for the memorization and oral recitation of that lineage. Words were so special because they bore the remains of one's ancestors and loved ones. It was important to him that words be handled with care, that they be ordered and precise and caring. He called this the "property" of his life's inheritance. There was no room for carelessness for to be careless would be to let part of oneself die. I said that I could not conceive of being so thoroughly known. "Our property is much more alienable," I said, almost idly, before I heard its import. He agreed that there was something essentially anti-individualist, even anti-democratic, in this memorizing of one's legacy, but he insisted that wisdom has a particular worded shape; to alter it not only is blasphemous but brings irretrievable loss.

From time to time I try to imagine this world of which he spoke—a culture in whose mythology words might be that precious, in which words were conceived as vessels for communications from the heart; a society in which words are holy, and the challenge of life is based upon the quest for gentle words, holy words, gentle truths, holy truths. I try to imagine for myself a world in which the words one gives one's children are the shell into which they shall grow, so one chooses one's words carefully, like precious gifts, like magnificent inheritances, for they convey an excess of what we have imagined, they bear gifts beyond imagination, they reveal and revisit the wealth of history. How carefully, how slowly, and how lovingly we might step into our expectations of each other in such a world.

"I was not only hunting for my liberty," said William Wells Brown, "but also hunting for my name."

In Search of Pharaoh's Daughter

An old woman walks by and she clenches her purse
When asked my opinion, I'm expected to curse
Take a look at my life . . .
Where a man examines his life and lets out a sigh
He knows there is one way out—that escape is to die
Take a look at my life.

—Jamel Oeser-Sweat, "Heroism"

W hy are you doing this to yourself?" asked my mother dubiously when I began the process of adopting a child. "You're only forty. The right man could come along any day now. Women are having babies into their fifties these days." I had been hearing my mother say this since my thirtieth birthday, when women were said to be having babies well into their forties. Her quiet, unblinking slippage into the next decade made me realize that while *her* hope sprang eternal, I was starting to get stiff from all that sitting on the porch in ruffled sateen with the gardenia behind my ear.

My father was grumpier about the prospect: "I'll be a hundred years old before this child reaches college."

"No, you won't," I said sourly. "You'll barely be ninety."

The rest of my family was delighted but worried that I had not adequately taken into account how much having a child would cut into the indulgent Buppy lifestyle of which they so rightly accused me.

I have really hated disappointing everyone, but thus far motherhood has been the richest, most satisfying of rewards. While my son has indeed restricted my ability to eat in fancy restaurants, he has opened up the way to new and far better indulgences, like playing, like learning to be silly again. He has made walking the streets of New York unexpectedly interesting: people smile at me—at him—more. They establish eye contact. They talk in streams of uncontrolled amiability. The other day as I stood waiting to cross the street, a young man with a ruby-hennaed mohawk and a ring through his nose said very gently, "What a cute baby. God bless you." My son, bless him indeed for I can take no credit in it, brings out the best in other people, even a hard case like me.

Yet for all the touted and mythic joys of motherhood, as the columnist Barbara Reynolds points out:

> Across the USA, there are about 250,000 children without homes
> . . . In Alaska, the whales are being fawned over because of their
> intelligence, their lovability. Hourly reports measure the "terrible
> stress" on these endangered mammals . . . Our endangered home-
> less children are under greater stress. They are also intelligent and
> lovable, when given a chance . . . If we could bottle that national
> will and enthusiasm poured on the whales and sprinkle it on
> children in dangerous waters, they would be more grateful than
> Jonah was when a great whale spit him out rather than devour him.

In contrast, consider a small piece of the material world: when arson destroyed a home in an all-white section of Queens, New York, which had been scheduled for the placement of six "boarder" babies, then police commissioner Benjamin Ward said, "I do know most of the babies are minority babies. Maybe that's inside."

> "Are they still going to be here when they grow up?" asked Richard
> Blasi, 11 years old. He meant the six babies . . . "This is heart-
> breaking," said Gretel Strump, a 46-year resident of the block.
> "Listen, we have nothing against babies. But the mothers, the dope
> addicts. My husband says, we will never be safe any more. It's
> nothing but dopists."

> "I know it's a selfish kind of feeling but I moved here because it is
> the way it is," Mrs. Sawicki said. "I have my daughter here. These
> houses are worth a lot of money. There's got to be a better place
> for them than smack in the middle of here."

(I can't help noticing that the word "better" is quite a loaded term in the context of that sentence. Better does not seem to mean better for the babies, but better for the Sawickis: someplace "else," someplace where the daughters and houses are worthless. So better for the Sawickis means worse for the babies and vice versa. Better from the reference point of the babies, in other words, means not better at all, but worse.)

> Fliers handed out to residents in opposition to making the house into any sort of a group home said, "We do not want our stabilized residential areas turned into garbage. We do not need more CRIME, VIOLENCE, BURGLARIES, TRANSIENT PEOPLE OR PROSTITUTION."

(Again the language is quite remarkable: the mere presence of six babies is a kind of reverse Midas-touch, a noxious contaminant, a garbagey breeding ground for flies, prostitution, and all the world's vices.)

> The battle over the house began when the owners put it up for sale. John W. Norris, the head of a local civic association, the Auburndale Improvement Association, said the owners asked $325,000, about $100,000 more than the market price for other houses on the block.
>
> In September, a private foster-care agency offered to buy the house and use it as a group home for six to eight girls ages 14 to 16. Human Resources Administration officials said the buyer, the Jewish Child Care Association of New York, changed their minds because of the community outcry.

> The city signed a rental agreement last Friday to pay $2,400 a month for the house, which neighborhood residents said would bring about $1,100 on the open market.
>
> Mr. Koch did not say why the city had agreed to that rent, other than to cite "supply and demand."

There is a peculiar and powerful inversion at work, in which "worthless" children drive up the price to corrupt or unattainable heights; the poorer and blacker the child, the higher the price

216

rises. Meanwhile the more valuable legitimate daughters get to live in the high-rent district for cheap.

The market valuation of children reflected in this story is reiterated at every level of social and legal thinking. Recently, I was rereading an article by that great literary mogul of the University of Chicago's School of Law and Economics, Judge Richard Posner, and his associate Elizabeth Landes. In their short opus "The Economics of the Baby Shortage," newborn human beings are divided up into white and black and then taken for a spin around a Monopoly board theme park where the white babies are put on demand curves and the black babies are dropped off the edge of supply sides. "Were baby prices quoted as prices of soybean futures are quoted," the authors say, "a racial ranking of these prices would be evident, with white baby prices higher than nonwhite baby prices."

The trail of the demand curve leads straight into the arms of the highest bidder; the chasm of oversupply has a heap of surplus at the bottom of its pit. In this house of horrors, the surplus (or "second-quality") black babies will continue to replicate themselves like mushrooms, unless the wise, invisible, strong arm of the market intervenes to apply the wisdom of pure purchasing power. In a passage that some have insisted is all about maximizing the kindness of strangers, Landes and Posner argue:

> By obtaining exclusive control over the supply of both "first-quality" adoptive children and "second-quality" children residing in foster care but available for adoption, agencies are able to internalize the substitution possibilities between them. Agencies can charge a higher price for the children they place for adoption, thus increasing not only their revenues from adoptions but also the demand for children who would otherwise be placed or remain in foster care at the agency's expense. Conversely, if agency revenues derive primarily from foster care, the agencies can manipulate the relative price of adopting "first-quality" children over "second-quality" children to reduce the net flow of children out of foster care.

What these authors conclude, in an unsurprising rhetorical turn, is that the current "black market" for adoptive children must be replaced with what they call a "free baby market."

When this article first appeared almost twenty years ago, it created a storm of controversy. Since Judge Posner has reaffirmed its premises many times, most recently in his book *Sex and Reason*, the article has remained a major bone of contention. I will leave to economists a full-fledged critique of the models presented (as well as of the more sophisticated models and analyses of adoption markets proposed by the economist Gary Becker, from whom Posner borrows heavily). My purpose in resurrecting this piece here is to examine (1) the degree to which it is a reflection of what goes on in the world of not just adoption but reproduction in general; (2) the degree to which market valuation of bodies, even when for ostensibly noble purposes, exemplifies what is most wrong with community as well as family in America; and (3) the possibility that a shift in focus could help us imagine a more stable, less demeaning, and more inclusive sense of community.

When I decided to adopt, I was unprepared for the reality that adoption is already a pretty straightforward market. I was unprepared for the "choices" with which I was presented, as to the age, race, color, and health of prospective children. I was unprepared for the fact that I too would be shopped for, by birth mothers as well as social workers, looked over for my age, marital and economic status, and race. All that was missing was to have my tires kicked.

"Describe yourself," said the application form. *Oh lord*, I remember thinking, *this is worse than a dating service. What's appealing about me, and to whom? Responsible nonsmoking omnivore seeks . . . what? Little person for lifetime of bicycle rides, good education, and peanut butter sandwiches? Forty and fading fast so I thought I'd better get a move on?* "You can't tell them you're forty," a friend advised. "No one will ever pick you." Okay, I sighed. "Very well rounded," I wrote.

"Describe where you live." At the time, I was still at the University of Wisconsin, even though I was visiting at Columbia, and traveling almost every week to places like Indiana and Georgia in a frenzied ritual of academic legitimation. I struggled, as I straddled worlds, with which side I should present in my "Dear Birth Mother" letter. *Chic New York apartment with expansive square footage, north-south exposure, and a refrigerator stocked with the leftovers of fifteen different types of ethnic take-out food? Your child will grow up riding the subways and knowing the finer shades of the chardonnay-and-caviar lifestyle of the middlebrow and not-so-famous? Or should I just offer a well-childproofed home in that friendly dairy center of the universe, Wisconsin, land o' butter, cream, and lakes?* "Your child will taste the world," I wrote.

"What age, what sex?" asked the social worker. "Doesn't matter," I said, "though I'd like to miss out on as little as possible."

"If you're willing to take a boy, you'll get younger," she replied. "There's a run on girls."

"What races would you accept?" asked the adoption agency. "And what racial combinations?" There followed a whole menu of evocative options, like Afro-Javanese, Sino-Germanic, and just plain "white." I assume that this list, so suggestive of the multiple combinations of meat offered at, say, Kentucky Fried Chicken, would make Elizabeth Landes and Richard Posner very happy indeed. They advise:

The genetic characteristics of natural children are highly correlated with their parents' genetic characteristics, and this correlation could conceivably increase harmony within the family compared to what it would be with an adopted child. Nevertheless, there is considerable suitability between natural and adopted children and it might be much greater if better genetic matching of adopted children with their adoptive parents were feasible—as might occur, as we shall see, under free market conditions.

219

"Any," I wrote, knowing that harmony genes abound in my ancestral bloodlines—yet wondering if the agency really meant to address that question to black parents. Would they truly consider placing "any" child with me if this agency happened to have a "surplus" of white babies? Would I get a Korean baby if I asked? And for all of the advertised difficulties, what does it mean that it is so relatively easy for white American families not just to adopt black children but to choose from a range of colors, nationalities, and configurations from around the world? (And I do mean *relatively* easy—for all of the publicity about the "impossibility" of white people adopting black American children, doing so is still in most instances far easier than going to Eastern Europe or China, for instance. While there are well-publicized instances of white families who are barred by local social service office policies, in most states a waiting period of about six months is the biggest institutional hurdle they will face. In addition, there are a good number of reputable private adoption agencies that facilitate and even specialize in "interracial" adoptions.)

What does it reveal, moreover, about the social backdrop of such transactions that if I "chose" a "white" child, it might reveal something quite alarming about my own self-esteem? What does it mean that if a white parent chose a black child, many people would attribute it to an idealistic selflessness that—however misguided and threatening to cultural integrity some blacks might consider it—is not generally perceived as proceeding from a sense of diminishment? Is race-neutral adoption the answer—even to the extent of barring "mild preferences" for same-race placements, as the law professor Elizabeth Bartholet has suggested? While I very much agree with the impulse behind that solution, does the social reality of unbalanced race relations and racial power suggest some constraints on complete color-blindness as a possibility?

A number of studies claim to show that black children fare just fine when adopted into white families—and I have no doubt that this is true on any number of levels—but I am troubled by some of the conclusions drawn from such representations: the claims that such children have "unique" abilities to deal with white people, or that they are "more tolerant." I always want to ask, more tolerant of what, of whom? More tolerant *than* other blacks? Or than whites? More tolerant *of* whites? Or of other blacks?

I am particularly troubled by the notion that black children in white families are better off simply because they may have access to a broader range of material advantages by having white parents and living in the largely white and relatively privileged world. Such an argument should not, I think, be used to justify the redistribution of children in our society, but rather to bolster a redistribution of *resources* such that blacks can afford to raise children too. Moreover, assertions that black children actually do better in white homes play dangerously against a social backdrop in which slavery's history of paternalistic white protectionism still demands black loyalty to white people and their lifestyle as a powerful symbolic precedent for deeming black social organization "successful." Such assertions do not take into account the imbalance in the way state agencies intervene in the lives of poor women and women of color—particularly in view of the disproportionate rate at which children of color are removed from their homes and put into foster care or up for adoption, with little provision of the kinds of facilitative family counseling that are available at higher ends of the socioeconomic ladder.

In any event, I wonder how many social science studies there are about how white children fare in black homes.

"What color?" asked the form. *You've got to be kidding.* I looked quizzically at the social worker. "Some families like to match," she said. *You mean, like color-coordinated? You mean like the Louisiana codes? Like ebony, sepia, quadroon, mahogany? Like matching the color of a brown paper bag? Like red, like Indian, like exotic, like straight-haired, like light-skinned? Like 1840, is that what this means?* Like 1940, sighed my mother, when I mentioned this to her. *(And is this what the next generation will be sighing about, so sadly, in 2040?)*

"I don't care," I wrote. And with that magical stroke of the pen, the door to a whole world of plentiful, newborn, brown-skinned little boys with little brown toes and big brown eyes and round brown noses and fat brown cheeks opened up to me from behind the curtain marked "Doesn't Care."

"This is a cheap shot," says my friend the economist. "How can anyone criticize or take scholarly issue with the breathy mother-love of such descriptions? And what does any of this have to do with the price of tea in China?" It's a good question, I guess, and all I can do is remind the reader that I am trying, quite intentionally, to explode the clean, scientific way in which this subject is often discussed. And if it has little to do with tea or soybeans, just maybe the positioning of mother-or-any-other-love as some kind of irrelevant externality has a little something to do with the price of children in America.

My son, because he is a stylish little character, arrived at my home in a limousine. (Credit for this must be shared with the social worker, who was a pretty jazzy sort herself.) I had a big party and a naming ceremony and invited everyone I knew. I was so happy that I guess I missed that price tag hanging from his little blue knitted beanie. A few weeks later I got a call from the agency: "Which fee schedule are you going to choose?"

"What's this?" I asked the adoption agent, flipping madly through Landes and Posner for guidance: "Prospective adoptive parents would presumably be willing to pay more for a child whose health and genealogy were warranted in a legally enforceable instrument than they are willing to pay under the present system where the entire risk of any deviation from expected quality falls on them."

"Are you going with the standard or the special?" came the reply. There followed a description of a system in which adoptive

222

parents paid a certain percentage of their salaries to the agency, which fee went to administrative costs, hospital expenses for the birth mother, and counseling. Inasmuch as it was tied exclusively to income, in a graduated scale, it clearly met the definition of a fee for services rendered. This, it was explained to me, was the standard price list.

"And the special?" I asked. After an embarrassed pause, I was told that that referred to "older, black, and other handicapped children," and that its fees were exactly half of those on the standard scale. Suddenly what had been a price system based on services rendered became clearly, sickeningly, a price system for "goods," a sale for chattel, linked not to services but to the imagined quality of the "things" exchanged. Although, as the agency asserted, this system was devised to provide "economic incentives" for the adoption of "less requested" children, in our shopping-mall world it had all the earmarks of a two-for-one sale.

I was left with a set of texts resounding in my brain, rattling with the persistence of their contradiction—a medley of voices like descriptions of Americans adopting children in Latin America and of having to hide for fear of kidnapping until they were back on the plane to the United States because "desirable" children are worth a great deal of money on the open adoption block. Or like the *New York Times Magazine* cover story of a white American couple who adopted a little girl from China: when the couple finally returned from Wuhan to New York City with the child, they felt as if they "had walked off with something of incalculable value—a baby—with the approval of everyone involved. What a coup, what a blessing—what a relief!"

What links these narratives for me is the description of a powerful emotional state that styles itself as theft, as a coup, a walking off with something right under the approving noses of everyone: "Sara and I regarded each other with a deep sense of disbelief." I am troubled; the theft of one's own body is a kind of trickster's inversion of one's life reduced to chattel status. But the acquisition of another for a sum considered as either a "deal" or a "steal," if not outright slavery, resembles nothing less than bounty hunting.

A friend of mine who has given birth to two children assures me that biological parents feel exactly the same way—exhilarated, disbelieving, unworthy of the life with which they are suddenly charged. I am sure that is true—I too feel great amazement at my own motherhood. But my point is that the ideology of the marketplace devalues such emotions, either by identifying them as externalities in and of themselves, or by using them to infuse, even impassion, certain price structures, uncritically crystallizing into dollars-and-cents what we might be better off trying to understand as the sort of "priceless" relation of which Walt Whitman spoke in "I Sing the Body Electric":

> A man's body at auction
> (For before the war I often go to the slave-mart and watch the
>   sale,)
> I help the auctioneer, the sloven does not half know his business.
> Gentlemen look on this wonder,
> Whatever the bids of the bidders they cannot be high enough for
>   it,
> For it the globe lay preparing quintillions of years without one
>   animal or plant,
> For it the revolving cycles truly and steadily roll'd.

How will my son's "price" at birth relate to what value doctors put on his various parts if he ever stubs his toe and shows up at a hospital? Will he be valued more as a series of parts in the marketplace of bodies or more as a whole, as a precious social being with not just a body or a will but a soul? ("Oh I say these are not the parts and poems of the body only, but of the soul, / O I say now these are the soul!") Will his fate be decided by a fellow human being who cares for him, or will his "outcome" be negotiated by some formulaic economic tracking policy based on his having health insurance or a job? Will his idiosyncratic, non-

224

market value be visible in the subconscious, well-intentioned decisions of a nice suburban doctor who has never known, spoken to, lived or worked with a black person in a status position of anything close to equality? Will "ethics" be able to consider this complicated stuff, or will we decide the whole topic is too risky, too angrifying, so that forced neutrality and pretend-we-don't-see-ness will rule the day? Who will rule the fate of this most precious bit of "living property," as Harriet Beecher Stowe called the status of blacks?

Writes the cultural theorist Mark Seltzer, "the precarious difference between person and thing appears . . . as the difference between consuming and being consumed . . . the competition for personhood in the market is the choice between eating and being eaten." How will our children, figured as the tidy "consumption preferences" of unsocial actors, be able to value themselves?

I was unable to choose a fee schedule. I was unable to conspire in putting a price on my child's head.

> When Luong Hung looks in the mirror, he says, shame ripples through his body. His sad-eyed visage, his tightly curled dark hair, are daily reminders of the relationship between his Vietnamese mother, a waitress in Saigon during the war, and his father, a cargo pilot he knows only as John.
>
> "I feel ashamed that my mother was with a black man, and now I have to carry that," said the slender 26-year-old refugee, his knees almost touching his chest as he perched atop a child-sized plastic chair in his Bronx apartment. "I wish I were a white Amerasian."

A picture of Mr. Hung shows him wearing a tee-shirt with a gigantic dollar bill on it. *Were baby prices quoted as soybean prices . . . I ruminate.*

One feature of the market as politics is that where consumer demand is high, succumbing to the pressure to produce more rationalizes market actors; where, on the other hand, the soy surplus is great, rational growers stop growing. It is no wonder that as long as one's head is locked within the box of this paradigm, a deference like Judge Posner's to the fundamentally absurd notion of a purely private preference for white babies might not reveal itself immediately as insidiously eugenic. The language of the market is so clean and impersonal, after all—it hardly hurts a bit when Landes and Posner start thinking up incentives to actually *produce* more white babies, not merely incentives for white women to "give up" more of their babies for adoption. Giving things up and other artifacts of a gift economy, after all, have little place in the logical order of a productive market economy. Most alarming of all, the troublesomely excessive supply of black and other socially discarded categories of babies—that is, the babies for whom there is this relatively low "demand"—inspires Landes and Posner to pursue not merely a set of incentives to "consume" or "take" them, but rather *dis*-incentives to produce them at all.

> Mr. Hung said all he knew about black Americans came from a movie about the antebellum South he saw in his youth.
>
> "I heard in Vietnam that black people were slaves," he said. "I didn't want to be a slave."
>
> He still may be hostage to his decidedly derogatory view of black Americans, fearfully associating them with crime and homelessness. When asked if his time here has helped persuade him otherwise, he nodded affirmatively.
>
> "Of course it changed," he said. "In the United States there is freedom. I don't have to live in the black community."

How does one create oneself apart from such power? How does one know oneself in a world of such double-edged symbolism? What is the escape route to the future for "cheap" black bodies, for those whose existence is continually devalued or written out of the social compact altogether? One "option," I suppose, is the sad odyssey of the singer Michael Jackson—his trajectory from the sweet brown-faced nine-year-old on the cover of his first album to the strangely effaced shell who exists apparently only in the mirror of society's harshest illusion.

226

Another version of that path may be the one pursued by the rap singer Lichelle "Boss" Laws. Her career is most interesting: from her beginnings as a middle-class former cheerleader and college student, who attended private schools all her life, and who began her career doing profanity- and violence-free rap at campus functions while dressed in "little cute matching [outfits]," to her present calculatedly hard-core image of swilling malt liquor on stage, toting automatic weapons, and singing about shooting her boyfriend dead. Being herself ("sweet as pie," proclaims one publicist) didn't sell, so she toughened up her act. "The sad truth is the harder the rapper's image, the more music they sell," says a rap music producer. "In promoting her career as a gangster rapper," the *Wall Street Journal* says, "Ms. Laws has made much of her experiences of living on the streets. She says she sold drugs and hung with the notorious street gang the Bloods. She also says she spent some time in jail. She didn't; and the stories about her life on the streets can't be verified." But as Ms. Laws opines, "I'm both a gangster and a smart business person. I know what I'm doing, and I know how to make it in this business."

This tactic is familiar to too many blacks: success by dissembling, dissembling styled upon the "Boo, I scared you" potential of our fearsome demographic selves. The *New York Times* essayist Brent Staples writes about his dawning realization, while a student at the University of Chicago, that white people were afraid of him:

> I'd been a fool. I'd been grinning good evening at people who were frightened to death of me. I did violence to them just by being. How had I missed this? I kept walking at night, but from then on I paid attention . . . I tried to be innocuous but I didn't know how. The more I thought about how I moved, the less my body belonged to me; I became a false character riding along inside it.

Staples went through a period of whistling Vivaldi so people could hear him coming and "they wouldn't feel trapped"—in effect he hung a bell around his neck, playing domesticated cat to a frightened cast of mice.

> Then I changed . . . The man and the woman walking toward me were laughing and talking but clammed up when they saw me . . . I veered toward them and aimed myself so that they'd have to part to avoid walking into me. The man stiffened, threw back his head and assumed the stare: eyes ahead, mouth open. I suppressed the urge to scream into his face. Instead, I glided between them, my shoulder nearly brushing his. A few steps beyond them I stopped and howled with laughter. I came to call this game "Scatter the Pigeons."

The gangster rapper who carves up her sweet-as-pie self into high-priced images of a low-down market. The gentle journalist who stands on the streetcorner and howls. What upside-down craziness, this paradoxical logic of having to debase oneself in order to retrieve one's sanity from the remaindered edges of market space.

The Rooster's Egg

I started out believing that life was made just so the world would have some way to think about itself, but that it had gone awry with humans because flesh, pinioned by misery, hangs on to it with pleasure. Hangs on to wells and a boy's golden hair; would just as soon inhale sweet fire caused by a burning girl as hold a maybe-yes maybe-no hand. I don't believe that anymore. Something is missing here. Something rogue. Something else you have to figure in before you can figure it out.

—Toni Morrison, *Jazz*

The transformation of slavery's rationales from one discourse to another has been, as I have said, an extraordinary force in the shaping of the modern world. While the master-slave dialectic about which Hegel wrote so evocatively is an ancient philosophical paradox, the life-and-death struggle with which the legacy of the actual slave trade marked contemporary political life is resoundingly modern. Karl Figlio, the author of a historiography of scientific medicine, has described the changing perception of the body at the end of the eighteenth century: "it involved a degradation of the notion of a self extended into a unique and inviolable corporeal volume, to one in which the self only loosely possessed a body."

The issue of self-possession as it has evolved in ethical discussions on issues from abortion rights to euthanasia is central to the determination of what we mean by justice in today's world. Ownership of the self still vacillates for its reference between a Lockean paradigm of radical individualism assuming a dualism between the body as commodity and the person as transactor and an older paradigm in which ownership of the self is understood in terms of the ability to defend one's inalienable corporeal integrity against oppression and abuse. Our system of jurisprudence is constantly negotiating the bounds of our communal civic body in the context of disputes about the limits of our physical edges (such as experimentation with fetal tissue, sales of body parts, and sterilization), the limits of identity (male/female, citizen/noncitizen, and so on), and the limits of life itself (wrongful death cases, right to die, and executions). Law negotiates these boundaries by constructing verbal guideposts and a whole range of representational lenses and filters through which we see each other.

At the center of the resolution of any of this, I think, is the conundrum posed by the slave who doesn't own her body, but at the same time owns nothing but her body. The uniquely dislocating magnitude of the actual eighteenth- and nineteenth-century slave trade, viewed as a kind of forced migration that created a domino effect of worldwide uprootedness, set in motion the social forces of a kind of global grief that has colored the question of self-possession with excruciating literalism ever since.

Toni Morrison's great novel *Beloved* is based on the story of a runaway slave whose fate is described by Paul Gilroy in *The Black Atlantic:*

> Taking advantage of the winter which froze the Ohio river that usually barred her way to freedom, Margaret Garner, a "mulatto, about five feet high, showing one fourth or one third white blood . . . [with] a high forehead . . . [and] bright and intelligent eyes," fled slavery on a horse-drawn sleigh in January 1856 with her husband, Simon Garner, Jr., also known as Robert, his parents, Simon and Mary, their four children, and nine other slaves. On reaching Ohio, the family separated from the other slaves, but they were discovered after they had sought assistance at the home of a relative, Elijah Kite. Trapped in his house by the encircling slave catchers, Margaret killed her three-year-old daughter with a butcher's knife and attempted to kill the other children rather than let them be taken back into slavery by their master, Archibald K. Gaines, the owner of Margaret's husband and of the plantation adjacent to her own home. This case initiated a series of legal battles over the scope of the Fugitive Slave Act, Margaret's extradition, her legal subjectivity, and the respective powers of court officers in the different states.

The bizarre legal locutions determining whether Margaret Garner and her child lived free or died (she was returned to her master and then sold; her daughter's body was taken and buried in ground "consecrated to slavery") required a conceptual butchery that could only be accomplished by a deeply socially embedded schema of self-partialization that was body-centered (as to blacks) and will-driven (as to whites). It is with great care, therefore, that we should look for its echoing repercussions in our world today, for 1856 is not very long ago at all. It is with caution that we must notice that with the advent of a variety of new technologies, we presumed free agents are not less but increasingly defined as body-centered. We live more, not less, in relation to our body parts, the dispossession or employment of ourselves constrained by a complicated pattern of self-alienation.

Increasingly, I hear about cases that reason away parts of living human bodies as "assets" that may be willfully disposed of; I read about judicial pronouncements that refer to women's wombs as "fetal containers"—as though we were packing crates or petri dishes or parking lots. Increasingly, whole ranges of social complication, paternalistic intrusion, and outright coercion are placed beyond the bounds of either legal or humanitarian remediation by simply being labeled the outcome of either "bad choice" or "irrational acts." And that, of course, makes it nobody else's business but our own.

A good liberated agent should, according to this new-age script, be able to sell her assets or rent the space of her available containers or make improvements on the premises with nary a second thought. Needless to say, many of us do have second thoughts, but we are told by the Orwellian powers-that-be (and just who *are* these powers again?) that if some bodies are valued more than other bodies, then it's not the fault of calling ourselves assets or containers, it's just that when one enters the weird territory of law-and-economics-speak as applied to the property of bodies, then certain preexisting valuations just become all the clearer, more apparent.

Who can argue with that logic? Certain races are worth more in the marketplace. Pretty faces are worth more in the mating game. Certain hairstyles and clothing fashions just don't sell. And if it all sounds more like a meat market than one of ideas—too bad, that's life and that's death, so stop your bellyaching, go out and get a job, buy a better nose job, a better baby, a better skin tone, a better life. Just say yes, dial rent-a-womb *now* and give that unwed teenage mother-to-be a job.

I want to recast and even intentionally mystify the underpinnings of certain valuations that inform those life-paths purporting to be choices—valuations that I think are too often nothing more and nothing newer than medieval obsessions, a kind of obsessive eugenics. Perhaps it is only in their mysterious contradictory power over us that these valuations can be seen as the real irrationality in our lives—almost religious beliefs and even hatreds, rather than "simply economic" or "observably scientific" taxonomies. My other aim here is to attempt to trace a connection between the bizarre, even hallucinatory self-partialization that afflicts these times and the relentless abstraction and word-violence of particular socio-legal taxonomies.

Let me quote Paul Gilroy again:

The value of this project lies in its promise to uncover both an ethics of freedom to set alongside modernity's ethics of law and the new conceptions of selfhood and individuation that are waiting to be constructed from the slave's standpoint—forever disassociated from the psychological and epistemic correlates of racial subordination. This unstable standpoint is to be understood in a different way from the clarion calls to epistemological narcissism and the absolute sovereignty of unmediated experience which sometimes appear in association with the term. It can be summed up in Foucault's tentative extension of the idea of a *critical* self-inventory into the political field. This is made significantly in a commentary upon the Enlightenment: "The critical ontology of ourselves has to be considered not, certainly, as a theory, a doctrine, nor even as a permanent body of knowledge that is accumulating; it has to be conceived as an attitude, an ethos, a philosophical life in which the critique of what we are is at one and the same time the historical analysis of the limits that are imposed on us and an experiment with the possibility of going beyond them."

Flipping through the pages of a book on dreams, I once read: "In archaic times, a person who stood outside the law of a culture was considered dead by ordinary people." It was instantly riveting, this idea of illegitimacy as a form of death, of legality as its own life force. It made me think of a weird case in Los Angeles some years ago, in which an elderly woman, desiring immortality, entered into a contract with some cryonics practitioners to have her old gray head severed and then frozen until such high-tech moment as it could be defrosted and attached to younger, healthier body parts. Predictably, her decapitation precipitated murder charges against the cryonics practitioners. Their defense was an interesting one: they asserted that the prosecution could not prove murder except by an autopsy. That particular path to Truth, however, would necessitate defrosting her head during our still-archaic times, thereby, they alleged, enacting the true murder by depriving the head of its chosen means of immortality.

My remembrance of this case was reawakened by Carolyn Walker Bynum's book *Fragmentation of the Body,* in which she aligns the cryonics case within an entire Western tradition of debate about the life and resurrection of dismembered bodies. Professor Bynum looks at medieval theological debates—legal debates no less serious than our own—about what will happen on Judgment Day if, for example, the leg of a Moor is grafted onto the body of a white man. (Since this particular experiment coincided with only the very crudest beginnings of European medical art, the subject of resurrection presented itself with necessary immediacy.) What will happen if a man fathers a child, then eats said child, the

234

child's body thus becoming part of the father? Whose body will rise on Judgment Day? Will one body rise or two?

As outdatedly macabre as these cases may sound, consider the legalities of resurrection in the recent case of Angela Carder, a young woman who had battled cancer for many years. When she became pregnant, her condition worsened, and eventually she lapsed into a coma that doctors deemed terminal. It is unclear from where the idea first cropped up to save the "life" of her "pre-born child," but however and whenever, Angela Carder ultimately was subjected to the Solomonic intervention of a court-ordered caesarian, over the objections of her husband, her family, her doctors, and the lawyers appointed to represent her—everyone, that is, save the hospital's insurers, apparently determined to slice the mother in half in order to show who best loved the child.

Angela Carder died within days of the operation; her twenty-six-week-old fetus died within hours.

Another case that captures the degree to which life and death in our society are not merely physical but sanctioned events is that of Nancy Cruzan, a young Missouri woman who, after being injured in an accident, remained in a coma for eight years, kept alive by means of a feeding tube. After an internationally publicized battle, Cruzan's family and friends finally obtained a court order permitting the removal of her feeding tube. What I found particularly interesting were the comments of the nursing staff at the hospital, who had known only her comatose body. They cried and spoke of her as their friend. They expressed willingness to nurse her forever, as long as her body housed its soul—perhaps longer, inasmuch as some of their protestations made Nancy Cruzan's body sound like a reliquary. Of what is this body a symbol, I wondered from the mythos-spinning of my own agnosticism. What do they imagine her soul to be that they pray at the altar of her prostrate form, washing away patiently the daily corruption of the body's composition?

It is true that the hospital where Cruzan's body lay was Roman Catholic, as were the nurses, but I do not mean my comments as an observation about their belief in particular. Rather, I am interested by the way the Christian notion of a community demarcated by the form of a communal body makes itself felt in our general sociological and legal discourse. The symbol of Nancy Cruzan's helpless innocence not only served a religious need but also underlay much of the secular debate about the medical ethics of her treatment. In this sense, Cruzan's body was no longer her own, nor even her nurses' (in the body of Christ) but ours (in the corpus of law).

In the transformation from worshipful community to industrialized collective, however, something insidiously complicated has taken place. If there is, in our culture, nothing we love so much as a suffering body to idealize, then we should not underestimate the ability of our profane, mechanical age to transform that metaphor into a biotechnological enterprise. If we are fascinated with the holiness of our incorporeality, we should be aware that new technology sells us a brand of tenuous corporeality—bodies hovering in that deliciously exotic state just between life and death.

The new technology is itself so incorruptible in its clean metallic plasticity, in its nonbiodegradable promise of immortality. I wonder sometimes if it is not the Leviathan of technology itself we are empowering even as we rush to create new rights to life, to death, and to "pre-life." I wonder, in fact, if any of this has anything to do with "real" life, at least as lived in a wakeful consciousness. The contemporary adoration of the fetus, for example, has taken on a legal life of its own. The fetus has become an abstract, technologically separable life-that-is-not-life: the pure future of infinite potential combined with an impeccable past, the absence of a present presence. Ironically, the contemporary fascination with cheap, efficient suicide machines uses almost the identical imagery to rationalize assisted euthanasia; and at the same time it employs precisely the visions of helpless innocence invoked by Nancy Cruzan's attendants who so strove to prolong her bodily functions. Dr. Jack Kevorkian, moreover, has specifically linked the appeal of assisted suicide, particularly in intensive care units and on death row, to the death-defying promise of recyclable organs that can be inserted elsewhere in the social body.

This impossible hunt for purity. The terms of its pursuit demand that all else is impure; all else therefore justifies a quantum of rage at the autonomous corruptions erupting all about, and at the imperfect communion of bodies that is, ultimately, the only fate we can ever own. Perhaps what connects these stories is, in the words of a friend of mine, that "there are no bodies (nobodies?)—only ciphers for the will of other entities. They do not exist except as markers of narrative transactions."

There is a crazily complex system of self-recuperative valuation still brought to our present-day markets for babies, bodies, and body parts—markets that have been given quasi-religious overtones, as though the soul were lodged in alienable body fragments that could be purchased, attached, consumed, and that would then ignite, revivify. Harvest and transplant mark a ritual of cannibalism-as-communion made sacred by the miracle of technology, a duty whose service is attended by the ministry of medicine. Soul becomes a physical byproduct, something that can be mined and excavated, worn, rendered immortal by the profane circulation of excision and transplantation. In this equation, immortality of our corporate selves is not the equivalent of the immanence of the spirit, but instead equals mortality extended by an indefinite trail of pieces and parts, an engulfment of organs, an extrusion of limbs. Life everlasting, mortality without end.

Let me end with a strange story that unfolded one day as I sat glued to the television as usual, thinking about world politics and scanning the afternoon talk shows for moments of redeeming social value. On one of these shows, the featured guest was a travel agent who was describing herself as "ugly." Her problem was apparently that she was slightly overweight, had dark skin, and was blessed with a broad nose that turned under rather than up at the end. She was extremely proficient at her job, but found herself passed over for higher-paying "client-contact" jobs in the front office, because her employer felt that image was one of the qualifications for front-office jobs. "Image" was supposedly related to consumer tastes and "expectations." The "ugliness" with which she was afflicted, in other words, turned out to be the inability to please hypothetical clients desiring the exotic—clients whose keenly acculturated consumer appetites were purportedly better whetted by flat tummies, little noses, golden but not brown skins, and long hair tousled as though by soft tropical rainfall.

Lawyer that I am, I was immediately certain that this was a program about employment discrimination. Sounded like a bias case to me. I am always *so* wrong. In the seat where the feminist lawyer Gloria Allred should have been sitting was another panelist, the requisite psychologist—the expert whose presence always assures us that closet cannibalism with a taste for lizard blood (or whatever) really is a treatable condition but the first step of Reaching Out is up to you . . . In this particular instance, the eager psychologist was reassuring the Ugly Black Travel Agent that more self-assertion, more self-confidence, and more aggressive sales techniques were all she needed to turn the situation around. "Just say yes to yourself," she glowed happily.

Eager for comparative data, I switched channels. In two flicks of the wrist, I was beamed aboard the world of another well-known talk show. The famous talk-show host, it turned out, was having a plastic surgery sweepstakes: prizes were being awarded for the most complete surgical makeover by a member of the audience. Again there was a panel of people all of whom were testifying about how they were going nowhere in their jobs, but then they decided to get liposuction, rhinoplasty, a nice Armani suit with big shoulder pads and some cheek implants—and now they're running the company. Over by the edge of all these testimonials, sitting in more or less the same seat in which the psychologist had been on the first program, was an eager plastic surgeon. He too was preaching the virtues of self-assertion and self-confidence that flow from the choice to go under the knife. "Just say yes to yourself," he glowed repeatedly.

As I searched for a moral in this morass, it occurred to me that what linked my discomfort about the two shows was the underlying espousal of the very worst kind of assimilationist platitudes. I don't simply mean that they were advocating assimilation into a particular cultural aesthetic or ideology, although that was obviously an important part of what was going on. What made it "the very worst kind" of assimilationism was that it was also assimilation out of the very right to coexist in the world with that most basic legacy of our own bodies. What made it so bad was the unselfconscious denial of those violent social pressures that make so irresistible the "choice" to cut off that perfect replica of one's grandmother's nose in favor of a trendier, more "acceptable" model.

Both programs redirected attention away from the powerful, if petty, call to conform—absolutely, in these cases—that is the perpetual risk of any socializing collective, whether family or polis. And rather than acknowledging the extent to which this is an interactive problem, both styled the issue as a mere matter of individual appearance, attitude, control. Neither effectively addressed how the politics of prettiness comes to be so dominating that ordinary people's economic survival depends on anesthetized self-mutilation, or that "image" has shaken itself free of illusion and become a power-concept. Put on a happy face, was the bottom line of both programs—literally, according to the second show, and figuratively, in the first.

While I have to confess that I am a passionate fan of afternoon talk drama, I worry that this general philosophy of happy

239

self-denial is perhaps what makes such shows so popular among mainstream Americans. Consider, for example, the following description of the Oprah Winfrey show:

> Although she has a frank-talking, even combative manner, Ms. Winfrey does not seem to be looking for trouble. When a white woman in the always well-integrated audience mentioned that her decision about whether to help a person being physically attacked would depend on the size and color of the attacker, Ms. Winfrey did not inquire into exactly what was being implied. The daily scenes . . . of blacks and whites engaging in spirited discussion about something besides race and dividing along racial lines is refreshing.

TV blacks as "combative" but not confrontational. TV whites as racist but "refreshing." TV-land as the mirror of America: simulated confrontations about race that we can all, black and white, pretend never happened; masturbatory moments of mock fear in which a white woman can express her fear of large black people to a large black person and no one will mind, not even the large black person, because after all the only reason the white woman and the large black person are even standing side by side is that we live in a world in which size and color Make Absolutely No Difference—certainly not one in which large black people frequently find themselves lost in the invisible vacuum, the self-denying silence, between the predator's rage and the mammy's indulgence.

What are the limits of this attribution to "choice" to eliminate oneself just before the emptiness swallows one up? At least some public urgency about such matters came to the fore in the recent media brouhaha about a black woman, married to an Italian white man, who gave birth to a "healthy boy with fair hair and blue eyes." The mother had been implanted with a white woman's egg to ensure that their offspring would be "spared the misery of racism." While the father described the matter as one of "practicality," the Italian Health Minister, Maria Pia Garavaglia, was

240

quoted as saying, "Desires are not rights. A child is not a consumer good."

I remember when I first heard about the so-called Baby M case (the first case of surrogate motherhood to receive widespread national and international attention) I had a dream that I was in one of those gigantic silos in which chickens are mass-produced. As I looked up into the dizzying height of the vast industrial space, all I could see were black women, like brood hens, sitting on thousands of little nests, a little white egg nestled beneath each one of them.

What I did not anticipate at that time was that black women would not only emerge as the vehicles through which more efficient white-baby-production would be fostered, but would be out there busying *themselves* with the acquisition of more profitable racial properties. The improbability for me is premised on the strange mixture of mammy imagery and a most efficient breach of the bounds of "white race." "Uh-oh, I'll bet that's really got them scared," laughed a friend of mine. "Us really *having* 'their' children." She paused, grew serious, and then said, "Uh-oh. This is really *scary*." This scenario, after all, is enabled by nothing less than the transformation of the social difficulty of being black into an actual birth defect, an undesirable trait that technology can help eliminate.

"Why won't somebody say that we are legitimizing a call for an Aryan race, or the beautiful and perfect only child?" asks Italian Health Minister Garavaglia. . . . Such complicated imagery of desire for survival, of wanting continuity even in disguise, of wanting to pass into new life even where a part of one has already died.

Sometimes I feel as though we are living in a time of invisible body snatchers—as though some evil force had entered the hearts and minds of an entire epoch and convinced them that they should shed their skin, cut off their noses, fly out of their bodies, leave behind their genetic structure as they climb up the DNA ladder to an imagined freedom. It is as though some invisible hand were nudging us toward a nice obliging mass suicide, disguised as a fear of looking into one another's faces without masks, disguised as fear not of difference but of being not enough "the same as . . ." The body has become a receptacle for the tracks of a cruel iconography. We have reached a point of high-tech internalized fascism, where it is very hard to live in the world without a conformed exterior and a submissive will.

There is a Benetton advertisement circulating in European publications in which a photograph of Queen Elizabeth II of England has been subjected to computer imagery so as to darken her skin and depict her as a black woman. According to the British newspaper *The Sun*, "a Royal aide said the Queen was 'deeply upset.' The aide added: 'It obviously cheapens the monarchy.'" The article goes on to say that Benetton has given new faces to other well-known figures: the Pope becomes Chinese, Arnold Schwartzenegger becomes "a negro," and, not surprisingly, Michael Jackson becomes a white man. (Sounds of protest from Mr. Jackson—that haunting Kabuki trickster who has Elvis rolling in if not actually rising from the grave, whose white skin is just a disease, who owns the rights to Paul McCartney's songs, who tortures McCartney slowly by slicing up the music into a peacock's fan of sneaker and soft drink jingles—sounds of protest from Mr. Jackson were apparently not forthcoming.)

At what cost, this assemblage of the self-through-adornment, this sifting through the jumbled jewelry box of cultural assets, selected body parts, and just the right accessories? Suspect profiles have been given demographic reality and market outcome in the politics of race and gender, displacing the lived body with alien shape, the aura that dazzles, the shadow that follows, the disfigurement that devalues. In battling the power of great social stereotypes, individual will has purified itself into a glimmering will-o'-the-wisp: simultaneously signifying the whole self *and* the light-headed cleanliness of disembodiment. In this atmosphere of cultural anorexia, survival becomes a matter of leapfrogged incarnations, the body's apparition a mere matter of fleshly rearrangements, the purchase of self-negation all flash and desperate hoarding, symbolizing No-one.

Notes

Notes are keyed by page number.

Scarlet, the Sequel

6 Jason DeParle, "Counter to Trend, a Welfare Program in California Has One Idea: Get a Job!" *New York Times,* May 16, 1993, p. 14.

7 Diana Pearce and Emily Knearl, "Teen Pregnancy, Welfare, and Poverty," Women and Poverty Project, Wider Opportunities for Women, Washington, D.C., n.d.; Campaign for Media Fairness on Welfare, "Ten Facts Everyone Should Know about Welfare," New York, n.d.

8 Todd Purdum, "The Newest Moynihan," *New York Times,* Aug. 7, 1994, p. 29.

10 Charles Murray, "The Time Has Come to Put a Stigma Back on Illegitimacy," *Sacramento Bee,* Nov. 7, 1993, p. FO1.

"A business consultant whose clients include Rupert Murdoch, [Murray's friend Irwin] Stelzer once arranged for Murray to spend a month in England writing about the British underclass for The Sunday Times." Jason DeParle, "Daring Research or 'Social Science Pornography,'" *New York Times Magazine,* Oct. 9, 1994, p. 48.

12 Jason DeParle, "Daring Research or 'Social Science Pornography,'" p. 48.

13 Richard Posner, *Sex and Reason* (Cambridge, Mass.: Harvard University Press, 1992), p. 430.

Ibid., p. 433.

Ibid., p. 196.

14 Gisela Bock, "Antinatalism, Maternity and Paternity in National Socialist Racism," in *Maternity and Gender Policies: Women and the Rise of the European Welfare States, 1880s to 1950s,* ed. Gisela Bock and Pat Thane (London: Routledge, 1991), p. 236.

Pansy Quits

17 Walter Benn Michaels, *The Gold Standard and The Logic of Naturalism* (Berkeley: University of California Press, 1987), p. 202.

18 Nancy Fraser and Linda Gordon, "A Genealogy of Dependency," *Signs: Journal of Women in Culture and Society,* Winter 1994, p. 311.

Eduardo Cadava, "Emerson's 'Boston Hymn,'" *Arizona Quarterly* 49, no. 3 (Autumn 1993).

21 James Kilpatrick, *The Southern Case for School Segregation* (New York: Crowell-Collier Press, 1962).

Jack Greenberg, telephone conversation with author, May 1994.

23 Quoted in Patricia Williams, "Among Moses' Bridge-Builders," *The Nation,* May 23, 1994, p. 694.

26 "White Teacher Apologizes for 'Enslaving' Two Blacks during Lesson on History," *Jet Magazine,* March 8, 1993, p. 11.

29 Richard W. Perry, letter of June 1, 1994, on file with author.

41 W. E. B. Du Bois, "On Being Crazy," *The Crisis,* June 1923.

Radio Hoods

43 Thurgood Marshall, of a generation that had fought to have the word "negro" dignified by the use of a capital "N," had recently made a public statement that he would continue to use "Negro" rather than "African-American."

45 "See, Rush Told You So," *Economist,* Nov. 6, 1993, p. 28.

46   Andy Herz, letter of Dec. 15, 1993, on file with author.

47   James Bowman, "The Leader of the Opposition," *National Review,* Sept. 6, 1993, p. 44.

48   Stephen Roberts, "What a Rush," *U.S. News & World Report,* Aug. 16, 1993, p. 27; Kurt Anderson, "Big Mouths," *Time,* Nov. 1, 1993, p. 66.

49   Bowman, "Leader of the Opposition," p. 46.

   Tom W. Smith, "Ethnic Images," General Social Survey Topical Report no. 19 (Dec. 1990), Opinion Research Center, University of Chicago.

50   Quotations from Anderson, "Big Mouths."

   Bowman, "Leader of the Opposition," p. 48.

   Anderson, "Big Mouths," p. 64.

   Michael Dobbs, "Master of Radio Invective Eyes Official Soapbox," *Washington Post,* April 8, 1987, p. A3.

51   "See, Rush Told You So," p. 28.

52   Anderson, "Big Mouths," p. 64.

54   Rochelle Sharpe, "In Latest Recession, Only Blacks Suffered Net Employment Loss: Firms Added Whites, Asians, and Hispanics Overall, But They Deny Any Bias," *Wall Street Journal,* Sept. 14, 1993, p. A1.

   Elaine Ray, "Another Depression," *Boston Globe,* Sept. 24, 1993, op-ed page.

55   Romesh Ratnesar, "University Failing to Meet Minority Grad Student Goal," *Stanford Daily,* Nov. 12, 1993, p. 1.

   Judith Michaelson, "Talk Radio: At the Mike, If Not White, Lean Right," *Los Angeles Times,* Aug. 23, 1993, p. F1.

56   *Time,* Feb. 7, 1994, p. 37.

   A. M. Rosenthal, "Bigots and Journalists," *New York Times,* Feb. 4, 1994, p. A23.

Unbirthing the Nation

58   Brent Staples, *Parallel Time: Growing Up in Black and White* (New York: Pantheon, 1994).

Notes

61 Mitchell Duneier, *Slim's Table: Race, Respectability, and Masculinity* (Chicago: University of Chicago Press, 1994), pp. 123–124.

62 John Edgar Wideman, *Fatheralong: A Meditation on Fathers and Sons, Race and Society* (New York: Pantheon, 1994), pp. 21–22.

Quoted in Duneier, *Slim's Table*, pp. 129–130.

64 Ibid., p. 130.

65 Ellis Cose, *The Rage of a Privileged Class* (New York: HarperCollins, 1993), p. 8.

68 Langston Hughes, "The Dream Keeper," in *The Dream Keeper and Other Poems* (New York: Random House, 1960).

70 *Johnson and Graham's Lessee v. William M'Intosh*, 21 U. S. 543 (1823).

71 Mike Davis, *City of Quartz* (New York: Vintage, 1992), p. 233.

Ariela Gross, letter of March 14, 1994, on file with the author.

73 Susan Orlean, "Figures in a Mall," *New Yorker*, Feb. 21, 1994, p. 48.

74 John Fiske, *Media Matters: Everyday Culture and Political Change* (Minneapolis: University of Minnesota Press, 1994), p. 123.

77 Ken Auletta, "The Electronic Parent," *New Yorker*, Nov. 8, 1993, p. 68.

"See, Rush Told You So," *Economist*, Nov. 6, 1993, p. 28.

James Bowman, "The Leader of the Opposition," *National Review*, Sept. 6, 1993, p. 44.

79 For discussion of these issues, see Donald Bogle, *Toms, Coons, Mulattoes, Mammies, and Bucks: An Interpretive History of Blacks in American Films* (New York: Viking, 1989); Donna Haraway, *Primate Visions: Gender, Race, and Nature in the World of Modern Science* (New York: Routledge, 1989); and Mark Crispin Miller, *Boxed In: The Culture of T. V.* (Evanston: Northwestern University Press, 1988).

M. Ethan Katsch, *Electronic Media and the Transformation of American Law* (New York: Oxford University Press, 1989), p. 242.

80 "No 'Miss Saigon' for Broadway," *Washington Post*, Aug. 9, 1990, p. D1.

81 Ellen Holly, "Why the Furor over 'Miss Saigon' Won't Fade," *New York Times*, Aug. 26, 1990, p. H7 (emphasis in original).

Mervyn Rothstein, "Equity Panel Head Criticizes 'Saigon' Producer," *New York Times*, Aug. 16, 1990, p. C15.

Ibid.

83 Matthew L. Spitzer, "Justifying Minority Preferences in Broadcasting," Social Science Working Paper 718, Division of the Humanities and Social Sciences, California Institute of Technology, March 1990, p. 25.

Shelby Steele, *The Content of Our Character: A New Vision of Race in America* (New York: St. Martin's Press, 1990), p. 11.

84 Ibid.

Ibid. p. 12.

William Glaberson, "One in Four Young Black Men Is in Custody, a Study Says," *New York Times*, Oct. 4, 1990, p. B6.

Steele, *Content of Our Character*, p. 13.

85 Dennis Hunt, "Black Radio Debates the Inclusion of White Artists," *Los Angeles Times*, March 26, 1989, calendar, p. 5.

Spitzer, "Justifying Minority Preferences in Broadcasting," p. 67, n. 106.

White Men Can't Count

96 Peter Kilborn, "Women and Minorities Still Face 'Glass Ceiling,'" *New York Times*, March 16, 1995, p. A22.

97 Ibid.

98 Ibid.

Lani Guinier, "Becoming Gentlemen: Women's Experiences at One Ivy League Law School," *University of Pennsylvania Law Review*, 143, no. 1 (1995).

Steven Holmes, "Programs Based on Sex and Race Are under Attack," *New York Times*, March 16, 1995, p. A1.

100 Diane Lewis, "Black Workers' Ranks Drop in Boston Banks," *Boston Globe*, March 17, 1995, p. 1.

102 Jules Lobel, *A Less Than Perfect Union: Alternative Perspectives on the U. S. Constitution* (New York: Monthly Review Press, 1988), p. 270.

103 All quotations from "amorphous" to "stereotypes" are from *Metro Broadcasting et al. v. FCC,* 110 S. Ct. (1990).

104 Leonard Zeskind, "For Duke, Just a Start?" *New York Times,* Oct. 9, 1990, p. A25.

See John Franklin and Alfred Moss, *From Slavery to Freedom: A History of Negro Americans,* 6th ed. (New York: Knopf, 1988).

106 *Metro Broadcasting.*

107 Ibid.

Town Hall Television

119 Jane Furse, "Whoopi Cooks Up a Storm," *New York Daily News,* Dec. 1, 1993, p. 3C.

Anita Creamer, "Costumes Can't Hide Right and Wrong," *Sacramento Bee,* Nov. 2, 1993, p. D1.

Los Angeles Times, March 28, 1988, cited in John Fiske, *Media Matters: Everyday Culture and Political Change* (Minneapolis: University of Minnesota Press, 1994), p. 147.

120 David Mills, "What's So Funny?" *Washington Post,* Oct. 26, 1993, p. F1.

Clarence X

123 *The Autobiography of Malcolm X* (New York: Grove Press, 1965), pp. 458–459.

Ibid., p. 454.

124 Ibid., p. 457.

125 *Today Show,* Thursday, Nov. 7, 1991.

127 Nell Irvin Painter, "Hill, Thomas, and the Use of Racial Stereotype," in *Race-ing Justice, En-Gendering Power,* ed. Toni Morrison (New York: Pantheon, 1992), pp. 201–202.

129 Peter Applebome, "Duke: The Ex-Nazi Who Would Be Governor," *New York Times,* Nov. 10, 1991, p. A1.

Virginia Lamp Thomas, "Breaking Silence," *People Magazine,* Nov. 11, 1991, pp. 111–112.

Autobiography of Malcolm X, pp. 306–307.

130   Thomas, "Breaking Silence," p. 111.

Don Terry, "In Louisiana, Duke Divides Old Loyalties," *New York Times,* Oct. 31, 1991, p. 1.

Applebome, "Duke."

133   "Speeches," *New Yorker,* Nov. 4, 1991, p. 35.

134   *Hudson v. McMillian,* 112 S.Ct. 993 (1992).

Autobiography of Malcolm X, p. 75.

135   Margaret Fernandez, letter of Feb. 25, 1992, on file with author.

A Hearing of One's Own

138   Quoted in David Gates, "Keep Your Eyes on the Prize," *Newsweek,* Oct. 18, 1993, p. 89.

Clint Bolick, "Clinton's Quota Queens," *Wall Street Journal,* April 30, 1993.

139   "Withdraw Guinier," *New Republic,* June 14, 1993.

Neil A. Lewis, "Clinton Selection for a Rights Post May Be Withdrawn," *New York Times,* June 2, 1993, p. A17.

John Leo, "A Controversial Choice at Justice," *U.S. News & World Report,* May 17, 1993, p. 19.

Ray Kerrison, "Loony Lani Is Symbolic of Clinton's Crazy Reign," *New York Post,* June 4, 1993, p. 18.

140   Lani Guinier, "The Triumph of Tokenism: The Voting Rights Act and the Theory of Black Electoral Success," *Michigan Law Review,* 89 (March 1991), p. 1109, n. 151. Ellipses indicate deletion of citations, not of any of the text of the footnote.

Paul Gigot, "Hillary's Choice on Civil Rights: Back to the Future," *Wall Street Journal,* May 7, 1993.

Stuart Taylor, Jr., "DOJ Nominee's 'Authentic' Black Views,'" *Legal Times,* May 17, 1993.

Editorial, "A Civil Rights Struggle Ahead," *New York Times,* May 23, 1993.

Kerrison, "Loony Lani."

141 Ibid.

David Boldt, "C'mon, Bill, Don't Lose Your Touch or They'll Cut You Off at the Pass," *Philadelphia Inquirer,* May 30, 1993, p. C7.

142 Patricia Williams, "Lani, We Hardly Knew Ye," *Village Voice,* June 4, 1993, p. 25.

143 R. W. Apple, Jr., "President Blames Himself for Furor over Nominee," *New York Times,* June 5, 1993, p. A1.

Barbara Amiel, "America, Anita and the Feminine Thought Police," *London Daily Mail,* May 2, 1993.

144 Kerrison, "Loony Lani."

145 Don Feder, "Multiculturalism: Racism's New Twin," *Boston Herald,* Aug. 19, 1991, p. 21.

147 Lani Guinier, *The Tyranny of the Majority* (New York: Free Press, 1994).

149 Quoted in Susan Robeson, *The Whole World in His Hands: A Pictorial Biography of Paul Robeson* (Secaucus, N.J.: Citadel Press, 1981), p. 121.

Henry Louis Gates, Jr., *The Signifying Monkey* (New York: Oxford University Press, 1988), pp. 167–169.

Quayle Has a Cow

152 Daniel Wattenberg, "Boy Clinton's Big Mama: The Lady Macbeth of Little Rock," *American Spectator,* Aug. 1992, pp. 25–26.

154 I am indebted to Greta Edwards-Anthony for bringing this information to my attention.

155 Christine Stansell, *City of Women* (New York: Knopf, 1986), p. 175.

Faye Ginsberg and Anna Lowenhaupt Tsing, ed., *Uncertain Terms: Negotiating Gender in American Culture* (Boston: Beacon Press, 1990).

157 Dan Quayle, May 19, 1992, in a speech in San Francisco to the Commonwealth Club of California.

159   Philippe Ariés and Georges Duby, *A History of Private Life*, vol. 5: *Riddles of Identity in Modern Times* (Cambridge, Mass.: Harvard University Press, 1991), pp. 542–543.

160   Joan Hoff, *Law, Gender, and Injustice* (New York: New York University Press, 1991), p. 50.

Ibid., p. 6.

Ibid., pp. 34–35.

161   Marilyn Quayle, Republican National Convention speech, 1992.

165   For further thoughts on this subject, see bell hooks, "Feminism: A Movement to End Sexist Oppression," in her *Feminist Theory: From Margin to Center* (Boston: South End Press, 1984).

166   Jeff Jacoby, "An Off-Key Note at Symphony Hall," *Boston Globe*, April 21, 1994.

Black-Power Dream Barbie

186   Studs Terkel, *Race: How Blacks and Whites Think and Feel about the American Obsession* (New York: New Press, 1992), p. 346.

188   Jonathan Kozol, "Romance of the Ghetto School," *The Nation*, May 23, 1994, p. 705.

191   Calvin Hernton, "The Sexualization of Racism," in *Sex and Racism in America* (Garden City: Doubleday, 1965); see also Gunnar Myrdal, *An American Dilemma* (New York: Harper and Brothers, 1944), pp. 587–588.

197   James Boyle, "A Theory of Information: Copyright, Spleens, Blackmail, and Insider Trading," *California Law Review*, 80 (1992), pp. 1467–68.

198   Anthony Lane, "Instant Karma," *New Yorker*, May 30, 1994, p. 98.

201   Stephen Kinzer, "European Leaders Reluctant to Send Troops to Rwanda," *New York Times*, May 25, 1994, p. A6.

202   "NBC Producer's Racial Remark Causes Furor," Reuters News Service, Oct. 15, 1993.

203   Robert Kaplan, "The Coming Anarchy," *Atlantic Monthly*, Feb. 1994.

Notes

204   Paul Johnson, "Colonialism's Back—And Not a Moment Too Soon," *New York Times Magazine,* April 18, 1993.

206   Kaplan, "The Coming Anarchy."

208   Roger Rosenblatt, "A Killer in the Eye," *New York Times Magazine,* June 5, 1994, p. 41.

In Search of Pharaoh's Daughter

215   Barbara Reynolds, "Save the Whales, but Don't Lose the Kids," *USA Today,* Oct. 21, 1988, p. 11A.

"Arson Damages Disputed Foster Home in Queens," *New York Times,* April 22, 1987, pp. 1, B5.

"Infants, Anger, and Fire Engines in the Night," *New York Times,* April 22, 1987, p. B5.

216   Ibid.

Ibid.

"Arson Damages Disputed Foster Home," p. B5.

217   Elizabeth Landes and Richard Posner, "The Economics of the Baby Shortage," *Journal of Legal Studies,* 7 (1978), 344.

"The thousands of children in foster care . . . are comparable to an unsold inventory stored in a warehouse" (ibid., p. 327).

Ibid., p. 347.

218   Richard Posner, *Sex and Reason* (Cambridge, Mass.: Harvard University Press, 1992).

219   Landes and Posner, "Economics of the Baby Shortage," p. 336.

220   Elizabeth Bartholet, *Family Bonds: Adoption and the Politics of Parenting* (Boston: Houghton Mifflin, 1993), pp. 110–117.

222   Landes and Posner, "Economics of the Baby Shortage," p. 341.

223   Bruce Porter, "I Met My Daughter at the Wuhan Foundling Hospital," *New York Times Magazine,* April 11, 1993, p. 46.

225   Mark Seltzer, *Bodies and Machines* (London: Routledge, 1992), p. 140.

David Gonzalez, "For Afro-Amerasians, Tangled Emotions," *New York Times,* Nov. 16, 1993, p. B1.

226   Ibid., p. B2.

227 Brett Pulley, "How a 'Nice Girl' Evolved into Boss, the Gangster Rapper," *Wall Street Journal,* Feb. 3, 1994, pp. 1, A8.

228 Brent Staples, "Into the White Ivory Tower," *New York Times Magazine,* Feb. 6, 1994, pp. 36, 44.

The Rooster's Egg

230 Karl Figlio, "The Historiography of Scientific Medicine: An Invitation to the Human Sciences," *Comparative Studies in Society and History,* 19 (1977), 277.

231 Paul Gilroy, *The Black Atlantic* (Cambridge, Mass.: Harvard University Press, 1993), p. 65.

234 Ibid., p. 56.

Hans Peter Duerr, *Dreamtime* (New York: Basil Blackwell, 1985), p. 61.

Carolyn Walker Bynum, *Fragmentation and Redemption: Essays on Gender and the Human Body in Medieval Religion* (New York: Zone Press, 1991).

237 Letter of March 1991 from Professor Wahneema Lubiano, Department of English, Princeton University, on file with author.

240 Walter Goodman, "3 Queens of Talk Who Rule the Day," *New York Times,* July 29, 1991, p. C14.

Ronald Singleton, "A Child to Order; Black Mother Chooses White Test-Tube Baby So He Won't Suffer from Racism," *London Daily Mail,* Dec. 31, 1993, p. 3.

241 "Black Mother, White Baby," *San Francisco Examiner,* Jan. 1, 1994, p. A11.

Ibid.

242 Robert Jobson, Royal Reporter, "Ma'amy: Fury as Benetton Blacks Up the Queen," *The Sun,* March 26, 1993, p. 1. (While I recognize that *The Sun* is a tabloid of questionable reputation, it also enjoys a daily circulation of at least three and one-half million; its copy at least offers a general reflection of a fairly widespread popular consensus on matters like race.)

Acknowledgments

I would never have been able to write this book without the love, feedback, and support of my very patient family and community of friends, including but by no means limited to: Beatrice Belcher, Derrick Bell, Abena Busia, Eduardo Cadava, Paulette Caldwell, Jerome Culp, Brent Edwards, Greta Edwards-Anthony, Margaret Fernandez, Martha Fineman, Liz Fust, Jackie Goodrich, Dwight Greene, Ariela Gross, Louise Harmon, Michael Harris, Cynthia Hewett, Bonnie Honig, Stella Kao, Joseph Kass, Sarah King, Sarah Krakoff, Maivan Lam, Wahneema Lubiano, Pearl Mattenson, Beverly Moran, Ewa Morowska, Kirin Narayan, Gar Patterson, Ann Pelligrini, Richard Perry, Deborah Post, Celina Romany, Kim Schepperle, Vicki Schultz, Reva Seigel, Bruce Shapiro, Jane Shaw, Bernestine Singley, Lane Vanderslice, Amy Virshup, Letitia Volpp, Matthew Wilkes, Carol Williams, Damon Williams, Maria Williams, Ruth Williams, Elizabeth Wolf, and Joe Wood. I would like to express my particular thanks to the editorial staff of Harvard University Press. In addition, I would like to acknowledge research support received from the Center for Advanced Study in the Behavioral Sciences, Columbia University, and the National Science Foundation.

Portions of this book have been previously published by the Anti-Defamation League of Boston, *Civilization Magazine*, the *Harvard Law Review*, the *New England Law Review*, *Ms. Magazine*, *The Nation*, *The Village Voice*, and *The Women's Review of Books*. "Clarence X" was first published in *Malcolm X: In Our Own Image*, edited by Joe Wood (New York: St. Martin's Press, 1992).

Index

Index

Index

Index